IMMIGRATION UNDER NEW LABOUR

Will Somerville

LEARNING
RESOURCES
CENTRE

To Zoë and "Reggie"

First published in Great Britain in 2007 by

The Policy Press
University of Bristol
Fourth Floor
Beacon House
Queen's Road
Bristol BS8 1QU
UK

Tel +44 (0)117 331 4054
Fax +44 (0)117 331 4093
e-mail tpp-info@bristol.ac.uk
www.policypress.org.uk

© Will Somerville 2007

British Library Cataloguing in Publication Data
A catalogue record for this book is available from the British Library.

Library of Congress Cataloging-in-Publication Data
A catalog record for this book has been requested.

ISBN 978 1 86134 967 5 (paperback)
ISBN 978 1 86134 968 2 (hardback)

The right of Will Somerville to be identified as the author of this work has been asserted by him in accordance with the 1988 Copyright, Designs and Patents Act.

The statements and opinions contained within this publication are solely those of the author, and not of The University of Bristol or The Policy Press. The University of Bristol and The Policy Press disclaim responsibility for any injury to persons or property resulting from any material published in this publication.

The Policy Press works to counter discrimination on grounds of gender, race, disability, age and sexuality.

Cover design by Qube Design Associates, Bristol.
Front cover: photograph supplied by kind permission of www.stanpix.co.uk
Printed and bound in Great Britain by Cromwell Press, Trowbridge.

Contents

List of figures and tables

Figures

Tables

Acknowledgements

I would like to thank several people for their help and ideas: Philip Trott, partner and head of the Immigration Department at Bates Well and Braithwaite; Neil Gerrard, the Member of Parliament for Walthamstow, and the only MP who has had the distinction of serving on all the Commons committees for immigration and asylum over the last 15 years; and Hiroyuki Tanaka, policy analyst at the Migration Policy Institute and Sara Beth Goodman of George Washington University, both of whom read the entire text.

There are also a number of people who have commented on individual chapters and to whom I owe a large debt. They are Rosie Donachie and Razia Karim, Commission for Racial Equality; Don Flynn, Barrow Cadbury Trust; Liz Britton, Opinion Leader Research; Betsy Cooper, St John's College, Oxford; Nancy Kelley, Refugee Council; Rachel Pillai, Institute for Public Policy Research; Elizabeth Collett, European Policy Centre; James Hulme, New Local Government Network; and Hannah Lewis.

About the author

Will Somerville is currently a senior policy analyst at the Migration Policy Institute, a think tank based in Washington, DC. He works on a number of pan-European and transatlantic projects. He has previously held jobs at the Commission for Racial Equality (CRE), where he led on asylum and immigration policy; the Centre for Economic and Social Inclusion; the Prime Minister's Strategy Unit in the UK Cabinet Office; and the Institute for Public Policy Research (ippr).

He has managed over 20 research and consultancy projects and has over 25 publications to his credit. Recent publications include *Reinventing the public employment service: The changing role of employment assistance in Great Britain and Germany* (Anglo-German Foundation, 2004), *New Labour's migration policy: problems of performance and priorities* (JCWI, 2006), *The integration of refugees and new migrants* (COMPAS, 2006) and several articles for *The Guardian*. He has also edited five welfare rights and best practice books, the latest being *Working in the UK: Second edition of the Newcomer's Handbook* (CESI, 2006).

He holds a first-class degree in History (BA Hons) from the University of Leeds and a Masters in Social Policy and Planning (MSc with distinction) from the London School of Economics and Political Science, where he was awarded the Richard Titmuss Prize for Academic Excellence.

Preface: The Blair Years

In less than a decade, Britain has reinvented itself completely in terms of how it understands immigration's economic value to the country and, hence, how the government relates to the issue. As a result, from one of the many European laggards on immigration thinking and action – plodding, uncertain, backward-looking, and investing scarce administrative and political resources in micro-managing processes expressly intended to minimise immigration – the Blair government turned Britain into a veritable hotbed of policy innovation, extraordinary activism and a commitment to growth through immigration. The transformation has been massive, relentless and completely transparent – and hence available for everyone to agonise over, criticise and witness the bureaucratic struggles endemic to managing an activist immigration policy.

As a result, Britain today stands head and shoulders above the rest of Europe in how it conceives of immigration and its value to the country. It remains the only European country with a well-developed and flexibly administered points system and is a key magnet for international students. However, even the occasional review of the British media points to the strong and growing reaction to immigrants, the focal point of which has been the volume of immigration. With levels of net immigration nearly quadrupling under New Labour, a trend also reflected across Europe but mostly at sharply lower growth rates, the economic benefits of migration may be threatened by deep social and cultural unease.

Immigration under New Labour covers a decade of migration policy making in Britain. By the time it 'hits the shelves', Prime Minister Tony Blair will have left office, making the book the definitive statement on Mr Blair's immigration revolution. Indeed, an apt description of the book might be 'Immigration: the Blair years', as it covers the period from May 1997 to May 2007.

The book serves several purposes and will be useful to four main audiences. First, for the student of migration, whether serious or casual, the book is an excellent primer on British migration policy, providing a brief historical introduction and illuminating some of the key trends in migration policy under 'New Labour'. Second, the volume will be a useful reference book for scholars interested in contemporary migration. Britain under Blair has seemingly made policy experimentation on immigration both the highest form of art and a serious science. It has been unafraid to borrow concepts from other countries, adapt them to British policy priorities and objectives, apply them with nothing short of policy 'gusto', evaluate them closely, and change them, again and again, on the basis of evaluation results and experience. Will Somerville's volume is the first book-length work to document this activism in a meaningful fashion.

The key point of the book, and one that has been painstakingly researched, is that there has been radical fundamental change in British migration policy in a decade. The development of economic migration, a more restrictive approach to asylum seekers, a set of new integration tools and an emphasis on security are recorded in detail. Institutional changes – all the way up to the new Border and Immigration Agency – are also covered. While preparing a work of what amounts to contemporary history cannot properly evaluate the effects of policy change, the extent of change is undeniable, and Will Somerville documents it thoroughly.

But the book is more than a reference tool. It also questions some of the fundamental tenets of the more pedestrian accounts of migration policy development in Britain. Specifically, *Immigration under New Labour* seeks to explore, albeit in rather tentative ways, how British immigration policy has been formulated in the more fragmented policy environment of the modern state. The book examines and attempts to marry the internal political factors, such as the networks of influences, with external factors, such as globalisation, that have led to changes in British economic migration policy. Similarly, it examines how Blair and the electorate have influenced asylum policy. Thus the book will also be of value to migration scholars who are theorising the dynamics of migration policy development.

The fourth audience for *Immigration under New Labour* is straightforward policy analysts. The final part evaluates migration policy using the government's own targets (so-called Public Sector Agreement targets, introduced by Labour to move attention to outcomes). In doing so, it reveals the gap between aspiration and reality as well as the progress that has been made. Most importantly, it points to the important finding that British policies and strategies are increasingly pro-active rather than simply reactions to events.

Will Somerville has had the 'perfect' vantage point to write this book. His varied career has encompassed the think tanks ippr and the Migration Policy Institute, the Prime Minister's Strategy Unit under Tony Blair, and the Commission for Racial Equality when it was chaired by Trevor Phillips. As a result, he has been able to meld an insider's perspective with that of an outsider, and he has done so in a fluid and highly readable way. *Immigration under New Labour* will be worthy reading for anyone interested in migration, regardless of their specialisation or country of interest.

Demetrios G. Papademetriou, PhD
President, Migration Policy Institute
14 May 2007

Introduction

Overview

This book is an inquiry into the development of migration policy in the United Kingdom from May 1997 to May 2007. The aim of this book is to survey, analyse and evaluate such developments in order to present new insights into this period of policy making.

Lurid headlines on every aspect of migration have been a consistent feature of the last decade, from worries over asylum seekers to concerns over unprecedented economic migration from Eastern Europe. Such headlines reflect the passions and deep anxieties that migration has aroused. MORI (2007), for example, has ranked race and immigration as among the top three most important issues facing Britain in nearly every one of its monthly opinion polls since 2003.

Labour – in power throughout this time – has made efforts to respond to such concerns. In October 2001, David Blunkett stated to Parliament that he wanted 'to introduce radical and fundamental reform' (*Hansard*, 29 October 2001, col 627). Three years later, Tony Blair said 'we have begun a top-to-bottom analysis of the immigration system' because the issue had reached a 'crunch' point (Blair, 2004a) and six months after that, Charles Clarke could be heard on the BBC Radio 4 Today programme, laying out the need for 'urgent reform' to the immigration and asylum system (BBC News, 2004). Then, in 2006, John Reid stated that a 'fundamental overhaul' of the Immigration and Nationality Directorate must be carried out (BBC News, 2006a)

Labour has gone beyond rhetoric; it has put migration at the centre of its legislative programme. In the ten-year period under consideration, Labour passed four parliamentary Acts, and at the time of writing a fifth Bill is going through Parliament.

The backdrop to such passions and pronouncements has been the increasing numbers of immigrants. The absolute and net numbers have both risen. For example, the *inflow* of migrants coming to the UK for more than one year rose from 326,100 in 1997 to 582,100 in 2004 while the *net inflow* increased from 46,800 to 222,600 (Home Office, 2006f, p 95). Net immigration is predicted to continue at 145,000 per year (GAD, 2007). The following graph lays out net immigration flows to the UK over the last 35 years.

According to the 2001 Census, the UK has a foreign-born population of 4.9 million or 8.3 per cent of the total population (ONS, 2007). The

Figure 1: Net migration to the UK, 1971–2005

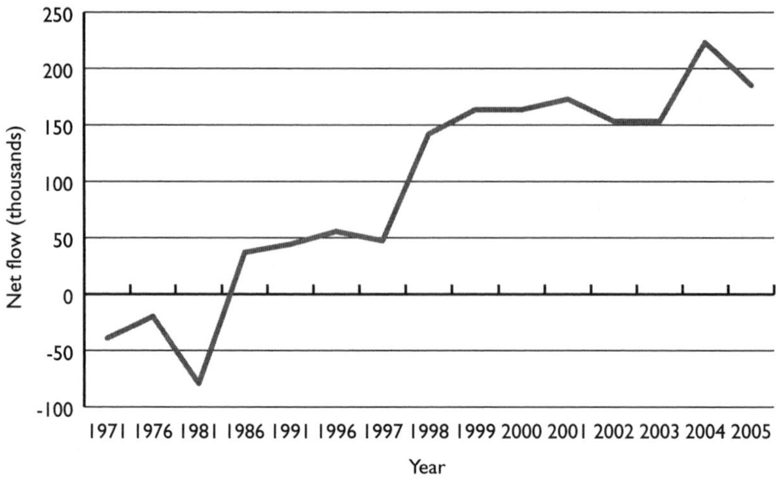

Source: International Passenger Survey

Labour Force Survey, which provides country of birth and nationality data and is the only source for the foreign national population working in the UK, indicates that in 2005 there were 1.5 million foreign nationals in the labour force, constituting 5.4 per cent of total employment (Salt and Millar, 2006, p 338). John Salt's analysis shows that European nationals remain dominant, accounting for 44.8 per cent of the foreign workforce (Salt, 2006, p 45).

The following table shows the top eight foreign-born groups living in the UK by country of birth. Together, they account for more than 40 per cent of the foreign-born population in the UK.

Table 1: Foreign-born living in the UK, by country of birth, 2006

Country	Proportion (%)
India	9.9
Ireland	7.2
Pakistan	4.8
Germany	4.7
Poland	4.0
Bangladesh	3.8
South Africa	3.4
United States	2.9

Source: Labour Force Survey, adapted from Salt, 2006, pp 68–9

A set of questions emerges from such a context. Has immigration policy changed? If so, how has it developed and has it been as radically reformed as might be assumed from such political statements? What have been the driving forces behind any such changes? And how can we judge Labour's record? To answer these questions, the book is structured into three parts.

'Policies within a policy': the different dimensions of migration policy

Part One details the extent of policy change under Labour. The first five chapters each focus on a particular theme:

- Economic migration
- Security
- Integration
- Asylum
- Delivery

The five policy themes or 'domains', determined by the responses in the interviews conducted for this book, reoccur as 'analytical units' throughout the book and thus deserve further explanation. Abstracting migration policy into a series of analytical units presents several problems, such as whether to break it down by 'level of power' (local, national, supranational); by 'group' (asylum seeker, worker, student, family member); by citizenship status (insider and outsider); and so on.

The majority of the literature takes a broadly chronological approach. Hansen (2000), for example, follows a linear chronological course in his study of post-war migration. Those who make (non-temporal) analytical divisions tend to follow Tomas Hammar's (1985) famous distinction between immigration policy at the 'gate' (immigration control) and immigrant policy in society (integration). Christian Joppke (1999), for instance, makes such a distinction in his comparative analysis of the UK, Germany and the United States. The benefit of dividing the analysis into themes is that it is easier to follow the internal dynamics of policy development. However, in summarising the developments in component parts, it is easy to lose sight of the fact that the themes are closely interlinked and interdependent.

Policy development between 1997 and 2007 can be summarised as the liberalisation of the economic migration system; increased restrictions on those seeking asylum; more control measures for unauthorised immigrants together with expanded security measures; as well as a reorientation of the official position on 'integration'.

The direction of policy has been paradoxical: on the one hand, a commitment to economic migration, and on the other, the development of a tough security framework that allows no unauthorised or 'illegal' migration and fast end-to-end processing of asylum seekers. In addition, anti-discrimination measures have been reinforced and at least partly amalgamated under an agenda of 'integration'. The *major change* under the Labour government has been the commitment to economic migration policy, which has been accepted across the political divide. The rhetorical commitment occurred early, in 1998, but concrete policy change only took place from 2001. Nonetheless, this position has meant that limitation has been put to one side: Labour's 'managed migration' has broken one half of the key settlement made in the 1960s and 1970s.

Categorising and understanding the influences on policy

Part One describes the various changes in immigration policy under Labour, whereas Part Two examines why such changes occurred. The analysis presented in Part Two is based on interviews with key experts, who identified a wide range of influences on migration policy making. Differing views on what caused change illustrate just how complex the policy process is, as well as the difficulties in extracting what is central and what is peripheral, even for those who develop policy on a day-to-day basis.

In locating the argument within the literature, this book takes its cue from the paradox outlined above – of expanding migration on the one hand and increasing restrictions on the other. An examination of the political science literature suggests that there is an (outdated) view that the UK is regarded as something of a 'special case'. Of all developed countries, Britain is typically characterised as a country of 'zero-migration' (Layton-Henry, 1992; Joppke, 1999; Hansen, 2000). In other words, of all liberal democracies, Britain had succeeded in restricting immigration where other countries had failed.

In explaining this apparent anomaly, several commentators have pointed towards the lack of constitutional checks and balances on Britain's political executive, which allows the executive to override the legal system more easily than other in countries, in order to exclude migrants. There has also been a general acceptance in accounts of migration development that the 'Westminster Model' of government – a combination of strong parliamentary sovereignty, a first-past-the-post election system, a strong Cabinet, and executive dominance of the legislature – is prevalent. Zig Layton-Henry (1992), Christian Joppke (1999), and Randall Hansen (2000) all work within a paradigm that Britain is a 'zero-migration' country, which plays strongly in their analysis of what influences policy. However, as laid out above, the UK is no longer a country of 'zero-migration', both in reality and in the goals and intention of policy.[1]

The argument developed in Part Two is therefore different from most other accounts of changes in migration policy, largely because it takes note of the policy changes since 1997. It accounts for the forces of globalisation as well as the role of the European Union and the legal system in influencing policy. In particular, this book argues that a more plural system of governance, or a 'differentiated polity model', exists (Bevir and Rhodes, 2001; Marsh et al, 2001, p 6; Rhodes et al, 2003). By taking a different view of governance and of power relations this book argues that theories of policy networks (Smith, 1993) are useful in supplementing our understanding of policy change. This is not to discount the influence of politics on policy development (see Hill, 2005, for instance), but to add to our understanding of policy change.

Finally, accounts of migration policy have generally left out the impact of those working within the systems of migration, the 'street-level bureaucrats' (Lipsky, 1979; but see Jordan and Duvell, 2003). This book attempts to correct the gap by integrating the impact of officials into the account of UK migration policy change.

Part Two categorises the influences in a triptych of macro-, meso- and micro-level policy inputs. Three chapters are dedicated to 'macro' forces:

- Globalisation
- Law
- The European Union

The qualitative evidence also places emphasis on what might be defined as 'meso' level factors. Chapters 10 to 13 examine:

- Networks
- Personalities and parties
- Attitudes
- The media

Chapter 14 is dedicated to the issue of how officials affect policy, particularly in terms of how they influence policy implementation.

Evaluating policy change

Part Three is an evaluation of Labour's record. Policy analysts make an important distinction between analysis *of* policy and analysis *for* policy, with the difference riding on whether the analysis is descriptive or prescriptive (Gordon et al, 1977, pp 26–30). Part 3 marks the beginning of a more prescriptive analysis, evaluating Labour's interventions according to their publicly stated aims, with a view to measuring success and failure.

Methodology

This book provides a synthetic, country-specific analysis of migration policy through both primary and secondary research. Desk research was carried out using secondary quantitative and qualitative sources to draw parallels and bring together the extensive existing evidence base. This was supplemented by 22 in-depth, face-to-face interviews to explore the key themes of policy change and the drivers behind them.

The study draws mainly on published secondary literature. The author carried out a literature review, which took the form of an extensive review of key journals; the analysis of a range of 'grey' or unpublished literature (mainly from NGOs); the analysis of material on migration websites; and a thorough review of government reports and documentation. There is a rich and diverse set of articles, papers, books and reports on various aspects of migration to the UK and migration policy making in the UK. While this study is not confined to any particular academic discipline, readers will note a strong bias towards political science.

The analysis is also based on primary sources, most notably legislation and parliamentary debate (as recorded in *Hansard*). Other primary sources include Home Office press releases and media accounts of change, statements and speeches by Ministers of the Crown, and a thorough investigation of departmental strategies, targets, and Public Sector Agreements (PSA), as well as their accompanying technical notes.

This book also employs a range of statistics from the International Passenger Survey (IPS), the Labour Force Survey (LFS) and Census data 2001 to support the conclusions reached. However, the shortcomings of the quantitative evidence must be acknowledged. Migration statistics are 'fragile' and many aspects are considered inadequate (Dobson et al, 2001; Stewart, 2004).[2] A 2003 government review, conducted to clarify a number of issues in respect to migration statistics, planned to link the Department for Work and Pensions (DWP) and Home Office databases to track migrants by March 2004; and by December 2005 there would be 'better statistics on the social and economic aspects of migration' (ONS, 2003). However, following pointed criticism by, among others, the Bank of England Monetary Policy Committee, further recommendations to improve the statistical base were set out (ONS, 2006).

This book also draws on 22 one-to-one interviews with migration 'experts' involved in the policy making process. Carried out in June– August 2006, the semi-structured interviews aimed to elucidate the policy development process since 1997 and tease out the key changes. The interviewees were asked what they considered to be the most important themes or dimensions of migration policy, and in what priority. They were also asked what led to policy change and how Labour's performance can best be judged.

The experts chosen for interview were drawn from four main areas: the legal profession (working in private practice, pro-bono human rights work, asylum appeals work, and for the government), business (employer associations and individual employers of both high-skill and low-skill labour), the civil service (typically from the senior cadre, and all Grade 7 or above), and from Parliament (which included Members of Parliament, parliamentary assistants and constituency case-workers). Of the 22 interviewees 19 were based in London, which indicates an obvious geographic bias, although several of those interviewed had views on the European policy-making apparatus. The other interviewees were based in Edinburgh, Cardiff and Brussels.

In addition, the text has also benefited from comments from colleagues, from an unpublished exploration of migration policy across the UK public sector conducted by the author in 2002,[3] from first-hand experience of migration policy making,[4] and from preparatory work completed for two editions of *The Newcomer's Handbook*, published in May 2004 and October 2006.[5]

A note on definitions

Migration is discussed in this book as the movement of people from one country to another. This simple definition of migration becomes more complicated when one disaggregates to the level of the individual migrant. Migrants have been defined variously according to their place of birth, their nationality, their status as accorded to them by the state, and how long they intend to stay in the country. For example, the International Passenger Survey (IPS), the major survey used to record the numbers of migrants entering and leaving the UK, defines immigrants as those who resided outside the UK for more than a year, and intending to reside in the UK for more than one year. Such a definition does not capture all migrants – for example the movement of Eastern European migrants, who may move for short periods of time, may not be recorded. In general, this book employs a wide definition, placing migrants in the wider concept of mobility and population (Salt and Clarke, 2005).

However, it is useful to define four broad categories that often emerge in policy discussion at the outset.

1. Migrant workers (or economic migrants) are generally defined as those awarded a work permit or Immigration Employment Document (IED) together with those who have residence rights in the UK and have moved to the UK in order to work (this includes nationals from the European Economic Area (EEA), plus nationals from outside the EEA who have gained residency rights in another EEA country).
2. Students (international students outside of the EEA area) are likely to come under a student visa, but may come under other schemes (such as the Science and Engineering Scheme).
3. Those seeking family reunion may come under a range of different visas (for example, joining work permit holders or students). It is important to note that different categories and statuses have different entitlements to jobs, welfare and services.
4. The final 'category' of migrants – forced migrants – requires particular consideration because the definition has unique policy implications and is often confused. The legal 'foundation stone' is the 1951 Convention Relating to the Status of Refugees. The 1951 Convention defines refugees as those fleeing across national borders 'owing to a well-founded fear of being persecuted for reasons of race, religion, nationality, membership of a particular social group or political opinion' (Article 1(2)). This book follows this narrow, but precise, legal definition when discussing refugees as it is the point of departure for UK policy makers. However, the 1951 Convention does not specify the definition of an 'asylum seeker'. An 'asylum seeker' is a modern construction and refers to the status forced migrants have *before* a decision on whether or not they are refugees.

It is worth noting that the above definitions are labels that mean different things to different people: the terms are contested. For example, popular definitions of refugees or migrants do not easily distinguish between causes of flight or types of people (Finney and Peach, 2005).

What this book is not about

Policy on immigrants, not emigrants

'Migration policy' is a vast subject and this book sacrifices some detail in order to provide a wider perspective, favouring breadth over depth. The book focuses on policies that attempt to control immigration and the behaviour and activities of immigrants; it does not examine policies for emigrants.

Emigration, however, is an important subject, as an estimated 5.5 million British nationals live abroad (Sriskandarajah and Drew, 2006, p viii). There may be implications for the education and training system if skilled professionals emigrate, or implications for the social security system if benefits are paid abroad (pensions paid to UK citizens living broad are projected to reach £6.5bn by 2050 (Sriskandarajah and Drew, 2006, p 70)). More important is the simple fact that emigration is the flip side of immigration. Thus the net inflow (of people, skills and so on) is dependent on the level of emigration. Given that a numerical assessment of flows is a key policy driver, this is clearly important, but while such implications are significant, there are few 'policies' on emigration beyond consular services abroad and web-based advice, with one striking exception. There is a subsidised return policy, the Voluntary Assisted Return and Reintegration Programme (VARRP), targeted at failed asylum seekers, and the Assisted Voluntary Return for Irregular Migrants (AVRIM), aimed at unauthorised migrants. Both programmes are run by the International Organisation for Migration (IOM) and largely funded by the UK government.

The general lack of emigration policies can perhaps be explained by the absence of any direct effects from emigration on UK society and institutions and because such policies would be difficult to implement, given that the right to leave a state is considered absolute. Regardless of the reasons, this book does not address emigration policies for the simple fact that there is a lack of them and the overwhelming focus of policy in this period is immigration.

The family 'gap'

Family migration is a crucial component of immigration flows to the UK. The most recent figures (2004) indicate that family migration (either accompanying migrants or those joining migrants already in the UK) totals approximately 18 per cent of the total inflow. However, observant readers may notice that family migration is given less attention in this book than other immigration streams. This is largely because family migration policy is 'content light' and, unlike asylum or economic migration, few policy changes have been enacted over the last decade.

Three factors may be significant to understanding the relatively few policy developments in this area. First, the right to accompany or join as a family member has long been considered a fundamental right (and the potential disincentive effects of abrogating such a right are patently obvious). Second, family migration, while making up about fifth of the inflow to the UK, has been a relatively stable component of the migration inflows. (Family migration has been steadily increasing but has remained proportionately stable.) Finally, by international standards, family migration makes up a relatively small proportion of the inflow. For example, in France or the United States, family migration constitutes approximately three-fifths of the inflow.

Nevertheless, some important policy changes to family migration have occurred, such as the increase in the minimum age to gain a spousal visa, or arrangements to prevent forced marriages. Such changes are discussed in the chapters on integration.

History

The following account of migration policy provides a brief background and context to the book. It divides the history of policy change into five periods: the long lead up to modern immigration control in the twentieth century; the inception of modern controls, from 1905 to 1948; the period from 1948 to 1976, when the dominant policy model was debated, formed and entrenched in law; the period encompassing the long period of uninterrupted Conservative government; and finally, changes since 1997.

It is important not to lose sight of the dominant motifs in each of these slices of history. There has never been a continuity of themes across ages. At the risk of oversimplification, these periods can be characterised by different preoccupations. The main concern between 1709 and 1905 was first with demographics (the importance of population size to national power) and later with protecting the population from hostile foreigners. The first half of the twentieth century can be seen in the context of the expansion of the democratic franchise and the growth of nationalism. From 1948 to 1976, policy makers were preoccupied first with the aftermath of war and the last throes of the British Empire and, increasingly from the 1960s, the issue of race relations. The period 1976–97 was one of relative stability, consistent with the immigration settlement formulated between 1948 and 1976, but also of a changing immigrant profile. The period 1997–2007 has been marked – particularly from 2001 – by a preoccupation with the consequences of a globalising world and with managing migration.

1709–1905: from demographics to border protection

There were three phases to policy over the two centuries up to 1905. The first parliamentary debates on immigration concentrated on whether foreigners were entitled to similar rights to those of natives and began as early as 1660, although the first major piece of legislation aimed at foreigners, the 1709 Naturalisation Act, was not passed until the following century. Some of the Act's influential supporters, such as the writer Daniel Defoe, are more likely to be remembered today but it was the first piece of legislation where the acquisition of legal rights equivalent to those of the native-born was made law. Before 1709, an immigrant could only gain citizenship by a private Act of Parliament or a grant by the Crown. The Naturalisation Act allowed foreigners to own property and to avoid paying the specific 'alien' taxes.

However, the debate in Parliament was not about individual rights but about the pros and cons of encouraging large numbers of foreigners to come to the UK. It was predicted, correctly, that the passing of the Naturalisation Act would result in a large population inflow to the UK (mainly German Protestants), who would bring skills and contribute to economic expansion (O'Reilly, 2001, p 494). The 1709 Act was, in effect, the earliest attempt to use migration to expand the economy. The migration of German Protestants that followed the Act was not, however, a happy one, and few of them settled in the UK, discrediting the policy approach. Consequently, the demographically driven immigration policy of the early eighteenth century was not pursued.

This period was nevertheless noted for the large inflow of another group of skilled foreigners – Huguenots – who emigrated from France in the wake of the Edict of Nantes (1685). From 1670 to 1710, an estimated 40,000 to 50,000 Huguenots arrived in England and they continued to immigrate over the course of the eighteenth century. The driver of their migration – religious persecution – shows that seeking asylum has a long history in the UK.

The next identifiable phase in discussions on foreigners occurred nearly a hundred years later when policy towards controlling the movement of foreigners became inextricably tied up with public protection. A combination of the growth of the nation-state in Europe and the increasing power and reach of Napoleon led to the establishment of early border controls. The earliest forms of passport and visa systems were developed in this period. Their purpose was to keep out non-nationals who were *hostile* to the country (Torpey, 1998; Torpey, 1999). For example, the requirement for foreign nationals to hold identification documents has its origins in the 1793 Aliens Act (Gardner, 2006, p 2).

However, British *nationality* was not restricted by borders: instead all British subjects had a right of abode in the UK and this was not dependent on whether they lived in the UK or not. This principle (of British nationality belonging to all 'subjects of the Crown') remained a fundamental assumption of policy until the 1960s, and was at the heart of the 1948 Nationality Act.

The third phase of policy happened over the course of the nineteenth century, which witnessed a gradual move away from a laissez-faire approach to immigration controls and into an era of immigration control regulations based on the protection of a British identity. This change coincided with the decline of Empire and the enfranchisement of new sections of the population (Flynn, 2005a). Throughout this period the major group of immigrants were the Irish, who were 'pushed' by the potato famine of the 1840s and 'pulled' by jobs, particularly in labouring. By 1861, the Irish numbered 602,000, comprising 3 per cent of the total population.

1905–48: rising nationalism

The first half of the twentieth century was a period that formalised 'restrictionist' policies. The origins of current immigration policy can be traced to the 1905 Aliens Act. The 1905 Aliens Act prescribed that foreigners could only land at authorised ports and gave immigration officials powers to refuse entry to those aliens deemed 'undesirable'.

The 1905 Aliens Act also created an immigration inspectorate to oversee immigration control, which was the first, embryonic infrastructure dedicated to enforcing migration controls. However, the 1905 Act was not concerned only with enforcement; it also provided exemptions for those seeking asylum (on the grounds of religious or political persecution) and guaranteed a right of appeal.

The 1905 Act was not driven by any overt threat (such as Napoleon) but by a stream of migrants. Jewish immigration had increased between 1880 and 1905 (Garrard, 1971) and the 1905 legislation was the culmination of an anti-Jewish campaign. By 1910, 1,378 Jews had been barred from entry as a result of the legislation (Flynn, 2005a). The 1905 Act showed that the criteria for exclusion in migration policy had widened. Originally, exclusion was based on hostility to the country on the grounds of national security, but the 1905 Act also excluded those seen as 'undesirable' for reasons of ethnic and cultural difference.

The 1905 legislation was cemented in the 1914 Aliens Restriction Act and, after the Great War, in the 1919 Aliens Restriction (Amendment) Act. The 1914 Aliens Restriction Act was a wartime Act, enacted under wartime conditions. However, it built on provisions in the 1905 Act. The 1914 Act restricted aliens' rights of entry and exit *to* the country, and movement and place of residence *within* the country. The Act also enacted 'Orders' that aliens must register with the authorities, which, for example, enabled the round-up of German nationals (Dummet and Nicol, 1990, p 107). It was originally anticipated that the 1914 Act would be repealed at end of the war. Instead, the Aliens Restriction (Amendment) Act 1919 was passed, which extended the 1914 Act for one year and repealed the 1905 Act in its entirety. The Act was then renewed on a yearly basis without significant parliamentary debate.

Despite the controls enacted in 1905, 1914 and 1919, in comparison with later periods, this period was liberal in terms of visa control. Immigration policy was embedded in the structures and systems of the Commonwealth and the UK's role (and perception of itself) as the head of the Commonwealth. This also applied to emigration, which was encouraged in order to populate the Commonwealth.

This system changed with the Second World War which, as it did in many other social policy areas, led to great change. The most important post-war difference was the increasing, although by no means predominant, flow of migrants from New Commonwealth countries. This should not be seen as a solely post-war phenomenon, as there was a significant migration in the inter-war period and during the Second World War, when many Commonwealth citizens fought for Britain. For example, at the start of the Second World War 60,000 British merchant seamen were from the Indian subcontinent, many residing in small communities in port cities (BBC, 2002).

Post-war immigration from New Commonwealth countries had its roots in labour shortages, a result of economic growth at a time when the labour supply had been decimated by war deaths and the flu epidemic. However, immediately after 1945 and in spite of the shortage, the Ministry of Labour actively worked to *repatriate* rather than *use* New Commonwealth workers. Their solution was instead to recruit from Europe, designing the European Voluntary Worker Scheme

(EVW) scheme. The EVW Scheme was aimed at the dispossessed and displaced workers in Europe's post-war cities and camps (Kay and Miles, 1992, pp 162–4). The scheme 'attracted' (there was a significant element of compulsion) 180,000 people – but remained inadequate to the scale of labour market needs.

In essence, the EVW was the UK's first low-skill economic migration programme, a 'policy partnership' between the state and employers. However, the scheme was unsuccessful as it suffered from implementation problems. These problems included reluctant civil servants (who disliked the compulsory element of the scheme and were attached to a laissez-faire approach); reluctant employers, who could not recruit directly from whom they wanted; trade union and international pressure; as well as a shrinking pool of willing workers. The EVW scheme was attracting few workers by 1949 and controls were lifted on 1 January 1951. The UK did not develop any other low-skill schemes in the following years, apart from in the agricultural industry, where the Seasonal Agricultural Workers Scheme (SAWS) was established. Interestingly, this programme has always had a strong 'educational' component that few would countenance in policy development of modern low-skill schemes today.

As a consequence of labour shortages and the end of the EVW as a viable option, some employers turned to the New Commonwealth as a source of labour. This led to a toxic public reaction encapsulated in the hostile reception given to West Indian workers arriving on the *Empire Windrush* in 1948 (Phillips and Phillips, 1998). But the effect on *policy* was not to be felt until later, in the debates of the 1950s and the legislation passed in the 1960s. The legislation passed in the same year as the arrival of the *Windrush*, the 1948 British Nationality Act, had little to do with immigration, and much to do with empire. Immigration control was not the driving force behind the Act (Joppke, 1999).

The British Nationality Act 1948 set out to reaffirm Britain as the leader of the Commonwealth. It recognised all citizens, including those of the newly independent Commonwealth countries, as British subjects (Spencer, 1997 pp 53–5). The 1948 Act thus granted citizenship to all members of the Empire (an estimated 600 million people). This Act served as a 'last throw' of a liberal laissez-faire die, with inclusive (citizenship) rights available to all British subjects (Hansen, 2000). Subsequent citizenship and nationality legislation would only be addressed through the lens of immigration control.

1948–76: from the end of empire to the politics of race relations

The analysis above showed that New Commonwealth immigrants came for jobs but, from the arrival of the *Empire Windrush* in 1948 onwards, such immigration became increasingly framed in the context of 'race relations'.

However, the focus on migration from the Caribbean and Asia can obscure the fact that it did not form a major part of the immigration flows in this period. For example, as many as 121,172 former Polish soldiers, with their families, came to the UK following the 1947 Polish Resettlement Act, complemented by 24,000 German, Ukrainian and Italian former prisoners of war and over 25,000 other immigrants (Herlitz, 2005, pp 16–17). Furthermore, flows were not confined to the immediate post-war period. In 1956, for example, 17,000 refugees were accepted following the Soviet invasion of Hungary.

Notwithstanding the size of the flows, official discourse implicitly assumed 'colonial', 'New Commonwealth' or 'coloured' immigration to be undesirable (Spencer, 1994; Spencer, 1997). The policy response, led by Labour's Clement Attlee, centred on how to restrict New Commonwealth immigration (Goulbourne, 1998, p 51).

The official discourse remained anti-New Commonwealth throughout the 1950s, and increasingly focused on the growing social problems of 'race relations'. The 1958 Notting Hill race riots are often seen as a key moment in the development of the view that Britain had a 'race' problem (Parekh, 1988, p 13). But debates were not restricted to New Commonwealth immigrants coming to the UK. Cabinet minutes and parliamentary debates included extensive discussions over other Commonwealth issues, notably the independence movement. For example, Sudan and Ghana, countries that gained independence in 1956 and 1957 respectively, figured largely in discussions. Thus the restrictive discourse was not reflected in hard policy until the 1960s. The period of migration policy 'stasis' ended in 1962.

The 1962, 1968, and 1971 Immigration Acts

The 1962 Commonwealth Immigrants Act was passed with the goal of preventing further non-white immigration to the UK (Dummett and Nicol, 1990; Hatton and Wheatley Price, 1999; Layton-Henry, 1992). The Act imposed controls on the movement of Commonwealth and colonial citizens to the UK with a system of work vouchers based on three skill tiers ('A', 'B' and 'C'). Caribbean and Asian migrants were channelled into category 'C' (the low-skill category), which was heavily restricted (Flynn, 2005a).[6]

The 1968 Commonwealth Immigrants Act, introduced by Labour, strengthened the 1962 Act. The main mechanism it used to do so was the concept of 'patriality', which entrenched differences in citizenship rights according to one's ethnicity through an ancestral connection to the UK (MacDonald and Webber, 2001, p 5). The legislation in 1968 coincided with the Kenyan Asian crisis and was designed to keep East African Asians out of the UK. It represented a key shift, in both Conservative and LabourParty thinking, away from respecting Commonwealth promises to a more nationalistic position (Hansen, 1999).

The capstone of the 1962 and 1968 Acts was the most comprehensive legislation of the last half century, the 1971 Immigration Act, which repealed, with a few minor exceptions, all previous legislation. The 1971 Immigration Act was a statement that Britain was a country of 'zero-migration', with strong control procedures, and immigration sanctioned only in selected cases. The Act proclaimed an end to economic migration and introduced new restrictions on family reunification. In effect, 'primary migration was definitively halted in 1971' (Hansen, 2000, p 222; see also Spencer, 1997, p 143).

The 1971 Immigration Act contains the *structure* of current immigration law. The first three parts of the Act were particularly important. Part 1 covers rule-making powers, in effect enabling the Home Secretary to make detailed rules on entry and exit; Part 2 covers those who have 'a right of abode' (permanent residence); and Part 3 those who do not.

The literature on the 1962, 1968 and 1971 Immigration Acts is substantial and there is insufficient space to appraise it here. Three points are nevertheless worth making. First, there is an assumption that the Acts themselves halted immigration from the Commonwealth. A more complete picture should factor in falling labour shortages (from 1958); increased emigration; and continued immigration, from South Asia and Europe, particularly after the UK joined the European Community in 1973. The attention paid to race also obscures Irish immigration. Census data from 1971 shows that the largest single country of birth for the foreign-born population in the UK was the Republic of Ireland. (This also holds true for the most recent Census, in 2001.)

Second, there is a debate in the literature over how racism was the driver behind these three Acts. The majority see the Acts as explicitly racist. For example, Spencer (1997) rejects the explanation that the 1962 Act was a response to falling labour shortages rather than to concern with the volume of 'coloured' immigration (see also Dummett, 2001, pp 89–136). Deakin (1970) similarly characterises the political and bureaucratic elite as advancing immigration control against a backdrop of wider public indifference.

Hansen (2000), on the other hand, strongly emphasises that policy was trying to constrain expansive rules set by the 1948 Nationality Act – a typical liberal democratic response to public attitudes that implies a racist public rather than a racist structure (see also Joppke, 1999; Geddes, 2005, p 723). However, the debates on 'race' can obscure two simple facts: that the goal was to restrict Asian and black immigration to the UK, which has never been acknowledged by any UK government, (Spencer, 1994, p 308), and that regardless of intention or responsibility, the *effect* of policy was racist.

Third, the policy in this period had *cross-party* support. Both major political parties introduced restrictive policies. For example, the Conservatives passed the 1962 Act and Labour the 1968 Act. Indeed, in political manoeuvrings before the 1962 Act, a backbench liaison committee favouring tougher measures – made up of both Labour and Conservative members – proved influential. In short, there was both intra- and inter-party conflict on immigration policy, but the settlement was a consensus (RSA Migration Commission, 2005, Annex E).

Race relations

Migration policy in this period did, however, have two sides, and was not simply about control with the aim of 'zero-migration'. There was also an acceptance of the need to challenge widespread racism, particularly in employment and in housing, where racial discrimination was rife (Little, 1947; Richmond, 1954). Shamit Saggar (1992) calls it the 'Hattersley equation': the commitment to limitation on immigration, with improved integration of ethnic minorities already in the UK. This dual approach (restriction and challenging discrimination) was officially formulated in the 1965 White Paper *Immigration from the Commonwealth* (HMSO, 1965).

Policy measures were given their most potent expression in anti-discrimination law, in a limited form in the 1965 Race Relations Act, in an expanded form in the 1968 Race Relations Act and in a much more comprehensive form in the 1976 Race Relations Act. The 1976 Act created the Commission for Racial Equality (which replaced both the Race Relations Board and the Community Relations Commission). The Commission for Racial Equality was given the power to investigate discrimination, set guidelines, and issue legally binding non-discrimination notices.

Commentators differ as to where the pressure for a liberal race relations regime of integration measures came from. Joppke (1999) regards it as an elite, top-down imposition, whose 'paternalistic taint' remains today. Sivanandan (2006, p 18) believes the opposite, a bottom-up approach driven by activists: cultural diversity came 'not from government edict, but from the joint fight against racial discrimination – on the factory floor and in the community'.

The two 'pillars' of immigration policy after the Second World War can thus be found in the 1971 Immigration Act and the 1976 Race Relations Act, passed with the broad support of the two major parties. Favell (1998) is struck by how unusual this was – a bi-partisan policy that was not unpicked by the Thatcher years. The policy – or rather policies – on integration and control won cross-party support that was to last for 40 years. As Hansen (2000, p 228) puts it: 'in the same way that strict immigration control has been the goal of every government, no government has considered the possibility of ... questioning the goal of anti-discrimination'. It is in this period – 1948–1976 – that we can say the dominant policy model was created and entrenched. The dominant model was a bifurcated one: emphasising the integration of immigrants (through a 'race relations' approach) and the restriction of immigration (a 'zero-migration' approach).

1976–97: new movements, same policy?

In the Conservative years 1979–97, policy continued in much the same vein, albeit with a stronger emphasis on limitation and restriction. However, the target of policy changed from the early 1980s, to 'new' movements that differed from previous post-war migration waves from Asia and the Caribbean (Munz, 1996; Koser and Lutz, 1998). More so than anything else, the issue of *asylum* rather than immigration per se became the concern. The fall of the Berlin Wall in 1989 and the break-up the Soviet Union, together with a swathe of conflicts, for example, in Somalia and (what was then) Yugoslavia in the early 1990s, led to flows to the UK. For example, the number born in the USSR and living in Britain increased by 16,000 between 1991 and 2001 and those born in the former Yugoslavia increased by 33,500 in the same period (Kyambi, 2005, pp 70, 72).

The legislation in this period bears the imprint of an attempt to curtail and control these new movements. Visa controls, including for Commonwealth citizens, grew rapidly from the mid-1980s. More significantly, the 1987 Immigration (Carriers' Liability) Act meant that carriers (particularly airlines) were liable to civil penalties if they carried passengers who did not have a valid visa to come to the UK. The strategy behind these Acts was to extend UK borders beyond the existing physical borders of sea, sharing the responsibility for control with carriers.

Policy making in this period has the hallmark of pragmatic response rather than strategic planning; the changing profile of the immigrant population meant policy was reactive. For example, four pieces of legislation were passed on the issue of Hong Kong during this period: the 1985 Hong Kong Act, the 1990 British Nationality (Hong Kong) Act, the 1996 Hong Kong (War Wives and Widows) Act, and the 1997 British Nationality (Hong Kong) Act. All were reactive: the 1990 Act followed the massacre in Tiananmen Square and provided for 50,000 persons to become British citizens, for instance, while the 1997 Act was a response to the potential statelessness of those in Hong Kong who were not ethnically Chinese.

As policy focused on restricting asylum seeking, there was a corresponding growth in the rights of asylum seekers and refugees. The connection between human rights and refugee law (and hence determination) grew in strength during this period, built through regional and international human rights treaties and jurisprudence. UK jurisprudence changed significantly in this period; key cases included the *Sivakumaran* case,[7] which established more precise standards of proof for refugee determination; the *Adan* case,[8] which established that persecution could be from both state and non-state actors; and the *Chahal* case,[9] which explicitly enforced the state's duty not to refoule (meaning to forcibly return a person to a country where they would face torture).

The 1993 and 1996 Acts

The policy changes under the Conservatives were encapsulated in the 1993 Asylum and Immigration Appeals Act. The Act included the new focus on asylum, incorporating – for the first time – the 1951 Refugee Convention. At the same time, the 1993 Asylum and Immigration Act created a 'fast-track' procedure for applications judged to be 'without foundation' and allowed detention of asylum seekers while their claim was being decided (Ward, 2004). The Act also subjected asylum seekers to 'separate and inferior provision in the fields of housing and social security' (MacDonald and Webber, 2001), revealing the main thrust of the Act to be restriction.

The next major piece of legislation, the 1996 Immigration and Asylum Act, introduced new measures and concepts designed to reduce asylum claims: the majority of provisions were 'designed to restrict severely the entry of asylum seekers, refugees, and immigrants' (Leigh and Beyani, 1996, p 3). This included an extended 'fast-track' appeals process; sanctions for employers; and welfare restrictions that removed the entitlement to subsistence benefits for most people subject to immigration control.

However, irrespective of the changed target of policy (to asylum seekers) the same bifurcated policy model remained dominant. For example, the work permit system was formalised in 1980, with set criteria for gaining a work permit based on local labour market conditions, but was barely changed from the system that had operated in the period 1948–76. More wide-ranging change, such as the 1981 British Nationality Act, incrementally added to the policy direction originally formulated in the 1960s. This direction was restrictive. The major exception was where the logic of the European Economic Area demanded otherwise, for example, on free movement provisions.

1997–2001: Labour's first term

The period 1997–2001 (when Jack Straw was at the Home Office) can be viewed as the first of two policy 'phases' under Labour. It involved some immediate changes in response to core supporters and then legislation to reduce asylum flows and clear asylum backlogs.

Upon election in 1997, Labour dropped the 'primary purpose rule', introduced by the Conservative government in 1980, which had aimed to ensure 'genuine' marriages.[10] However, subjective judgements by entry clearance officials, combined with the burden of proof lying on the applicant, meant that the rule was considered unjust. The policy change by the incoming Labour government was largely a response to community concerns voiced in constituency offices (see, for example, Hussain, 2001, pp 209–16).

The government then turned to clearing backlogs. The immigration system was under considerable administrative pressure from a growing number of (mainly asylum) claims, which can be seen from the chart below. (Figure 2 also shows that policy does not have a complete impact on asylum numbers, given that they grew steadily throughout the 1990s.)

The policy approach was encapsulated in the White Paper *Fairer, faster and firmer: A modern approach to immigration and asylum* (Home Office, 1998) which led to the 1999 Immigration and Asylum Act. The central

Figure 2: Asylum applications in the UK, excluding dependants, 1987–2005

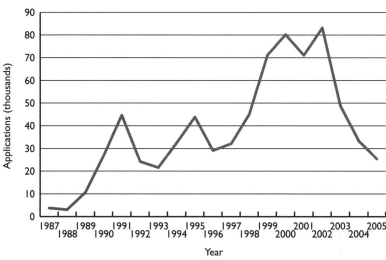

Source: Home Office

dynamic of the 1999 Act, while including a contract or 'covenant' with asylum seekers, was restriction (Harvey, 2001).

The 1999 Immigration and Asylum Act also significantly extended the use of civil and criminal sanctions in immigration matters. These included expanding existing offences of entering the country by deception (Part 1); sanctions on carriers, particularly road hauliers (Part 2);[11] and greater police powers, including the use of force, for immigration officers (Part 7).

Restrictions on the right of appeal were introduced in Part 4 of the Act, widening the procedure of certifying certain applications as 'manifestly unfounded', introducing one-stop procedures, and expanding the 'safe third country' concept (although a general right of appeal was also introduced to reflect the new Human Rights Act). The 1999 Act also inserted new sections into Part 3 of the 1971 Act, rendering rule-making powers even more flexible. The most significant changes were contained in Part 6 of the Act, which legislated for the introduction of a new agency to deliver welfare support (the National Asylum Support Service or NASS) for asylum seekers, while making them ineligible for social security benefits.

Cohen (2002b, pp 143–4) argues that the 1999 Act represents 'what is probably the greatest tightening of controls since 1905', with the removal of appeal rights, new powers for immigration officers to arrest, search and fingerprint, and the 'conspicuous feature' of growing surveillance of asylum seekers.

In 1997, the immigration system was under considerable administrative pressure and this first phase of policy development (up to 2001) can be considered an 'efficiency drive' combined with a tougher asylum settlement. However, this 'efficiency drive' was not accompanied by extra financial or staff resources.

2001–07: reattaching economics to migration policy

Labour's second term in office marked the beginning of the second (and new) phase of policy. This phase was *pro-active*, rather than reactive, and marked a change of direction. It also began with a new Home Secretary, David Blunkett, who was followed by Charles Clarke in December 2004 and John Reid in May 2006.

The policy approach can be found succinctly in the 2002 White Paper *Secure borders, safe havens: Integration with diversity in modern Britain* (Home Office, 2002a). The White Paper included the concept of 'managed migration', the idea that migration can be used as a positive economic asset that contributes to macro-economic health. The legislation that followed, the 2002 Nationality, Immigration and Asylum Act, and later the 2004 Asylum and Immigration (Treatment of Claimants, etc) Act and the 2006 Immigration, Asylum and Nationality (IAN) Act deviates little from the ideas in the 2002 White Paper. The legislation emphasised control, with an increasingly tough stance on asylum and measures to combat unauthorised immigration, but upheld the value of economic migration.

The 2002 Act did not reaffirm the 1999 Act's 'covenant' with asylum seekers, but set out to build a seamless management system, along with strong enforcement powers (Flynn, 2003). There was a series of restrictive asylum measures, such as provisions ending in-country appeals if certified as 'unfounded' (Ward, 2004, p 10) and an increase of surveillance and monitoring.

The 2004 Act further reduced asylum appeal possibilities, increased the potential for withdrawing support, introduced the idea of asylum seekers undertaking community work in return for accommodation, and widened third country removals (McKee, 2004).

The developments in Labour's third term continued along the same policy line. The key strategy document for this period was published in February 2005 as the Home Office five-year departmental plan on asylum and immigration 2005–10, entitled *Controlling our borders: Making migration work for Britain* (Home Office, 2005a). The five-year plan was followed by a major consultation on the detail of economic migration, *Selective admission: Making migration work for Britain* (Home Office, 2005d) and the following year by a policy plan, *A points-based system: making migration work for Britain* (Home Office, 2006a).

There was no White Paper before the 2006 Act, although the five-year plan can be considered a proxy White Paper. The 2006 Act was the first major legislation enacted by Labour that did not have an emphasis on asylum issues, but instead was focused on immigration. The 2007 Borders Bill (at the time of writing it is still a Bill) also seeks to implement some aspects of the five-year plan. Provisions include more police powers for immigration officers and a requirement that foreign nationals acquire biometric immigration documents (BIDs). Such BIDs would be the equivalent of identity cards intended for British citizens (Thorp, 2007).

The immigration legislation under Labour has also been complemented by other major Acts. The most notable include rights-based legislation, such as the 1998 Human Rights Act and the 2000 Race Relations (Amendment) Act, and legislation to combat terrorism, including the 2001 Anti-terrorism, Crime and Security Act and the 2005 Prevention of Terrorism Act. The following five chapters break down these legislative and policy developments into distinct themes.

Table 2: Policy and legislative timeline, May 1997–May 2007

Policy/Legislation	Type	Time
Fairer, faster and firmer: A modern approach to immigration and asylum	White Paper	1998
Human Rights Act	Parliamentary Act	1998
Immigration and Asylum Act	Parliamentary Act	1999
Race Relations (Amendment) Act	Parliamentary Act	2000
Full and equal citizens: a strategy to integrate refugees	Policy strategy	2000
Anti-terrorism, Crime and Security Act	Parliamentary Act	2001
Secure borders, safe havens: Integration with diversity in modern Britain	White Paper	2002
Nationality, Immigration and Asylum Act	Parliamentary Act	2002
Asylum and Immigration (Treatment of Claimants, etc) Act	Parliamentary Act	2004
Controlling our borders: Making migration work for Britain	Five-year departmental plan	2005
Improving opportunity, strengthening society: the government's strategy to increase race equality and community cohesion	Policy strategy	2005
Prevention of Terrorism Act	Parliamentary Act	2005
Integration matters: the national integration strategy for refugees	Policy strategy	2005
A points-based system: making migration work for Britain	Policy strategy	2006
Immigration, Asylum and Nationality (IAN) Act	Parliamentary Act	2006
Identity Cards Act	Parliamentary Act	2006
Racial and Religious Hatred Act	Parliamentary Act	2006
Fair, effective, transparent and trusted: rebuilding confidence in our immigration system	Reform strategy	2006
Enforcing the rules: a strategy to ensure and enforce compliance with our immigration laws	Policy strategy	2007
UK Borders Bill	Parliamentary Bill	2007

Notes

[1] This has been accepted in later work; see, for instance, Layton-Henry, 2004.

[2] The flaws include that there are no longitudinal studies that allow tracking over time and the life course and major differences in coverage, particularly in regard to emigration. Furthermore, refugees are not recorded separately as a group.

[3] The exploratory study included 20 semi-structured, one-to-one interviews with mid-management practitioners (between Grades 7 and 5 in the civil service, or their equivalent in executive agencies) in the housing, education, employment and health sectors, and two interviews with officials from the Immigration and Nationality Directorate (IND). The interviews were carried out in January–February 2002 and aimed to draw out the interaction and operation of welfare and immigration policies across the public sector.

[4] This has included work for the Strategy Unit, for the think tanks ippr and the Migration Policy Institute, for the Commission for Racial Equality and in evaluations of refugee and migrant worker projects carried out on a consultancy basis.

[5] *Working in the UK: The Newcomer's Handbook* is a welfare rights and best practice guide. The preparatory work included 50 phone interviews with migrant and refugee community organisations to explore issues on the front line for the first edition and, for the second edition, an e-mail survey using SNAP software that asked for views on the handbook from the 1,900 who purchased it, specifically on whether there were gaps in practice. The disappointing response rate (37) was followed by calls to key stakeholders.

[6] It is worth remembering that the focus was on migrant workers; migration for family reunion or asylum were not yet issues.

[7] *R v Secretary of State for the Home Department, ex parte Sivakumaran* [1988], available at http://www.refugeelawreader.org/files/pdf/112.pdf.

[8] *R v Secretary of State for the Home Department, ex parte Adan* [1998], available at http://www.parliament.the-stationery-office.co.uk/pa/ld199798/ldjudgmt/jd980402/adan01.htm.

[9] *Chahal v United Kingdom*, Judgment of the ECtHR, [1996] IIHRL 93, available at http://www.worldlii.org/int/cases/IIHRL/1996/93.html.

[10] The primary purpose rule required a couple to show that the spouse entering the UK was not doing so for the primary purpose of gaining entry to the UK.

[11] The 1987 Immigration (Carriers' Liability) Act was repealed but its provisions re-enacted and extended.

Part One
Policy themes (1997–2007)

ONE

Managed migration

Labour's policy on economic migration may well become one of its most lasting legacies. Labour has introduced a number of measures to facilitate the entry of migrant workers, particularly from 2001, that have comprehensively changed policy and marked a decisive break with the previous policy model.

The birth of the managed migration system

Economic migration is often referred to under the umbrella term 'managed migration', which was popularised by David Blunkett, who used the phrase 11 times in Parliament when he was Home Secretary. The extent of the changes to economic migration policy is not, however, easily read across from primary legislation. This has much to do with the structure of immigration law and regulation. As discussed in the introduction, the 1971 Immigration Act gave the Home Secretary extensive and flexible rule-making powers regarding immigration regulations.[1] Indeed, so regular are these changes, that many are not even press-released by the Home Office. More importantly, there are categories (such as au pairs or investors) within the Immigration Rules but most (such as work permit holders) 'defer' to a separately administered scheme (Trott, 2005, p 506). This broad distinction means that the majority of migrant workers enter under schemes based on easily amended guidance notes.

The exact date when a new, more pro-active economic migration policy was introduced is difficult to judge. However, the benefit of hindsight suggests that late 2000 and early 2001 was a crucial period. This is probably best shown by the absence of policy proposals prior to this time. For example, the 1998 White Paper only mentions economic migrants in reference to the abuse of the asylum system and exploitation.

A major government review of international migration and its impact on the economy was carried out in 2000. The review was prompted by thinking on the competitiveness of the UK economy, particularly by the Treasury and the Department of Trade and Industry (DTI), the early signs of which can be seen in the White Paper *Our competitive future: Building the knowledge driven economy* (DTI, 1998), which questioned whether there was room to lower barriers for skilled professionals and entrepreneurs. The White Paper was endorsed by the 1999 pre-budget report, which stated that the 'Government is therefore making it easier for skilled foreign workers ... [to] work in the UK' and would consider the recommendations of the DTI report (HMT, 1999, paras 3.98–3.99).

The review in 2000 was strongly influenced by Barbara Roche, then Minister for Immigration, and by Alan Johnson, then Minister for Competitiveness, and was completed late in the same year. In parallel to the review, the first scheme for the new economic migration system was introduced. The Innovators Scheme, a small-scale pilot, which can be seen as a 'policy bridgehead', was announced in the summer of 2000. The review was complemented by a wave of government-funded research evidence. This included a joint Cabinet Office–Home Office project (Glover et al, 2001).

The introduction of a pilot scheme demanded that Labour show their hand regarding their approach and the agreed line on economic migration was formally announced by Barbara Roche in a speech to the Institute for Public Policy Research on 11 September 2000. It was clear that the approach was centred on the highly skilled. In her speech, she said the 'UK was in competition for the brightest and best talents – the entrepreneurs, the scientists, the high technology specialists who make the economy tick ... [and] ... we need to explore carefully their implications for immigration policy' (Rollason, 2002, p 338).

Highly skilled economic migration

Labour has taken a two-pronged approach to highly skilled migration: one prong has been a conscious expansion of the work permit system and the other has been the creation of a new, points-based migration scheme.

The criteria for gaining a work permit, in addition to a job offer, were relaxed from October 2000: from a qualification (typically a degree) *and* two years' experience, to just the qualification. This allowed those who had recently graduated to gain a work permit. Furthermore, exceptions to the Resident Labour Market Test (the requirement that employers had to prove that no European Union national could do the job and which applied to all work permits) were introduced, for example for board-level managers (Papademetriou and O'Neil, 2000, p 233).

The expansion of the work permit system was further enhanced by an easing of some of the administrative rigidity to work permit categories, including intra-company transfers and multiple-entry work permits. Intra-company transfers were eased through a new, electronic application system and the self-certification of workers by major corporations was also piloted. Previous policy (introduced in 1991) had created a two-tier system, where it was easier for board-level employers to gain transfers, but this further simplified the process. In 2001, the government introduced multiple-entry work permits, designed for employees who worked for short periods of time in the UK for the same employer and found the business visitor visa process cumbersome.

In addition to a relaxation of the administrative criteria, the bureaucracy was also restructured. Senior civil servants and politicians made clear that the objective was to meet employer needs and ensured there was a strong customer (employer) focus. The unit responsible for issuing work permits was renamed Work Permits (UK)[2] and departmental responsibility was shifted to the Home Office in 2001.

The work permit system also incorporated the General Agreement on Trade in Services (GATS), a global treaty under the auspices of the World Trade Organisation (Lavenex, 2002; 2004). GATS was agreed in 1996, before Labour came to power, and is a scheme that only allows work in periods of three months in the fields of legal services, accountancy, tax advice, architecture, engineering, urban planning, advertising, management consultancy, and technical testing, among others. However, Labour's position on the current round of GATS negotiations,[3] which would extend agreements on skilled migrants, has been supportive, which may prove to further entrench certain global labour migration agreements into UK policy. Labour's support has been facilitated by the position of European Trade Commissioner, which has been held since 2004 by former Labour minister and Blair confidante, Peter Mandelson.

The success in expanding the system can be seen in the increase in the number of work permits awarded. The absolute number of work permit holders (and dependants) increased from 62,975 in 1997 to 137,035 in 2005 (Home Office, 2006f, p 44). Figure 1.1 shows approved work permits and first permissions (issued to foreign nationals living within, rather than outside, the UK). Approvals have more than tripled since 1995.

The second prong in Labour's approach to the highly skilled was the creation of a points-based system. This was new policy direction, not based on employer demand but instead on the supply side: the skills of the individual migrant.

Labour introduced two schemes, the Innovators Scheme and the Highly Skilled Migrant Programme (HSMP). These complemented

Figure 1.1: Number of approved work permits and first permissions, 1995–2005

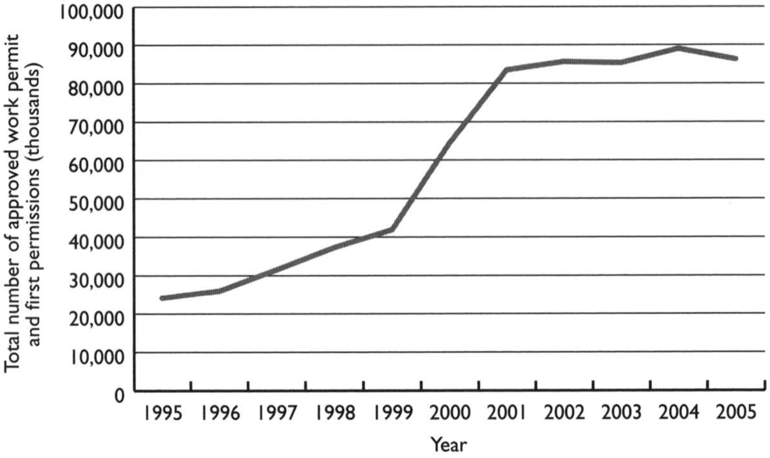

Source: Work Permits (UK); figures adapted from: Salt (2006)

other programmes on the 'supply side', including the Investors or Business Person schemes, which were focused on those with financial rather than human capital. Given the new departure in policy terms, it is worth examining these schemes in more detail.

Announced on 25 July 2000 by the Ministers for Immigration and Competitiveness (Home Office Press Release, 2000), the Innovators Scheme was the first tentative step towards a points-based approach. The scheme, originally set up as a concession outside the Immigration Rules, came into operation on 4 September 2000 and was aimed at attracting entrepreneurs to the UK. Policy makers envisaged that there would be 2,000 applications for each year of the project's duration. Over the course of the two-year pilot, however, the Innovators Scheme attracted just 112 successful applicants, well short of the anticipated numbers. This was largely because it was overtaken by events and, in particular, the creation of the HSMP.

The HSMP (originally called the Skilled Migrant Entry Programme) was introduced in December 2001, having been trailed in David Blunkett's speech to the Labour Party conference in October 2001. The HSMP initially required an applicant to reach 75 points on a scale that awarded points for 'human capital' (such as a person's skills or education) and for 'significant or outstanding achievement'. The first person to gain entry to the UK was David Scott, one of only 12 men to walk on the moon. This was seen as something of a coup as it symbolised what Labour was trying to achieve. The numbers entering under the

HSMP have risen steadily, from 1,197 in 2002 (it was introduced on 1 February of that year), to 4,891 in 2003; 7,358 in 2004 and finally 17,631 in 2005 (Salt, 2006, p 92).

The HSMP has developed over the years. After the first year of its operation, the threshold for entry was made easier. The pass mark was reduced to 65 points and the points total for certain categories was increased. In January 2003, for example, the number of points a prospective immigrant could receive for previous work experience was doubled (from 25 to 50 points). New points categories, such as the qualifications of partners (August 2003) and being under 28 years old (October 2003) were also added.

Several pronouncements from government officials from late 2004 and 2005 indicated that the pendulum had swung too far – that the threshold had become too easy to reach – but it was not until 7 November 2006, when evidence of fraud was discovered, that the HSMP was significantly changed.

New criteria, such as a mandatory language requirement, were added and existing criteria (such as previous employment experience, except for a small bonus if one had specific UK experience) were removed. The points earned for certain categories, such as education, were altered and the pass mark was increased to 75 points (out of an available total of 120).

In 2006, the Masters in Business Administration (MBA) provision was also added to the HSMP, illustrating that policy makers have continued to innovate. This provision allowed those passing the language requirement and gaining an MBA from a list of 50 schools worldwide to immediately gain the 75 points needed for entry to the HSMP.

The HSMP and the Innovators Scheme are major departures from previous economic migration policy, and were aimed at those without significant financial capital but with the potential to achieve.

Low-skilled economic migration

While there has been much attention paid to the highly skilled, there have also been major changes for the low-skilled. The most obvious innovation under Labour was the creation of new low-skill migration routes, called Sector Based Schemes (SBS). The SBS, announced in the 9 April 2003 Budget, were modelled on the Seasonal Agricultural Workers Scheme (SAWS) that had existed since the Second World War.

The difference was in the labour-market sector – the SBS were for the hotel and food-processing sectors – and in the more overt work focus (SAWS included an educational component, typically language learning, that the SBS did not). In 2005, the SBS attracted 7,401 persons, 40 per cent of whom were from Bangladesh and the Ukraine. The SAWS attracted 15,455 persons, 51.2 per cent from the Ukraine and Bulgaria (Salt and Millar, 2006, pp 351–2).

These specific low-skill schemes have not lasted. The SBS were phased out during 2006 and were ended in December 2006. The SAWS will also be phased out, with a projected end date of 2010.

The enlargement of the European Union

Labour has been strongly supportive of an enlarged Europe. This has had a direct impact on policy. The enlargement of the European Union on 1 May 2004 came with the caveat that countries were free to impose restrictions to protect their domestic labour market for a period of up to seven years. Crucially, Labour was one of only three countries that chose not to impose labour restrictions on nationals of the so-called A-8 countries, a decision perfectly in keeping with the new approach to economic migration.

This effect of enlargement has been profound. Between May 2004 and December 2006, 579,000 A-8 migrants registered with the government, 65 per cent of whom were Polish (DWP, 2007, pp 4, 8). Those who resided in the UK without authorisation prior to May 2004 were 'legalised' and a new work route was simultaneously established. The huge inflows also led to a new policy approach: there would no further low-skilled migration from outside the EU (Home Office, 2005a). Thus, the decision to support enlargement and to open borders within the EU directly altered policy, in particular ending the low-skill schemes.

The government did not permit the same labour market access rights to Romanian and Bulgarian nationals following EU accession on 1 January 2007. The political compromise has centred on opening up the labour market gradually. Highly skilled Romanians and Bulgarians can continue to access the UK through the HSMP and other work permit routes, and 'low-skilled' Bulgarian and Romanian nationals were given exclusive access to the SAWS (up to the quota of 19,500 per year) (*Hansard*, 24 October 2006, cols 82–84WS). Of course, all Romanians and Bulgarians are free to move to the UK, but not to work, except in self-employment. Thus, policy on enlargement has also affected other schemes, for example forcing the second major shake-up of SAWS in 2006.

The evolution of managed migration

The Home Office released a blueprint for the development of managed migration for 2005–10 in the form of a five year plan (Home Office, 2005a). In terms of economic migration, it laid out four tiers of economic immigration based on points accrued for skills, shortage occupations, and for students and 'others'. The basic premise was to bring the various categories of economic migrant (at least 22 categories and 80 routes) into one of four tiers based on clear criteria. The plan was followed by a consultation document, *Selective admission*, specifically aimed at the economic migration system (Home Office, 2005d). The simplified points system remained but was expanded to five tiers, related to a grading system of skills.

The outcome of the consultation, *A points-based system*, deserves further discussion as it lays out the future. Tier 1 is aimed at the highly skilled; Tier 2 at skilled workers with a job offer; Tier 3 at low-skill workers; Tier 4 at students; and Tier 5 at 'youth mobility and temporary workers' (Home Office, 2006a).

Tier 1 has subsumed the high skilled supply-side programmes, chiefly the HSMP, but also the Investors and Business Person schemes. It has also subtly changed tack on the nature of who the highly skilled are; the original focus (on those with outstanding achievement) has given way to a strong commitment to youth and to certificated qualifications. This has changed the ethos of the HSMP: from rewarding those of high potential to rewarding those with documented achievement. New provisions (such as the MBA provision) fit the new criteria of youth and qualifications.

Tier 2 incorporates the main body of the work permit system, with advice on shortage occupations provided by a new body. The proposed new body, the Migration Advisory Committee (MAC), will be independent but will not have a policy remit (Home Office, 2006g). The MAC is extremely similar to a proposal in 2005 for a 'Skills Advisory Body', which was to be a pseudo-independent body providing impartial labour market advice to the Home Office. The main difference with this proposal appears to be that the MAC will be complemented by a government-convened forum to examine the social impacts of migration. Such work will be carried out by a newly named Migration Impact Forum (MIF). The new MAC and MIF may therefore be better equipped to take the 'political heat' out the debate. Labour will not be constrained by the MAC, but it will be able to use it as a mechanism to justify particular decisions. Outside of shortage occupations or sectors, the work permit system would still operate, with a Resident Labour Market Test, where employers must prove that they cannot find someone inside the European Economic Area to do the job before applying for a work permit.

Tier 3 incorporates the remaining 'rump': economic migration for 'low skill' jobs. It has been envisaged as a highly restricted migration route. Its restriction is less to do with recognised low-skill shortages and more because it is assumed that low-skill labour will come from an enlarged Europe.

Tier 4 refers to students (discussed in more detail below) and builds on the existing system, largely in more coercive ways, such as by ensuring there are sponsors for students. Tier 5 is described as 'youth mobility and temporary workers' (Home Office, 2006a). This final tier might perhaps be more appropriately termed 'miscellaneous', as it includes five subcategories under temporary workers (Home Office, 2006a, p 35).

Overall, with its focus on points and sponsors (Tiers 2–5 will now require a domestic sponsor), the evolution of managed migration has moved away from an employer-led system to one that is government-led and more focused on control.

Students

Students are not economic migrants but are included under the managed migration 'schema'. Labour has committed to making the UK the most attractive place for international students to study, and policy has consequently become a hotbed of innovation. The numbers have increased dramatically. In 1997, the numbers coming to the UK for formal study (excluding short-term courses) totalled 85,300; by 2004 the numbers had risen to 136,100 (Home Office, 2006f, p 96).

Tony Blair has made a personal commitment to increase the numbers of international students. This has been formalised in two Prime Minister's Initiatives (PMI), the second of which was launched in April 2006. The 2006 PMI overtly aims to increase the numbers of international students by positioning the UK brand more effectively, ensuring a quality experience for international students, focusing on building strategic partnerships and targeting particular countries.

Students are an important part of the managed migration system because they contribute to a number of aims of the economic migration system. While studying, they provide an additional boost to the (low-skill) labour pool, and after finishing their studies they can be retained for high-skilled jobs. Innovative schemes have been created to attract and retain such students. These schemes are biased towards the level of qualification, the subject studied and where students wish to work.

The Science and Engineering Graduates Scheme (SEGS) allows undergraduate students studying certain subjects to remain in the UK for 12 months after graduating (without a job offer and with no restrictions on the type of work). The scheme was extended on 30 March 2006 so that all students graduating with a Masters or a PhD could apply (Somerville, 2006b, pp 46–7). Finally, Labour introduced the first regional scheme with the Fresh Talent: Working in Scotland Scheme (FT:WISS), which allows students who lived in Scotland while studying and who applied within a year of graduating to stay in Scotland for up to two years to work (Somerville, 2006b, p 54).

Moulding pathways for economic migration

Labour inherited an economic migration system made up of a large number of different schemes that had developed in a piecemeal fashion. From 2001, new schemes and measures to facilitate the entry of both low- and high-skilled economic migrants have been introduced (although the enlargement of the European Union after 2004 obviated the need for the low-skill routes). Furthermore, Labour has 'retuned' other migration pathways for the purpose of economic migration. For example, in 2002 changes to the Working Holidaymaker Visa were made to make it more work focused (Somerville, 2004a, pp 20–2).[4] Moreover, the 'transition' between visas has been eased. For example, students can now apply for a work permit, the HSMP or specialist schemes such as SEGS while studying.

In addition to such changes, unauthorised migrant workers have also been brought into the formal economy. While Labour has been strongly opposed to amnesties in public, several policy decisions have amounted to de facto regularisations. For example, the introduction of the SBS was in part justified by reducing unauthorised working, and the decision to allow A-8 migrants the right to work in the UK led to the overnight regularisation of all the nationals from those countries who had been working 'illegally' in the country prior to 2004.

Economic migration policy has therefore undergone profound change between 1997 and 2007 and, more to the point, was a pro-active policy change. The reactive policy changes of the 1980s and early 1990s gave way to a concerted, thought-out policy designed to maximise the potential economic gains of immigration.

Notes

[1] For an overview of the exact nature of the rule-making powers, see the adjournment debate on 12 June 2003 (*Hansard*, 12 June 2003, cols 919–26).

[2] It was previously called the Overseas Labour Service.

[3] GATS is negotiated by the European Commission and member states (so-called 'mixed competencies').

[4] The Working Holidaymaker Visa was substantively changed again in February 2005, away from an economic migration route. It is currently something of a hybrid (see Chapter 14).

TWO

Security: powers to combat the 'illegal' threat

This chapter examines the extent to which new security powers have been aimed at migrants and, secondly, examines the general measures and policies targeted at unauthorised ('illegal') migrants. The two aims of the chapter reflect the number of policy measures (particularly in the aftermath of the terrorist attacks of 9/11) intended to combat a cocktail of issues: unauthorised migration, border security, fraudulent asylum claims, crime, and terrorism.

The theme of 'security' therefore encompasses elements of anti-terror policy and elements of unauthorised ('illegal') migration policy. While the overwhelming majority of unauthorised immigrants do not pose a terrorist threat to the UK, they are discussed together under the theme of security because that is often how they are treated by policy makers. However, such a lens can distort reality, adding to the general view that they are interconnected. As a result, this chapter starts by trying to unpick the discourse of security.

Securitisation

The conflation of different policies under the rhetoric of security, particularly in the wake of the 11 September 2001 attacks, has led some commentators to suggest a *securitisation* of migration policy – in other words, a move by political actors to place the immigration issue on a security agenda to allow them to respond in extraordinary (often emergency-response) ways (Buzan et al, 1998; Zucconi, 2004).

Anti-terror rhetoric

When the political discourse is analysed, there is plenty of evidence to support the claim that policy has been securitised. For example, the major anti-terrorism Act in the period 1997–2007, and the one most closely associated with immigrants, is the 2001 Anti-terrorism, Crime and Security Act. The connection between asylum and terrorism was made explicit as the Bill was going through Parliament. Beverly Hughes, then Minister for Immigration and Citizenship, in reply to challenges that the Bill's scope was too wide, stated that 'all the measures are designed to enhance intelligence and information gathering, to restrict people suspected of involvement in terrorism, *to prevent abuse of asylum* [my emphasis] and to give law enforcement and security agencies powers to tackle the problems that we face' (*Hansard*, 19 November 2001, cols 112–13).

Tony Blair has also used the framework of secure borders and legal migration as an essential tenet of an anti-terror strategy. His final speech to the Labour Party conference as Labour leader was strongly centred on this balance. In framing his speech he said, 'the question today is different to the one we faced in 1997. It is how we reconcile openness to the rich possibilities of globalisation, with security in the face of its threats' (Blair, 2006a). While acknowledging the benefits of immigration to the UK, he asked 'how do we reconcile liberty with security in this new world?' before placing the onus on security: 'but I know that if we don't have rules that allow us some control over who comes in, goes out, who has a right to stay and who has not, then instead of a welcome, migrants find fear.... That is why Identity Cards using biometric technology are not a breach of our basic rights, they are an essential part of responding to the reality of modern migration' (Blair, 2006a). Blair has tended to single out asylum seekers. For example, his press announcement on 5 August 2005, after the London bombings on 7 July 2005 (committed by British citizens, born in Britain), laid out a 12-point plan to combat terrorism which included (Point 3) that asylum would be denied to anyone who had been involved with terrorism (Blair, 2005).

Other politicians have linked security and migration policy in comments entirely consistent with the rhetoric of the Prime Minister. Most bluntly, then Home Secretary David Blunkett stated to the House of Commons in 2001 that 'our moral obligation and love of freedom does not extend to offering hospitality to terrorists' (*Hansard*, 15 October 2001, col 923–4). However, of all the Labour Home Secretaries, John Reid stands out as the person who most fiercely proselytises the link between security and migration. His approach is neatly summed up by a speech in September 2006, where he emphasised the insecurity of the modern world and the fear it engenders: 'that fear and feeling of unfairness is most evident today in relation to mass migration. It isn't fair when desperate people fleeing persecution who need asylum are put at risk because criminal gangs abuse an antiquated asylum system. It isn't fair when someone illegally enters our country and jumps the queue ... That's why I favour tighter immigration controls and ID cards' (Reid, 2006).

Gordon Brown has focused less on connecting unauthorised migration with security and more on measures to undermine the finances behind terrorism. But he has also posited the view that policy to promote common values, identity and the integration of migrants is important as a counter-terrorism strategy. For example, in his first major speech on terrorism he stated that 'after July 7th ... we asked anew whether we had done enough to encourage and support the integration of people of different ethnicities and faiths into our country and suddenly dry debates about citizenship and Britishness had both a meaning and urgency for our times and for our generation' (Brown, 2006b).

From rhetoric to measures

The above examples of political discourse show that aspects of migration have been filed under the heading 'security'. But how far has political rhetoric translated into migration policy measures?

The 2001 Anti-terrorism, Crime and Security Act was, crucially, passed under emergency measures (the state of emergency was the threat of further terrorist attacks following 9/11). In practice, this meant parliamentary scrutiny was sacrificed for speed. The measures that most affected immigrants were concentrated in Part 4 of the Act and included that suspected terrorists who were immigrants could be interned regardless of the decision on deportation (and therefore potentially on a permanent basis). Independent review of such decisions was allowed by the Special Immigration Appeals Commission (SIAC), but no judicial review of their decisions was permitted.

Furthermore, there is something of a legislative 'pattern' between 1997 and 2007 where discrete portions of individual anti-terror legislation are devoted to asylum and immigration and vice versa, entrenching the connection between the two in law. The best example of this was in the passage of the 2006 Immigration, Asylum and Nationality (IAN) Act. The relevant migration measures in Tony Blair's 12-point plan to counter terrorism found their way almost verbatim into amendments placed in the House of Commons committee stage of the 2005 Immigration, Asylum and Nationality (IAN) Bill. The changes remained in the final legislation (sections 53–59 of the 2006 Act); for example, section 54 in the 2006 Act states that asylum would be denied to terrorists and to those who encouraged others to commit terrorism and is a direct echo of Point 3 of Blair's plan.

Other changes included the introduction of a 'good character' test for persons entitled to register for British citizenship. The 'good charactei test may remind readers that the security theme cannot be divorced from the theme of 'integration' (the subject of the next chapter). The debate about the 'failure' of multiculturalism and the need for measures such as citizenship tests and ceremonies is part of a move to treat immigrant integration as a way of moderating potential terrorism. Muslim communities in particular appear to be the target of such policy measures.

The political rhetoric on security has thus translated directly into some measures, but anti-terror policy is broader than legislative clauses in certain Acts. Hampshire and Saggar (2005) note that various control measures, on border controls, asylum restrictions, acquisition and removal of citizenship, and deportation orders 'amount to a significant expansion of the state's discretionary powers over migrants and non-nationals'. There is insufficient space to detail all such measures here, but an analysis of the UK's anti-terrorism strategy, known as Project Contest, with a view to examining the measures in the strategy targeted at migrants, is revealing.

Project Contest

The UK's anti-terrorism strategy was initiated by David Blunkett and developed during 2002. Blunkett reported progress on the development of the strategy to Parliament in 2003, saying that 'since the terrorist attacks in the United States on 11 September 2001, the Government has conducted a thorough and comprehensive review of all preventative measures to counter terrorism to better protect this country from the threat from international terrorism. We have taken major steps to enhance the security of the UK's borders' (*Hansard*, 16 October 2003, cols 319–20W). This review led to the formal anti-terror strategy to combat terrorism, known as 'Contest' or 'Project Contest', and was in place from 2003 to 2006. John Reid announced the next stages of the development of the Contest strategy to Parliament in July 2006, when he said further refinements to the strategy had been made. The counter-terrorism Contest strategy was published in July 2006 (Home Office, 2006e).

When John Reid presented the update to Parliament, he made little mention of migration, save for an analysis of threats that included a brief allusion to 'mass migration' (*Hansard*, 10 July 2006, col 1115). This may imply that there were no migrant measures in the strategy, but analysis of the detail reveals there were two sets of relevant measures: deportations and border controls.

The strategy states in relation to deportations that:

where the person concerned is a foreign national, and is a threat to the UK, deportation will usually be an appropriate means of disrupting terrorist activity. This is important in terms of ensuring public safety, as well as sending a strong signal that foreign nationals who threaten our national security cannot expect to be allowed to remain in the UK. (Home Office, 2006e, p 18)

Border controls are the second point, with the strategy focusing on the ongoing programme of electronic border management (e-borders) and biometric controls as well as an emphasis on information sharing. In addition, it is clear that the Contest strategy has 'absorbed' the Prime Minister's statement of 5 August 2005, where he laid out his response to the London bombings. Appendix A of Project Contest is dedicated to a summary of progress against the 12 points outlined in the statement (Home Office, 2006e, pp 30–2). In short, the strategy contains some anti-terror measures directed at migrants, but, importantly, these measures are not the major focus of the strategy.

It therefore appears there is valid evidence for the 'securitisation' of some aspects of the migration debate; particularly at the level of rhetoric, but also at the level of policy. There have been clear examples of anti-terror policy measures, introduced under 'security concerns', that target migrants (and especially asylum seekers). Furthermore, recent institutional changes, including the establishment of a streamlined Home Office with a focus on crime, terrorism and immigration, are likely to cement the new security framework.

However, it is important to keep these measures in perspective. As Christina Boswell (2007) has argued strongly, there has been an 'absence' of securitisation for much of migration policy.[1] This is particularly true of certain dimensions of migration policy, such as the theme of the previous chapter, economic migration policy. There has been no discussion of security measures (either in the political rhetoric or in policy measures) in respect to the Points-based System, for instance.

Unauthorised migration

The issue of unauthorised ('illegal') migration has been high on the agenda throughout the 10 years of Labour government. As asylum numbers have dropped, the issue has become even more important. The publication of an estimate of the size of the illegal (unauthorised) population – 430,000 or 0.7 per cent of the population (Woodbridge, 2005, p 1) – further heightened concerns.

The publication of the IND reform plan in July 2006, *Fair, effective, transparent and trusted: Rebuilding confidence in our immigration system* (Home Office, 2006d), together with the 'vision' of secure borders (Home Office, 2007b) and an enforcement strategy (Home Office, 2007a), both released in March 2007, heralded significant development of policies on unauthorised migration. The Home Secretary John Reid and Immigration Minister Liam Byrne have made unauthorised (illegal) migration their top priority.

However, while there are new elements to these recent reforms, such as proposed embarkation controls by 2014 (Home Office, 2006d), most are an acceleration of the thinking in the 2002 White Paper which approached the issue of unauthorised migration as one of 'tackling fraud' and 'organised immigration crime' (Home Office, 2002a, p 76).[2] In explaining organised immigration crime, the problem was acknowledged as complex, requiring new measures on illegal working and trafficking; more international cooperation and cooperation across government; prevention in source and transit countries; and enforcement and intelligence operations (Home Office, 2002a, p 77).

Labour has introduced a plethora of policy measures to deal with this multi-dimensional problem, from criminal laws increasing the penalties for trafficking, to the creation of a code of practice on non-discrimination for employers. There are four main 'groups' of measures:

1. Strategic enforcement measures
2. Identity management
3. Increasing employer compliance
4. Joining up, in and between governments.

Strategic enforcement measures

Enforcement against unauthorised migrants has developed since 1997, becoming more strategic in terms of whom measures are directed against. Operations have become overtly aimed at the 'worst' offenders – for example businesses that employ significant numbers of unauthorised migrants. Enforcement units have made a smaller number of high-profile, high-impact raids rather than general sweeps. This approach is referred to as 'intelligence-led' enforcement (Home Office, 1998, para 6.12). In 2007, the 'organising principle' behind enforcement measures was elucidated in the Home Office's enforcement strategy – action was directed towards those who caused the most *harm* (Home Office, 2007a, p 11; see also 2006d). This approach echoes the recommendations of the Home Affairs Select Committee report on immigration control, produced the previous year (Home Affairs Select Committee, 2006b).

The resources for enforcement have also increased, particularly from 2002. In 2003, funding for Reflex, the immigration crime taskforce, was trebled (Home Office Press Release, 2003b). The Serious Organised Crime Agency (SOCA), launched on 3 April 2006, has placed organised immigration crime as its second-top priority, apportioning 25 per cent of its operational effort to it (Thorp 2007, p 12). The 2006 review of IND led to further resources for enforcement, with the recruitment of 800 new immigration officers announced on 20 November 2006 (*Guardian*, 2006). Further increases in resources were promised in the 2007 strategy on enforcement: by April 2009, funding for enforcement and compliance is set to double (Home Office, 2007a, p 4).

Identity management

There has been a conscious investment in and promulgation of new technologies, introduced under the rubric of identity management. Examples include the Asylum Registration Card (an identity card for asylum seekers); biometric visas; and increased detection equipment in airports and ports, which includes devices such as scanners, passive millimetre wave machines, carbon dioxide probes, and heartbeat detectors (Home Office, 2006k, p 18).

Identity cards have become central to Labour's policy response to unauthorised immigration. The government waited until the consultation in the summer of 2002 to formally announce its support for identity cards but an earlier proposal of an 'entitlement' card found in the 2002 White Paper suggests Labour was considering such a solution much earlier (Home Office, 2002a, p 82). By 2004, the Regulatory Impact Assessment for the Identity Cards Bill highlighted their aim clearly: Objective (a) specifically refers to illegal migration and illegal working. The accompanying press release described identity cards as crucial to tackling 'crime, terrorism and illegal immigration' (Home Office Press Release, 2004). Furthermore, politicians have regularly used unauthorised immigration as a justification for identity cards. In November 2006, for example, Prime Minister Tony Blair led a concerted effort to sell identity cards on the grounds that they would combat illegal immigration and terrorism (BBC News, 2006c).

In December 2006, two 'action plans' were published which have provided much of the detail of future policy. The first, a *Strategic action plan for the national identity scheme* (Home Office, 2006j) was notable largely because it stated that the government would use three existing databases, rather than a new, stand-alone database, to store the information underpinning the identity card system (Thorp, 2007, p 22). More importantly, it made clear that the scheme would provide a 'comprehensive identity management service for all those who legally reside and work in the UK' (Home Office, 2006j, p 6). The goal of including all foreign nationals has become pivotal.

These developments were given substance with the publication of the second plan, the *Borders, immigration and identity action plan* (Home Office, 2006i), which lays out an approach of providing foreign nationals with a biometric visa that can be checked against national databases in the UK (pre-travel). The document can also be used to check entitlement to work and to benefits. This will be made compulsory in 2008 for all foreign nationals coming to the UK for longer than six months. Biometric visas for foreign nationals will be, in essence, a trial run of identity card technology. The Home Office has also set out milestones for implementation. By 2007, the criteria for the Visa Waiver Test (a test to decide which countries require biometric visa application processes) will be completed; by 2008, biometric visas will be introduced worldwide; and by 2011, 95 per cent of passengers will be checked in and out of the UK (Home Office, 2007b, p 4).

Increasing employer compliance

Labour has made a concerted effort to corral employers into supporting immigration control. There have been two stages to this effort between 1997 and 2007. First, an attempt to improve employment verification procedures (best viewed as a stop-gap measure to prevent unauthorised migrants gaining employment). Second, a more comprehensive policy approach aimed at tightening verification through a system of financial penalties for employers who do not comply.

The 2002 Act changed the rules on employing 'illegal' workers. The original rules, known as 'Section 8', were amended so employees had to show verifiable document(s), proving they were legal, in order to work.[3] The year after the new rules came into force (May 2004), the 2005 Immigration, Asylum and Nationality (IAN) Bill was presented to Parliament. The Bill devoted significant attention to the problem of illegal working and the role of employers, offering more comprehensive reform. The subsequent 2006 IAN Act contained a range of new obligations, restrictions and penalties (sections 15–26), such as annual employment verification checks on all employees to ensure they were legally allowed to work and, in particular, a civil penalty scheme, with employers facing a fine of £2,000 for each unauthorised worker, underpinned by a new offence of knowingly employing an illegal worker.

The new Points-based System plan also makes the concept of sponsorship fundamental to the operation of the system (Home Office, 2007a, p 13). This will involve a 'certificate of sponsorship' and progressively less bureaucracy for employers who meet the requirements. A new Employer Task Force has been established to consult on the changes, which will be implemented in stages (Home Office, 2007b, pp 10–11).

Coordination and cooperation

Labour has consistently emphasised greater coordination, both in government and between governments. The approach to joining up internally has centred on introducing measures to increase the conditionality of service provision. Examples include implementing regulations to restrict access to secondary healthcare and ensuring that schools teaching the children of unauthorised migrants must register that fact with the correct authority. Both measures have been greeted with a distinct lack of enthusiasm in the health and education sectors (Duvell and Jordan, 2003, p 312).

There has been less opposition to operational coordination with law enforcement agencies. For example, the Home Office established a major immigration crime taskforce called Reflex, designed to enhance multi-agency working and, from 2006, there have also been pilot programmes to test new ways that local government can work together with immigration enforcement (Home Office, 2005d, p 34). The joining-up of law enforcement agencies took a more formal form in 2006 under the banner of the 'Border Management Programme'. The programme falls short of Conservative Party proposals for a border police, but has formalised cooperation. The Home Office has made it clear that 'formal agreements on inter-agency collaboration' will be developed by July 2007, between the Border and Immigration Agency, HMRC, Police, SOCA, and UKvisas (Home Office, 2007b, p 20).

Labour has enthusiastically supported greater cooperation between governments on unauthorised migration, and has generated a series of inputs into policy, such as on ideas for expanding common border cooperation. For example, Home Secretary John Reid presented an (unpublished) working document on behalf of the UK, Germany and others to the informal JHA meeting in the second half of 2006 (German Presidency Press Release, 2007). This document included recommendations which found their way – in a different form – into the Presidency conclusions of December 2006 (EU Council, 2006). This type of cooperation has been a feature of Labour in Europe in contrast to the Conservative government's approach prior to 1997.

While measures have been passed by the EU Council on unauthorised migration, most of the policy development work has been carried out at the bureaucratic or operational level (EU Council, 2006). For example, there has been strong support for the development of the common border security agency, FRONTEX and for data exchange (EU Council, 2006, paragraph 24c). Labour has also supported exchanges of information (particular on biometric data) outside of the EU. For example, the UK is working with the 'Four Countries Group' (UK, USA, Canada and Australia) to develop a framework for data sharing that will be operational by 2009 (Home Office, 2007b, p 23).

Regularisation

There has been no official amnesty or regularisation and no senior minister has been able to float it as a serious policy option. Even Liam Byrne, the Immigration Minister, was immediately overruled by the Prime Minister for having had the effrontery to tell the Home Affairs Select Committee on 13 June 2006, 11 days into his job, that he was not ruling it out as a policy option. (It was – in effect – ruled out for him.)

Nonetheless, there is a further layer to policy. Policy decisions on EU enlargement, as discussed earlier, reduced the number of unauthorised migrants and were part of the rationale behind those decisions. More concretely, there have been two major backlog-clearing exercises since 1997 which have been amnesties in all but name. This included a major exercise for asylum seekers, which has now applied to 24,415 main applicants, with a further 8,540 considered under 'another Family ILR application' (Home Office, 2007d, p 11).

Summary

This chapter has examined the tangled issue of security and unauthorised (illegal) migration. Migrants have been brought further under the auspices of security powers and laws, but direct policy measures have lagged behind the rhetoric of ministers. Moreover, certain groups, notably asylum seekers, have been targeted by the new powers, rather than all migrants equally.

—

Unauthorised (illegal) migration has always been on the agenda but became a priority in 2005 with the publication of an estimate of 430,000 illegal immigrants residing in the UK. Labour has taken a range of policy steps to combat unauthorised migration, the majority of which have been outside of an overt anti-terrorism frame of reference. They include new enforcement and identity management policies, compliance measures, and greater cooperation and coordination, especially with other governments. There has also been an official position vehemently against regularisation, but it has been a dimension of policy decisions nonetheless. The current phase of immigration policy making has much to do with securing borders to prevent unauthorised flows, and this has become the top migration policy priority.

Notes

[1] Boswell does acknowledge that some restrictive security measures have impacted on asylum seekers and notes that the situation for the integration of Muslims is somewhat different (Boswell, 2007).

[2] The 2002 White Paper was published after 9/11 and shows that while unauthorised migration is linked to security concerns, it is also framed in the contexts of crime and border control.

[3] 'Section 8', from the 1996 Immigration Act, made it unlawful to employ someone without permission to work and placed a duty on employers to check workers' documentation.

THREE

Integration: a new pivot for policy?

In December 2006 Tony Blair stated, 'We like our diversity. But how do we react when that "difference" leads to separation and alienation from the values that define what we hold in common? For the first time in a generation there is an unease ... [that] ... our willingness to welcome difference ... is being used against us' (Blair, 2006b).

Questions of 'integration' have been high on the public and political agenda from 2001. Three issues in particular have been at the forefront of debates. The first, often prompted by Labour politicians, has been a debate on 'common values' (Geddes, 2003). The second, prompted by a famous essay by David Goodhart, is the seeming division between diversity and solidarity (Goodhart, 2004). The third, following the 9/11 and 7/7 terrorist attacks, is the concern over security and its implicit, if not an explicit, focus on Muslims.

This chapter examines the policy concerns that make up the 'integration' debate. It explores what integration means, unravels Labour's 'Janus-faced' approach to policy, and examines discrete elements of policy, including the subtext of much of integration discourse – Muslims.

'Integration' is a complex area in which to record policy changes. Integration policy was one of the two migration policy pillars during the period of immigration settlement between 1948 and 1976.[1] Then, integration policy was aimed at first-generation immigrants, whereas by 1997 it had become associated with ethnic minorities (second, third, and fourth generations). It is perhaps useful to start, therefore, with an interpretation of integration policy – later labelled as 'multiculturalism' – from this former period. The best shorthand description remains that of Roy Jenkins, the Labour Home Secretary, who pithily described multiculturalism in 1967 as 'not a flattening process of assimilation but equal opportunity accompanied by cultural diversity in an atmosphere of mutual tolerance'.[2] This interpretation is embedded in the concept of the 'race relations model' that was enshrined in several laws in the 1960s and 1970s, culminating in the 1976 Race Relations Act.

A number of commentators have suggested that the integration measures adopted by Labour mark a departure from Jenkins' multiculturalist model (McGhee, 2006, p 119; Robinson and Reeve, 2006). They cite policy developments that move toward assimilation such as the requirements to take an oath to the Queen as part of the citizenship ceremony, to pass a new citizenship test that requires knowledge of British institutions, and to possess a proficient level of English before a person can be naturalised. Such measures are part of a trend. In 2006 the requirement to have a certain level of English proficiency was extended to cover all those applying for long-term residence (irrespective of whether they apply for citizenship).

However, other commentators have pointed towards developments in a more multicultural vein, citing, for example, the passing of the 2000 Race Relations (Amendment) Act, which, for the first time, attempted to address institutionalised racism. These conflicting views of the direction of integration policy under New Labour are often labelled the 'two faces' of the Labour government (Back et al, 2002b).

Sociologists have often portrayed the differing views along a continuum between assimilation and multiculturalism. However, 'integration' is not so easily defined and has a series of overlapping meanings that have developed since the 1930s (Bosswick and Heckman, 2006, pp 2–6). Integration has been pilloried as a 'treacherous concept' (Banton, 2001, pp 151-2) or as a definitional mirage: it is 'one of the most dazzling phrases' (Bommes and Kolb, 2004, p 5). In short, integration introduces other frames of reference into the debate that do not fit easily on the multiculturalism–assimilation plane, particularly at the policy level.

Notably, in the UK discourse, integration policy includes 'social exclusion' and 'community cohesion'. In fact central government and statutory agencies have employed wider expressions such as social cohesion, community cohesion, active citizenship, civil renewal, and social inclusion when referring to the concept of integration. The still-developing terminology has led to intense debate on what indicators should be used to measure integration and on policy concepts, objectives and effects (Parekh, 1988, 2000; Favell, 1998; Rudiger and Spencer, 2003). The most recent authoritative literature review highlights 'a serious lack of data and other factual knowledge' with regard to integration (Castles et al, 2002, p ii).

Policy measures making up integration

The following section groups various policy measures under terminologies promoted by Labour; including race equality and race relations, community cohesion, social exclusion and inclusion, and citizenship. First, however, the UK's only targeted integration policy – that aimed at refugees – is examined.

Refugee integration

Labour's policy on refugee integration has taken the form of strategic policy development, specific resources and specific government machinery. There have been two strategies. The first, *Full and equal citizens: A strategy to integrate refugees* (Home Office, 2000), followed a consultation in 1999 and prepared the ground for specific funding of integration. The second, more comprehensive, strategy, in 2005, *Integration matters: The national refugee integration strategy* (Home Office, 2005c), proposed a coordinated case-worker system and refugee 'loans' that would aid integration. At the same time as *Integration matters* was released, the Department for Work and Pensions published *Working to rebuild lives* (DWP, 2005b), a strategy for increasing refugee employment which focused on improving the employment outcomes of refugees.

The Home Office, by dedicating specific resources to refugee integration, has brought voluntary and not-for-profit organisations into the mainstream delivery of services. The importance of the third sector was formalised in 2001 with the creation of a government-sponsored forum, the National Refugee Integration Forum (NRIF). The NRIF was reorganised in late 2005/early 2006 and abruptly abolished in October 2006.

It is not entirely clear why refugees have been singled out for particular attention but it is likely to be a combination of a moral argument, the reality that the dispersal of asylum seekers has brought more actors and regions into the debate, and that such work helps the government meet targets on ethnic minorities. However, the strategy expressly excludes asylum seekers, making clear that 'integration' starts only when a positive decision on an asylum application has been made.

Race equality and race relations

The key development in matters of race equality is the 2000 Race Relations (Amendment) Act. At the centre of the Act was the Race Equality Duty, a policy measure designed to eradicate institutionalised racism by obligating public authorities, including the police and immigration services, to take action to correct ethnic inequalities.

However, the extension of race relations legislation to immigration functions came with exceptions. Discrimination against immigrants, for example, can be authorised under section 19 of the Act and such authorised discrimination has been widely applied, for example, in asylum processing (for more details, see Coussey, 2004, 2005). However, despite these exemptions and implementation issues (for an overview, see Fredman and Spencer, 2006), it has become increasingly standard for local and national government to include the needs of migrants, especially refugees, in the planning and delivery of services.

In addition to the law, Labour has placed greater emphasis on race equality by assigning both a cross-cutting target on race equality and a cross-cutting race equality strategy *Improving opportunity, strengthening society* (Home Office, 2005b). The strategy is overseen by a board made up of senior figures from across the public sector.

The Commission for Racial Equality (CRE) remains at the centre of the institutions that work on racial equality. From 2003, the CRE has enthusiastically supported, even instigated, the terminology of 'integration'.[3] Trevor Phillips, who became chair of the CRE in March 2003, made integration[4] central to CRE business, both politically (he remains a New Labour insider) and in the media. The ethos of his tenure – one that attracted both criticism and plaudits – can perhaps be summed up as a 'whole society' approach. In particular, he has been strongly critical of policies that are perceived as promoting separation between communities. Famously, he was quoted as saying that multiculturalism is 'dead'.

More importantly, the government mainstreamed the integration agenda during Trevor Phillips' tenure. The CRE successfully pushed for new integration 'machinery' within government, initially proposing a 'new body' to deal with such issues. In May 2006, responsibilities for 'integration' moved from the Home Office to the Department of Communities and Local Government (CLG).

However, while the CRE has consistently pushed for anti-discrimination law to cover immigration functions (see, for example, CRE, 1985), it is rare that the Commission will publicly question the direction of *immigration* policy. For example, on the 25th anniversary of the CRE on 16 May 2002, the then chair, Gurbux Singh, suggested that we 'fail to give positive messages [on migration, and] we fail to challenge negative headlines' (Singh, 2002). The following day, Lord Rooker, Minister of State for Citizenship and Immigration, publicly denounced the speech as 'ill-informed' – the first Labour minister to chastise the CRE since Labour was elected (*Guardian*, 2002).

In further change, both symbolic and substantive, the Commission for Racial Equality is scheduled to cease in October 2007 when it will merge with other equality bodies to form the Commission for Equality and Human Rights (CEHR).

Community cohesion

The term 'community cohesion' became widely used in the aftermath of the 2001 riots in the northern cities of Bradford, Burnley and Oldham. The government-ordered report on the riots was written by the independent Community Cohesion Review Team, chaired by Ted Cantle (Cantle, 2001). The Cantle review was one of several reports published at the time, which also included a ministerial report (Home Office, 2001) and geographically specific inquiries into events in Burnley and Oldham (Burnley Taskforce, 2002; Oldham Independent Panel Review, 2001).

The Cantle report raised concerns of segregation, where communities lead 'parallel lives'. The concept, like that of integration, has been critiqued both as 'fuzzy', with little input in setting the definition from communities themselves (Temple and Moran, 2005, especially pp 9–10, 46–7) and as a political response to the riots (Burnett, 2004). Regardless, community cohesion soon moved from a concept to a discrete policy agenda, with the creation of the Community Cohesion Unit (CCU) in the Home Office and the issuance of guidance to local authorities, *Building a picture of community cohesion* (Home Office, 2003d), on how to mainstream community cohesion objectives (Robinson, 2005, pp 1411–12). While 10 measures were included in the guidance, the *key* indicator used for community cohesion has been a perception measure: the percentage of people who feel that their local area is a place where people from different backgrounds can get on well together.

More recently, community cohesion has broadened its scope to include *religious* as well as cultural differences. This change in focus was reflected in government institutions when the Community Cohesion Unit was renamed the Cohesion and Faiths Unit.

Social exclusion and social inclusion

Labour has employed the terminology of social exclusion more frequently than that of social inclusion. The government's Social Exclusion Unit defines 'social exclusion' as a series of linked problems such as substance abuse and teenage pregnancy, a multi-dimensional concept of deprivation. Labour's social exclusion policy (its approach to poverty and deprivation) can be summarised as moving people into the labour market (Levitas, 1998). Consequently, the government has adopted a number of reforms to reduce unemployment and economic inactivity (particularly for disadvantaged groups), and to 'activate' welfare benefits for both economic and social goals (Powell, 2002; Finn, 2003; Hills, 2004). The annual reports *Opportunity for all* record progress and audits action on the various reforms.

The relevance of these reforms to immigrants may not be immediately apparent, even though they are aimed at combating social exclusion, because *migrants* are not characterised as a group in need of support (with the exception of refugees). Instead, they are subsumed under the heading 'ethnic minorities' who receive other forms of targeted support. (Such support is usually area-based, but targeted employment support exists, such as the work programme spearheaded by the Ethnic Minority Employment Taskforce.)

Citizenship

Citizenship – its entitlements, parameters, and how it affects identity – is a major subject in its own right (Aleinikoff and Klusmeyer, 2002, p 1) and since 1997, as Nick Pearce (2005) has aptly described, the UK has undergone a 'quiet revolution in its citizenship policies'.

The major changes to citizenship policy were heralded by the 2003 report of the 'Life in the UK' advisory committee. The committee, established by David Blunkett and chaired by Sir Bernard Crick, issued a report that focused heavily on the *promotion* of citizenship (Home Office, 2003b). Most of the report's recommendations were accepted and policies such as citizenship ceremonies (first piloted in February 2004), citizenship tests (which came into force in October 2005), and a language requirement for naturalisation (a basic knowledge of English, Scottish, Welsh or Gaelic) were introduced.

Labour has actively promoted debates on nationality and what it means to be 'British'. Gordon Brown has suggested a national day of celebration, for example, (Brown, 2006a), while other measures such as section 56 of the 2006 Immigration, Asylum and Nationality Act permitted the Home Secretary to remove British citizenship from dual nationals more easily.

The emphasis on citizenship values is a new phenomenon. Citizenship policy after the 1948 Nationality Act, culminating in the 1981 British Nationality Act, aimed to realign nationality rights with immigration rights. Requirements for naturalisation were relatively consistent and involved a largely passive application process. However, citizenship policy under Labour has shifted the focus away from immigration control and more towards democratic civic participation by equipping migrants practically for 'Life in the UK'. The existing cultural guidance is largely pragmatic, with explanations of how Britain is governed, the law and individual rights.

Family migration

While family reunion constitutes a major immigration stream, few policies associated with family migrants have been enacted, compared with those for other immigrant groups. The policy developments related to family migration focus almost exclusively on values and, in particular, on chain migration.

Chain migration refers to the practice whereby new migrants sponsor family members to join them. The 'end' to chain migration was made explicit in the government's five-year plan, which stated that 'we will end the practice where those who have settled on a family reunion basis can themselves immediately sponsor further family members' (Home Office, 2005a, p 22). Policies concerning marriages have largely centred on stopping forced marriages. Direct measures have included the creation of a joint government strategy and a government unit – the Forced Marriage Unit – to investigate alleged cases. Labour has also committed to a consultation on a code of practice for couples applying for marriage that would involve an in-depth interview. Indirect measures have included increasing the legal age for a spouse to gain a visa from 16 to 18 (Ensor and Shah, 2005, p 5). The latest Home Office strategy indicates that the age will be raised again, from 18 to 21 (Home Office, 2007b, p 13). Perhaps most significantly, the Home Office has recently considered whether prospective spouses should pass a 'Life in the UK' test, which includes a language requirement (Home Office, 2007b, p 13).

However, the UK also has a softer face with regard to family migration. For example, unlike many other countries, it allows cohabiting partners to enter as family migrants. Furthermore, in 1997 family reunion was eased considerably when the government abandoned the primary purpose rule, as discussed in the introduction. The Human Rights Act (especially Article 8) has also given family rights a stronger legal base.

Muslim communities

It is not possible to discuss 'integration' without a brief appraisal of where Muslim communities 'fit' in the picture. Recent integration debates have increasingly centred on Muslim communities, and two pivotal aspects lie within this discussion – policies that have increased the rights of Muslims and responded to Muslim concerns, and measures designed to counter Muslims' (possibly radical) 'separateness' from UK society.

First, Labour has increased government engagement with Muslim communities. Particularly during its first term, the party maintained a consistently supportive position to the main umbrella body for Muslim organisations, the Muslim Council for Britain (MCB), which was created six months after the 1997 election victory. It also made a point of appointing several Muslim peers, such as Nazir Ahmed in 1998, to the House of Lords. Further, in the aftermath of the July 2005 bombings, Tony Blair consulted a group of Muslim community leaders and thinkers to seek their advice on designing policy initiatives that would provide a community response to the attacks. The final report, *Preventing extremism together* (PET), brought together a number of recommendations for government (Home Office, 2005g). Similarly, the Commission on Integration and Cohesion had a clear focus on Muslim communities.

More recently, the Department of Communities and Local Government (CLG) produced a strategy document that plots the short-term engagement policy. First, the government is committed to 'shared values' and hopes to instil such values by extending citizenship education into supplementary schools, for example. Second, it supports actions at the local level through a new funding mechanism for local responses to extremism. Third, it aims to 'rebalance' consultations by engaging with organisations explicitly on the basis of shared values (CLG, 2007).

Significantly, Labour has also acted on such dialogue, introducing several policy measures in response to Muslim concerns. In 2006, on the third attempt, Labour passed the 2006 Racial and Religious Hatred Act, legislation long promoted by Muslim advocates. Labour has also implemented several of the PET recommendations, albeit the minor ones.

However, the other side of the debate has been more prominent and has seen Labour posit a link between Muslim communities and several aspects of 'security'. Palpable concern over 'home-grown terrorism' and the perception that Muslim communities are 'segregated' underlies much of the preoccupation with 'core values'. For example, the ever-precise Foreign Secretary Margaret Beckett, in a speech on 'Trans-national Terrorism', stated that 'when fellow Muslims speak up against extremism and correct the skewed world-view of the terrorists, it is much more powerful', remarks interpreted as urging Muslims to do more to combat extremism from 'within'. She ended by saying it was necessary to 'stake out our common ground, our common values and defend them with resolve and with strength, then we will, together, defeat terrorism' (Beckett, 2006). Similarly, since 2005, politicians have increasingly sidelined the MCB, especially since Ruth Kelly took over at CLG.

The political rhetoric has revolved around ensuring that Muslims share 'core values', and do not support an anti-Western doctrine supportive of 'terrorism'. Tony Blair made this crystal clear when he suggested that there was 'a new and virulent form of ideology associated with a minority of our Muslim community. It is not a problem with Britons of Hindu, Afro-Caribbean, Chinese or Polish origin' (Blair, 2006b). Initiatives aimed at reducing 'segregation', such as Blair's 2006 proposal to make community funding contingent on community integration (Blair, 2006b) or measures to combat forced marriages, also try to address the integration of Muslims into the UK. Political efforts have been made to advocate 'similarities' instead of 'differences' between the Muslim and non-Muslim communities, epitomised in the debates over whether Muslim women should be allowed to wear the niqab. It is important to note that the extent of 'difference' on the UK's heterogeneous Muslim community remains an open question. (For an emphasis on difference, see Leiken (2005); for an opposite view: Maxwell (2006)).

The analysis of integration policy and Muslims goes beyond debates on migration, but the association of terrorism with Muslims, combined with perceptions of segregation and difference, is a crucial component to understanding shifts in integration policy.

The tidal quality of rights under Labour

The various components that make up integration policy – race relations, community cohesion and citizenship, among others – can be difficult to conceptualise 'in the round'. To get a purchase on the debate, the remainder of this chapter analyses immigrant integration from an individual rights perspective by discussing two conflicting developments in rights protection for migrants.

The advance of rights

The major advance has been in enshrining the European Convention on Human Rights (ECHR) into UK law in the form of the 1998 Human Rights Act (HRA). In particular, all migrants, but particularly asylum seekers, have certain rights vis-à-vis deportation. Article 3 (no one shall be subjected to torture or degrading treatment), contains the provision against *refoulement*, which prohibits the forcible deportation of migrants to countries that practise torture (Lambert, 1999). Furthermore, forced migrants are more likely to be awarded temporary protection status[5] as a result of the Human Rights Act.

More broadly, Article 1 of the European Convention of Human Rights (ECHR) guarantees rights and freedoms of everyone within state jurisdiction. The 1998 Human Rights Act, with its status of higher law, has entrenched these rights in the English legal system. It is often noted that the ECHR was binding in the UK and the HRA therefore simply enshrined existing obligations. There is a subtle assumption within this type of commentary that rights would exist without the HRA. This is not without merit, but does not credit the extent of the HRA's impact. Human rights arguments can not only be heard in all domestic courts in the UK but the structure of the HRA also allows all international human rights law to be heard – not simply jurisprudence from the ECHR. Given that the courts previously only allowed arguments to be used from English law ('common law'), this is a major departure.

Importantly, this was the intention of policy makers. Jack Straw, Home Secretary at the time, made the advance of rights explicit to the development of migration policy in his foreword to the 1998 White Paper in which he wrote, 'The government's approach to immigration control reflects our wider commitment to fairness … The Human Rights Bill currently going through Parliament will prove a landmark in the development of a fair and reasonable relationship between individuals and the state in this country' (Home Office, 1998).

There have also been other legislative developments that have increased rights protection. These include European directives (for example on Temporary Protection) and the 2004 Gangmasters (Licensing) Act. The latter Act was prompted by the exploitation of migrants and originated as a Private Member's Bill by the Labour MP Jim Sheridan, with the backing of a coalition put together by the Transport and General Workers Union. The measure gained wider support in response to the February 2004 Morecambe Bay tragedy, where 23 Chinese cockle pickers were drowned. The Act established the Gangmasters Licensing Authority in February 2005, which aims to improve conditions in the agriculture and fisheries sectors by regulating employers and ensuring adequate health and safety measures exist.

While not 'sanctioned' by policy makers, UK jurisprudence has increased rights, particularly for refugees. For example, the House of Lords decided in the 1999 *Islam and Shah* case[6] that women constituted a social group and faced gender persecution, widening the definition of a 'refugee'. This has been interpreted progressively by the Home Office to also include persecution on grounds of sexual orientation (UKLGIG, 2004). The 2004 *Ullah and Do* and *Razgar* cases[7] extended the scope of the application of the ECHR, widening the gateway of protection for asylum seekers (Symes, 2004).

Finally, as previously discussed, there have been various advances to anti-discrimination legislation, including the 2000 Race Relations Amendment Act and the 2006 Racial and Religious Hatred Act, and to family migration, such as the repeal of the primary purpose rule.

The retreat of rights

The majority of policy and legislation passed by Labour, however, has restricted rights and emphasised responsibilities. The general dynamic has been an abrogation of migrants' rights. For example, the 1999 Act introduced 'one-stop' appeal procedures[8] and the 2002 Act reinforced provisions preventing multiple appeals and ended in-country appeals if certified as unfounded (Ward, 2004).

Outside of primary legislation the Labour government has also introduced a series of policy measures aimed at increasing control, limiting settlement and reducing the number of asylum claims. For example, the Home Office five-year plan made refugee status temporary rather than permanent. From August 2005, refugee status has been dependent on conditions in the source country for the first five years. The government has also increased restrictions on entitlement to certain public services, such as the restrictions introduced in 2004 on non-urgent secondary care.

In parallel to legislation to protect vulnerable migrant workers under the 2004 Gangmasters Act, new restrictions have also been imposed. The 2006 policy, *A points-based system*, proposed imposing financial bonds on migrant workers, and welfare benefit restrictions were imposed on migrant workers from the A-8 countries (see Somerville, 2006b, pp 26–8).

Surveying UK policy developments does not provide a neat line of gradually increasing or decreasing rights. On the one hand, policy makers have acknowledged and strengthened the connection between human rights and migration policy, but on the other they have legislated for restrictions in the rights of migrants. These two contradictory forces have sparked friction and antagonism among different parties: but the government has placed a clear emphasis on security and focused less on rights.

Integration: a new interpretation?

The literature tends to make a temporal division between the first and second terms of the Labour government. The assimilation rhetoric and measures in government discourse are placed in the context of key events that took place in 2001: the riots in Bradford, Burnley and Oldham, those crossing from Calais to claim asylum in the UK and the eventual closure of the Sangatte refugee camp, as well as the terrorist attacks of 9/11 (Abbas, 2005). This is contrasted with the 'Cool Britannia' overtures of the first years of Labour government. As a result, a number of commentators have suggested a first-term policy of multiculturalism (1997–2001) and a second-term policy (2001–05) that veers towards assimilation (Back et al, 2002b; see also Schuster and Solomos, 2004).

This is a seductive analysis, but it overlooks two factors. First, it is useful to note that 'integration' is traditionally a term found in the literature on refugees rather than the ethnicity or race relations literature, where it is more likely to be equated by many with assimilation. Second, it is important not to confuse a notion of 1960s 'assimilation' with policy overtures in the 2000s. This is not to suggest that changes since 2001 have not been aimed at migrants (as many changes patently have) but to point to the basic assumption, shared across the political divide and accepted by public institutions, that both settled and new populations have a shared understanding that change is to be negotiated. This is most commonly noted with the shorthand phrase a 'two-way street' or 'two-way process'. However, this basic assumption was not shared by both sides in the 1960s and 1970s, when legislation was first passed through Parliament. The issue may be less one of assimilation for migrants and more one of assimilation of Muslims. Here, the charge has more than a kernel of truth.

Notes

[1] The other pillar was restricted entry to (largely) Asian and black immigrants.

[2] This standard interpretation of multiculturalism obscures the many ways the concept can be understood, including: a description of the make-up of a society; a vision of the way society should orient itself; specific policy tools for accommodating minority cultural practices; specially created governance frameworks to ensure the representation of immigrant and ethnic minority interests; and a variety of support mechanisms for assisting ethnic minority

communities to celebrate and reproduce their traditions (Vertovec and Wessendorf, 2005, pp 3–5).

[3] The CRE held a conference in July 2005 entitled The Integrated Society, for example.

[4] The CRE's interpretation of integration is based on three interlocking 'spheres' of interaction, participation and equality. Conceptually, this definition draws strongly on theories of social capital (Putnam, 2000).

[5] Known as Discretionary Leave (DL) or Humanitarian Protection (HP).

[6] *Islam v Secretary of State for the Home Department; R v Immigration Appeal Tribunal, ex parte Shah (Conjoined Appeals)* [1999].

[7] *R v Special Adjudicator, ex parte Ullah (FC); Do (FC) v Secretary of State for the Home Department* [2004] UKHL 26, available at http://www.publications. parliament.uk/pa/ld200304/ldjudgmt/jd040617/ullah-1.htm; *R v Secretary of State for the Home Department, ex parte Razgar* (FC) [2004] UKHL 27, available at http://www.publications.parliament.uk/pa/ld200304/ldjudgmt/ jd040617/razgar-1.htm.

[8] A general right of appeal was introduced to reflect the new Human Rights Act.

FOUR

The vicious circle of asylum policy

Policy towards asylum seekers has been among the most visible aspects of Labour's overall migration policy. Asylum has dominated debates in Parliament and among the judiciary. However, it cannot be considered in isolation. As Chapter 2 discussed, asylum seekers have been given more attention than any other immigrant group in policies on unauthorised migration and anti-terrorism.

Reducing the numbers of asylum seekers

Labour has made reducing asylum claims the key policy goal. Close observers of the process regularly refer to the 'numbers game' as a fundamental tenet of policy. This is perhaps unsurprising, as reducing numbers has been an ongoing discussion throughout the post-war period for *all* immigrant categories. However, under Labour, the concern has narrowed, applying to asylum seekers and the unauthorised, but not other groups, such as economic migrants or students. It is less surprising in the context of actual numbers.

Over the course of the 10 years under study, asylum applications followed a parabolic curve (see Figure 2 in the Introduction). Applications in 1997 (excluding dependants) totalled 32,500. By 1999, they had reached 71,160, and then 80,315 in 2000. A slight dip was followed by a peak of 84,130 in 2002, before a drop to 49,405 in 2003, 33,960 in 2004 and 25,710 in 2005 (Home Office 2006g, p 48). The most recent figures indicate a further decrease to 23,520 (Home Office, 2007d, p 2).

During its first term, Labour focused on reducing the number of *fraudulent* asylum claims. While the emphasis moved from fraudulent claims to the total number of asylum applications later on, in 2004, in effect policy was always concerned with reducing the overall total. From 2004, the policy priority formally became reducing the total number of claims after the Prime Minister made a personal commitment to halve the number of asylum applications 'within a year'.

The focus on reducing asylum claims is not, however, the only part of the 'numbers game'. The numbers game also includes the speed at which asylum claims are processed (the faster the better) and the numbers who are deported. The target on deportations has explicitly linked the numbers deported to the numbers claiming asylum. The so-called 'tipping point target' (where deportations of 'failed applicants' will be greater than unfounded claims) clearly shows that asylum seekers are the target group of this policy.

In general, Labour's policy on asylum can therefore be seen through a prism of reducing numbers and increasing control (ILPA, 2004). The most obvious manifestation of restriction has been in the curtailment of various appeal rights, which can be found in all four of the immigration Acts passed between 1997 and 2007. Surveillance measures have been crucial to this effort. Asylum seekers were the first group who were compelled to carry an identity card (the Asylum Registration Card) that includes biometric information, and their reporting arrangements often include either voice recognition over the telephone, electronic fingerprint checks or electronic tagging (or a combination of all three). Labour has also introduced rigorous reporting requirements for public servants. For instance, teachers are expected to record children of failed asylum seekers in their schools and pass this data to the Immigration and Nationality Directorate.

It is worth making three further points in relation to reducing numbers. First, restrictive policy measures on asylum are not 'new' to Labour. Restrictive measures can be traced to at least the 1993 Act, under the Conservative government. As Randall Hansen (2000, p 235) points out 'asylum policy appears to be in a cycle of unending restrictionism'.

Second, it was argued in the Introduction that the first term of the Labour government can be seen as an efficiency drive aimed at 'sorting out the mess' of backlogs inherited from the previous Conservative government. However, the rhetoric of bringing order to chaos was not matched with resources. Backlogs on asylum cases, for example, worsened during the period 1997–2001. This can be attributed in part to self-imposed spending restrictions from 1997 to 1999.

Third, in 2002, when the numbers of asylum claims peaked, a very public 'symbol' of those numbers became a media staple. The Sangatte refugee camp housed refugees sleeping rough in and around Calais but was widely seen as a staging post for asylum seekers coming to the UK. Run by the French Red Cross and opened originally in 1999 with a capacity of 600, the Sangatte refugee camp was hosting over 1,300 by mid-2002, when the crisis was at its height. A deal between David Blunkett, then Home Secretary, and his opposite number, Nicolas Sarkozy, in July 2002 agreed to close the camp by March 2003, but the visual images of chaos and desperation became indelibly linked to the surge in the numbers of asylum seekers. The political priority of reducing numbers was therefore strongly reinforced by the situation in Sangatte.

'Demagnetising' the UK

Central to the debate about reducing numbers has been the perception that 'pull factors' exist that make Britain a more attractive destination for asylum seekers than other countries. Consequently, a number of measures that reduce such pull factors have been introduced, typically centred on *lowering* support or *excluding* asylum seekers from services. It is important to bear in mind that the calculation that pull factors exist has been fiercely contested by independent research, which categorically refutes the claim that asylum seekers are 'pulled' to the UK by welfare benefits (Robinson and Segrott, 2002; Gilbert and Koser, 2003).

Labour did not introduce restrictions on welfare for asylum seekers, but has assiduously followed the course set by the previous Conservative government. The most far-reaching policy changes were made in Part 3 of the 2002 Nationality, Immigration and Asylum Act (sections 43–61). Taken together, this was a concerted (and effective) set of policy measures to reduce support for asylum seekers and includes infamous measures such as section 55 (withdrawing of support to 'late' applicants). More importantly, Schedule 3 ensured support was withdrawn from asylum seekers who were not successful in their claim for asylum, which has contributed to widespread destitution. Section 9 of the 2004 Act constituted a further development, legislating for the withdrawal of support from families with children under 18, although so far this measure has only been piloted in three areas between January and December 2005.

Welfare benefits for asylum seekers were set at 70 per cent of benefit levels and were initially introduced not in cash but in vouchers. Following a campaign led by Bill Morris, then General Secretary of the Transport and General Workers Union, cash replaced vouchers. However, for those on Section 4 'Hard Case' support (failed asylum seekers who temporarily cannot be returned to their country of origin), vouchers continue to be used (CAB, 2006).

Labour has also excluded asylum seekers from services and markets. In July 2002, asylum seekers' right to work was revoked, excluding them from the UK labour market.[1] Labour has also introduced policy measures that have excluded asylum seekers from public services, namely social housing (housing is organised through NASS) and non-emergency healthcare. For example, the unheralded changes to the Overseas Visitors Regulations, introduced in 2004, excluded failed asylum seekers from accessing secondary healthcare. Labour has also extended welfare restrictions to refugees. For example, for those granted refugee status, the previous entitlement to backdated benefits (which were owed due to the fact that asylum seekers were not paid at the full entitlement rate) has been stopped and replaced with a loan (the Refugee Integration Loan).

The extent of destitution among asylum seekers has been documented in independent research and was the subject of an extensive Select Committee report (JCHR, 2007, especially pp 30–3). Moreover, destitution has also been found in those processed through the New Asylum Model (Lewis, 2007), discussed further below.

Dispersal

'Dispersal' was among the most fundamental of Labour's reforms to asylum policy. Introduced in the 1999 Act, 'dispersal' relocated asylum seekers to various parts of the UK in order to relieve housing pressure on London. Unless an asylum seeker chooses the option of subsistence-only support (which does not offer help with housing costs), there is no choice of destination. In effect, asylum seekers are relocated by official sanction.

The numbers of those dispersed have been significant, totalling at least 100,000 since the policy was implemented in April 2000.[2] Furthermore, dispersal has been concentrated in three English regions in particular, the North West, West Midlands, and Yorkshire and the Humber, as well as in Scotland (Table 4.1).

The dispersal of asylum seekers has attracted much opposition. Ian MacDonald QC (MacDonald and Webber, 2001, p 13) described it as 'a dreadful scheme', for example. The subsequent implementation also attracted much local ire and opprobrium. Robinson et al (2003) suggests that opposition was particularly widespread between 2002 and 2003, when it resembled a moral panic. Grillo (2005) explores the reaction of residents in the seaside town of Saltdean and finds the almost hysterical opposition driven by a desire to defend middle-class privileges alongside a narrative of local (white) nationalism.

Dispersal has had four major consequences (see also Griffiths et al, 2006). First, it has created new government machinery (the National Asylum Support Service). Second, it has introduced people from a diverse set of backgrounds to areas unused to immigration, often

Table 4.1: Proportion of NASS-supported asylum seekers by region, 2000–05

Region	% supported to end of Dec 2001[1]	% supported to end of Dec 2002	% supported to end of Dec 2003	% to end of Dec 2004	% to end of Dec 2005
East Midlands	8	8	7	6	6
East of England	1	1	1	1	1
Greater London	4	5	6	4	4
North East	12	11	10	10	9
North West	20	19	16	16	17
South East[2]	2	2	3	2	1
South West	2	2	3	3	3
West Midlands	17	19	18	15	14
Yorkshire & Humber	21	19	20	23	22
Northern Ireland	0	0	0	0	0
Scotland	12	10	11	14	15
Wales	2	3	5	6	6

Source: Home Office Asylum Statistics 2000–2005

Notes:
[1] NASS was created April 2000
[2] Described as South Central in the Asylum Statistics 2001

without the necessary services to support or administer to their needs (Phillips, 2006). Third, it has filled previously unused or unwanted housing. Fourth, it has engaged new partners in the process, particularly local authorities, and has led to the creation of new voluntary groups and community organisations. These include, most obviously, service providers (particularly housing and advice networks) but also a significant number of MPs who had had no previous interest in asylum.

Exporting borders

Labour has successfully 'exported' the borders of the UK beyond their geographical limits. In part this has been achieved by legislative measures, for example the reintroduction of the 'white list' (which automatically presumes asylum claims from certain countries are unfounded), 'safe third countries' (where asylum seekers cannot claim asylum if they have previously passed through a 'safe' country, such as a European Union Member State) and 'safe country of origin' prescriptions. There have also been new penalties on traffickers.

Labour has effectively exported borders by placing new restrictions on those bringing asylum seekers to the UK. Building on earlier Conservative policy, such as the 1987 Act, Labour has introduced carrier sanctions (civil penalties on road hauliers and airlines), and 'juxtaposed' (reciprocal) controls, such as UK border points in Calais and Paris.

The Home Office describes a number of the measures it took to reduce unfounded asylum claims in its annual reports (for example, Home Office, 2003e, pp 93–4). They neatly summarise the new line of control abroad and include juxtaposed controls, new visa regimes, new detection equipment, the closure of Sangatte and greater manpower (airline liaison officers, strategically placed immigration liaison officers, and an immigration crime team).

Furthermore, Labour was also among the first governments in the EU to instigate the notion of 'extra-territorial processing' of asylum seekers. Such a move was signalled by the launch of a debate on whether the 1951 Refugee Convention should be redrawn. Jack Straw, then Home Secretary, suggested changes in an article for the *Telegraph* newspaper on 12 March 2000 and in a speech at the Institute for Public Policy Research on 6 February 2001 (quoted in Schuster and Solomos, 2001). The nature of such changes was formalised with the policy document *New international approaches to asylum processing and protection* (Home Office, 2003a), introduced when David Blunkett was Home Secretary. This proposed the 'internationalisation' of policy where asylum processing would take place in regions around the world. Labour attempted to persuade Europe of its agenda, including proposals for greater interception of migrants crossing the Mediterranean, at EU summits in Athens and Seville.

However, a response somewhere between tepid and outright opposition from other European countries meant that only a much-reduced version has been established, in Tunisia.

Europe matters more than it did

The extra-territorial debate shows that asylum policy developments can no longer be solely analysed at the national level. Developments in the European Union have been particularly important since 1997. Labour politicians have gone so far as to suggest Europe is part of the 'solution'. For example, Jack Straw indicated asylum was part of a

'Europe-wide problem' and that Britain should 'go along with' other civilised countries (BBC Politics, 1999).

The importance of Europe between 1997 and 2007 was partly a coincidence of timing. Labour came to power in the same year (1997) that the Treaty of Amsterdam was signed, a central provision of which was to move asylum into the 'first pillar' of European governance. In the plethora of different decision-making mechanisms of the European Union, the move to the 'first pillar' has meant that the EU has a legal competence to make binding law in asylum policy. However, the UK negotiated an opt-out to the Treaty of Amsterdam, although the reservation is not as rigid as might be assumed: it was drafted in a way that the UK has the option of participating on certain issues if it wishes. It is an opt-out to opt in.

Analysis of the regulations, directives and decisions indicates that the UK opted in to about half of those made between 1 May 1999 (when the treaty came into force and community law began to be made) and 30 April 2004 (Geddes, 2005, p 734). The balance was, however, skewed. Labour opted in to all seven of the asylum measures but only six of the 21 measures on border control and visas.

Labour's decision to comply with all seven asylum measures could suggest its strong support for the EU agenda. This is commensurate with its support for other EU asylum measures, such as Dublin II, which decided the rules for where an asylum claim could be made. However, the qualitative evidence for this study suggests that, in practice, Labour has been a less than committed partner in the EU's asylum harmonisation process, partly due to suspicion or lack of interest in the Home Office.

A lack of commitment may reflect an island mentality but it is also perhaps a result of the fact that the priorities and direction of EU and UK policies have complemented one another. Both have focused on controlling borders and reducing asylum claims. EU competence on legal migration has remained slight. This is not a happy accident: the UK, along with other major European countries, has contributed to the 'synchronisation' of agendas. For example, when opting in to directives, Labour's negotiators in the EU have aimed to lower the minimum standards of asylum support, consistently 'negotiating down' on reception measures.

However, the harmonisation toward a single EU standard has, on occasions, steered UK policy away from its own goals. For example, contrary to UK policy denying asylum seekers the right to work, introduced by Labour in 2002, European Directive 2003/9/EC, which came into force on 6 February 2005, allows asylum seekers to work if they have been in the UK for more than 12 months. The EU emphasis on the integration of asylum seekers similarly does not fit snugly into the UK policy framework. Overall though, measures agreed by the EU complement Labour's policy changes to 'export' borders.

A new 'path'

Changes in asylum policy may be viewed as an attempt to create a separate immigration path outside of mainstream services. This has come in two main forms: the exclusion of asylum seekers from mainstream services and the provision of new, tailored services.

The exclusion of asylum seekers from services built on Conservative reforms in 1993 and 1996 and largely eliminated entitlements to welfare benefits. Labour has gone further, such as by introducing measures to exclude asylum seekers from the labour market and reducing legal aid (GLA, 2005b).

The new 'services' for asylum seekers include new support mechanisms, the expansion of removal centres and the implementation of the New Asylum Model (NAM). The National Asylum Support Service (NASS), a rival mechanism for the social security and benefit system, provides welfare support to asylum seekers, in the form of either benefits (support only) or accommodation and benefits. Those who sign up for accommodation are forcibly dispersed.

Labour's policy on removal (detention) centres, where asylum seekers are held before deportation, has focused on increasing capacity and strengthening the link to the fast-track process (Home Office, 2005a, p 30). The number of detainees in removal centres has increased from 741 in 1998 to 1,950 in December 2005, of whom 1,450 were asylum seekers (Home Office, 2006f).

The NAM began operating in Croydon and Liverpool in June 2005, and there are now 25 teams based in Glasgow, Solihull, London, Liverpool, Leeds and Wales. NAM has been described as 'end-to-end management to enable us to see cases through from making a claim to removal or integration' by IND (Home Office, 2006c, p 2) and 'the most radical redesign of ... asylum processes in more than two decades' by Citizens' Advice (CAB, 2006). All new asylum cases came under the NAM from 5 March 2007.

NAM is basically a new approach to the refugee determination system, which segments asylum seekers into a series of different processing 'streams' and assigns a case-worker as the single point of contact throughout the asylum process. The criteria for entering a particular stream include how hard it is to deport an individual. While refugee determination has always been 'separate', the NAM reforms will ensure asylum claims are not 'lost' within the system, and are likely to speed up asylum determination.

Accommodation centres

The most effective way to illustrate the concept of a 'path' is to provide a brief account of a failed proposal. In 2001, Labour proposed that accommodation centres (large sites that would house all asylum seekers coming to the UK) be established. It was envisaged that both health and education would be delivered separately in such centres. Such a proposal was the ultimate embodiment of a 'separate' path, as it would cut off asylum seekers from all services in mainstream society.

The proposals on accommodation centres dominated parliamentary debate during the passage of the 2002 Nationality, Immigration and Asylum Bill. Questions were raised on nearly all aspects of the plan, from how the centres would be staffed (the government expected the staff to come from the local population) to whether there would be a statutory requirement for an anti-bullying policy (the government said not, and details would be agreed with each contractor).

The implementation of the centres was planned throughout 2002 and 2003. For example, in September 2003, the Home Office released a list of Frequently Asked Questions (FAQ) on accommodation centres (Home Office, 2003f). The questions included where they were to be geographically situated – planning permission had been granted for RAF Newton in Nottinghamshire and for the Defence Storage and Distribution Centre in Bicester, Oxfordshire – and what services they would deliver – education and primary care were to be delivered on site, along with 'purposeful activities and voluntary work'.

The intent behind policy was clear: separate asylum seekers on a 'path' to increase control and reduce numbers by fast-tracking decisions. However, accommodation centres were never implemented, chiefly because of large-scale opposition at the local level, such as the campaign in Bicester. Interestingly, the failure of the policy was unforeseen; Labour had expended parliamentary time and political capital and 'won' the battle to put it on the statute books. Instead, policy failure was a bona fide case of nimbyism in action, probably combined with ethno-racial distrust (Grillo, 2005).

Summary: reducing numbers through degrees of separation

It is clear that Labour has introduced an array of restrictions with the goal of reducing the numbers of asylum seekers. The metaphor of a path effectively describes policy changes on asylum from 1997 to 2007. Labour has created an insulated immigration path for asylum seekers where they are separated from mainstream society (and often from their communities, through relocation) until a decision on their status has been made. Policy has effectively excluded asylum seekers from mainstream support. Moreover, this separate path has been reinforced by externalising borders, so the starting point of this new path is outside the UK.

Notes

[1] EU Council Directive 2003/93EC circumscribed this policy, allowing asylum seekers to work if their claim is outstanding for more than one year.

[2] This is a personal calculation based on asylum statistics 2000–06 and average length of time supported in the National Asylum Support Service (NASS). Those receiving subsistence-only support are excluded.

FIVE

Delivery: non-stop reform

This chapter explores the delivery of migration policy – the institutions, structures and processes that 'realise' policy. Since 1997, the policy infrastructure has been significantly reorganised, in line with reforms to public services pioneered in the 1980s (such as the Next Steps programme). Labour's approach was comprehensively outlined in the White Paper *Modernising government* (Cabinet Office, 1999), which emphasised inclusive, evidence-based policy making and responsive, high-quality public services. As a result, in addition to reorganisation, several policies have been pursued to improve delivery: the state-funded delivery infrastructure has been diversified; there has been more 'joining-up' of government; new technologies have been introduced to improve efficiency and customer-service; and powers have been devolved.

New management techniques and financial imperatives have been the two most consistent drivers of reform. New management techniques, such as target-setting, have had a profound effect, especially on asylum reform. For example, the target on reducing numbers was the driver for setting up border controls in Calais. The targets on failed asylum seekers (unauthorised migrants) have also led to an increase in resources for enforcement since 2003.

Financial imperatives have also accounted for institutional change. Asylum processing, for example, has been speeded up partly because of the government's commitment to save £450m through 'bearing down on the cost of providing asylum support' by 2007/08 (Home Affairs Select Committee, 2006a, Annex B, Question 13). Similarly, efforts to reduce the legal aid budget to support asylum seekers have led to a fundamental reshaping of the asylum legal system. For example, a new structure, the Legal Services Commission, has taken control of legal aid funding and implemented a 'merits' test for appeal cases.

Among the most important changes to the delivery structure, driven again by financial imperatives, has been the development of a fee-charging regime. The regime, which originated from thinking on economic migration in the Cabinet Office and Home Office in 2002, initially charged low fees for work permits in 2003 with the aim of subsidising the processing costs. However, since then the floodgates have opened and the costs of obtaining a visa, a visa extension or visa switch, or to go through the naturalisation process, have rapidly increased.

The immigration fee-charging regime reached a high-water mark on 2 April 2007, when new, higher fee levels were set following a consultation in October 2006. The majority were radically increased. A work permit visa application, for instance, rose from £85 to £200, while an Indefinite Leave to Remain application increased from £335 to £750 (and for the premium service, £950).

The migration policy infrastructure

In fact, few areas of the migration delivery infrastructure have been left untouched by reform. The start of major institutional restructuring began when the spending freeze of 1997–99 came to an end, and reforms are continuing apace. On 2 April 2007, the Immigration and Nationality Directorate (IND) was hived off into a Next Steps agency and renamed the Border and Immigration Agency. Most recently, the Home Office has been streamlined, with many of its functions transferred to a new Ministry of Justice. Before providing detail of the changes between 1997 and 2007, the following section briefly outlines the delivery mechanisms of migration policy.

The Home Office is at the centre of the national state infrastructure (as opposed to the state-funded infrastructure) and is typically where migration policy is made. More specifically, the Immigration and Nationality Directorate, recently given arms-length agency status, is responsible for developing the detailed content of policy. The ministerial role (encompassing special advisers), discussed in more detail in Part Two, has become more prominent since 1997.

The Prime Minister's private office (and by extension the Cabinet Office) has had more influence on migration policy than prior to 1997, particularly in specific areas such as asylum. At the national level, nearly all government departments develop migration policy through the delivery of services to migrants as a group (for example language provision is the concern of the Department for Education and Skills and mental health provision for the victims of torture is the concern of the Department of Health).

Regional government and local authorities have little if any *policy-making* role. In Romain Garbaye's description, UK governance is a two-layer cake, with policy making taking place in only the national layer, which contrasts with the 'marble cake' of France (Garbaye, 2005, p 43). In practice however, regional and local institutions provide the crucial, front-line response to new migrants. For asylum seekers and refugees, services are relatively advanced, coalescing around 12 regional 'consortia' that supply services; for labour migrants, provision is extremely patchy. For instance, only a small number of local authorities have strategic plans in place to respond to migration. Finally, it is important not to overlook the role of private actors in policy delivery, part of an international trend (Lahar, 2000). The following analysis takes a thematic approach to institutional change and covers asylum, economic migration and integration.

Asylum

There have been three waves of reorganisation for the delivery of asylum policy. First, in 2000, a new agency, the National Asylum Support Service (NASS), took over asylum support. Systemic problems with NASS resulted in a second wave of reform, which devolved asylum support services and processes to the nine English regions and the devolved administrations of Scotland and Wales, bringing in local governance to a greater degree. The third wave of reforms has been centred on the New Asylum Model (NAM), which has streamlined and personalised the asylum determination process. In addition to these three waves of reorganisation, new infrastructure has been created in other areas, such as border control, where 'juxtaposed controls' (reciprocal border points) were established in Calais and Paris in France.

Economic migration

Reforms to the agencies dealing with visas (UK visas) and work permits (Work Permits (UK)) have made them more 'customer-focused', or employer-focused in the case of Work Permits (UK). The introduction of the fee-charging regime has provided resources for expansion and branding.

In the case of Work Permits (UK), major change took place when the unit moved departments in May 2001, together with David Blunkett, from the Department of Education and Employment to the Home Office. In the years following its move, it was expanded. When the Points-based System is introduced in 2008, however, decision-making on work permits is likely to be transferred from Work Permits (UK) (based in Sheffield) to Entry Clearance Officers (ECO) abroad (Home Office, 2006a).

Institutions have also developed in response to low-skill migrant workers. The statutory Gangmasters Licensing Authority was created to enforce the 2004 Gangmasters (Licensing) Act and regulate the relevant labour market sectors for migrant workers, for example.

Integration

The integration functions of government are somewhat difficult to identify as they cut across government, but several functions are particular to integration and cohesion. They included (in the Home Office between 1997 and 2006) the Active Citizenship Unit, the Civil Renewal Unit, the Cohesion and Faiths Unit, the Race Equality Unit, and the Social Policy Unit. However, even these units gave *immigrant* integration little specific attention, instead focusing (like the Commission for Racial Equality) on the overlapping subject of ethnic minorities. The Social Policy Unit, as the only unit within IND (the rest were elsewhere in the Home Office), was only concerned with refugee integration.

Two major changes can be noted between 1997 and 2007. First, there has been the creation of new units or bodies, such as the Community Cohesion Unit (subsequently renamed the Cohesion and Faiths Unit) in the Home Office, and the Forced Marriage Unit (created following the 2000 report *A choice by right* (Working Group on Forced Marriage, 2000)) in the Foreign and Commonwealth Office. More significant was the establishment of the independent Advisory Board on Naturalisation and Integration (ABNI), which develops support services for the citizenship and English language tests.

Second, there was a significant shift in 2006, when a government reshuffle moved the Home Office functions concerned with race, equality and faith into the newly named Department of Communities and Local Government (CLG).[1] Furthermore, in 2006 the CLG began hosting the secretariat of an independent Commission on Integration and Cohesion (due to report at the time of writing) and will be the 'parent' department for the Commission for Equality and Human Rights (CEHR), scheduled to begin operations in October 2007. (Previously the Commission for Racial Equality (CRE), which will form part of the CEHR, reported to the Home Office.) The equality functions have therefore moved away from the Home Office, although it is too early to tell what impact this will have on policy. Clearly though, a different Cabinet member will be championing this policy area.

Diversifying the delivery structure

A crucial change to the delivery of policy since 1997 is that the state-funded third sector has taken a prominent role in service delivery. On election, Labour adopted the terminology of government as an *enabler* of services and has encouraged non-state actors to become increasingly involved in service provision (Powell, 2002), a logic that has extended to the provision of immigration services.

Voluntary sector organisations have tended to provide welfare advice and service delivery for migrants and, particularly, asylum seekers and refugees. Their work increased significantly following the introduction of the dispersal policy in 2000 because numerous NGOs played a role in dispersing asylum seekers across the UK and providing services to meet their needs. In fact, organisations dealing with only asylum seekers and refugees (Refugee Community Organisations or RCOs) currently total more than 800 in number. Together with organisations (often based on ethnic lines) providing for labour migrants, the third sector increasingly resembles a shadow state, where government funding has expanded provision to meet the needs of migrants, making voluntary organisations deeply reliant on state funding and closely regulated by government, and therefore vulnerable to any policy change (ESRC, 2006b).

For-profit private sector companies have not become involved in welfare services, but rather in enforcement activities. For example, in 2005–06, private sector companies ran seven of the ten Immigration Removal Centres. Carrier sanctions have also ensured that transport companies play a role in immigration enforcement.

Unsurprisingly, delivery by the private and voluntary sectors has raised a number of ethical issues. Broadly speaking they include whether the private sector is 'fit' and 'accountable' to run services. For the voluntary sector, the dilemma is whether they have been co-opted into a government agenda that is inimical to the people they are supposed to serve. Cohen (2002b), for example, argues that engagement with the framework set up by the 1999 Act compromises the values and actions of the voluntary sector.

Joined-up government

Labour has emphasised joined-up government (JUG) – meaning better horizontal and vertical coordination across services – in all its policies. The intention to ensure joined-up government for migration policy was signalled early, in Labour's first White Paper (Flynn, 2005b; Home Office, 1998).

JUG has taken several forms, including stipulations on other parts of the public sector – for example, in pressing the health service to refuse primary care to failed asylum seekers – and in using existing machinery more effectively. Cabinet committees, such as MISC 20, have been used to drive through asylum changes at the highest level.

There have also been innovations. Government targets been used to encourage JUG (James, 2004). For example, the joint Public Sector Agreement target on visa processing (held by the Home Office and the Foreign and Commonwealth Office) has ensured efforts are more joined-up. Similarly, different departments have pooled budgets – the Department for Constitutional Affairs and the Home Office share an asylum budget, for instance.

Technology

The White Paper *Modernising government* dedicated an entire chapter to the 'information age government' (Cabinet Office, 1999, pp 44–54). Investing in technology has been a consistent thread in the reforms of immigration functions. For clarity, it is worth distinguishing between the application of technology in internal and in external functions.

Increased investment in technology for internal functions (systems, processing) pre-dated Labour's election victory. The Casework Programme was initiated in 1996 under the Major administration and implemented up until 2000. The Casework Programme was designed to improve the efficiency of decision-making underpinned by new computer software to speed up case-work decisions. The system was unsuccessful, causing delays and negative effects on the quality of service as well as 'administrative chaos' (Public Accounts Select Committee, 2000; Jordan and Duvell, 2003, p 299).

In general, the application of new software to Home Office systems has been problematic.[2] Individual failures include the passport fiasco of 1998; the collapse of the Siemens contract on developing an integrated case-work system in 1999 (Public Accounts Select Committee, 2000); the admission by David Blunkett that there had been a failure of asylum counting in 2001 (see, for example, Duvell and Jordan, 2003, p 305); and the failure to record details of foreign prisoners who should be deported, which ultimately led to the resignation in 2006 of then Home Secretary, Charles Clarke.

The main investment in technology has been in external functions, such as increased surveillance or biometric controls. The extent of change – the immigration system has come to rely on technology – was shown clearly in the four Acts passed by Labour, which have all included legislative clauses to enable the use of such technology and to establish what data can be used and by whom.[3] For example, a quarter of the 2006 Immigration, Asylum and Nationality Act (sections 27–42 of 63 sections) is dedicated to information-sharing, fingerprinting and a code of practice governing disclosure.

Most investment has aimed to increase surveillance and improve border controls through new technologies. E-borders, for instance, offers a system of electronic visas (i-visas) and biometric technology (iris and fingerprint) at border control points. Iris-recognition technology was first introduced in Heathrow Terminals 2 and 4 in June 2005 and the technology currently operates in all Heathrow, Gatwick, Stansted, Birmingham and Manchester Terminals (Home Office Press Release, 2006b). Another example from the e-borders project was the project to pilot passports with facial biometric data (Home Office, 2004c, p 69).

However, not all technological advances have been aimed at control. The managed migration system will also rely on technological advances. In the future, work permit applications will be made through a website that will carry up-to-date information on how to apply and the criteria immigrants need to meet (Home Office, 2006a).

The investment in technology is driven by two goals: improved security, particularly in terms of border integrity, and more efficient, less costly controls.

Devolution

Several interviewees highlighted the shift in governance towards the regions and to Scotland and Wales. There are several examples of such a shift, such as the regionalisation of NASS and of NAM referred to above, the likely operational set-up of the Border and Immigration Agency, and the services for refugee integration, which are held jointly by the GLA and IND in London, and led by the Scottish Refugee Integration Forum in Scotland.

Above all, though, interviewees pointed towards Scotland and the introduction of the Fresh Talent scheme, a regional economic migration programme described in Chapter 1, and strongly promoted by Jack McConnell, then First Minister for Scotland. However, migration policy remains a 'reserved matter'. In other words, all policy changes must defer to Whitehall. A shift in governance power has occurred, but it must be viewed in perspective.

Summary: non-stop, unplanned reform

This account of organisational change indicates a linear, logical progression. The reality has been chaotic, unplanned change, often at short notice. For example, in 2004, a review of how IND allocated resources and managed immigration enforcement showed that there were no less than nine major change initiatives impacting on the work of just one area, the Enforcement and Removals Directorate (Atos Consulting, 2004).

This has been noted by the players themselves. David Blunkett, while Home Secretary, was critical of the Home Office and noted that IND was chaotic. He believed that there were parallel policies running, noting that officials referred to 'Home Office policies' that were different from his own (Pollard, 2005, pp 254–8). In fact, the 'chaos' of parts of immigration policy in the Home Office has been used as a justification for reform. For example, John Reid, two weeks after becoming Home Secretary, famously stated that 'our system is not fit for purpose' (Home Affairs Select Committee, 2006b, Ev 155, 23 May 2006). This led the Home Office to adopt a new strategic direction and action plan.

The policy infrastructure remains in a state of flux today. The 2006 IND reform plan set out a radical simplification of migration rules and proposed 'agency' status for IND (Home Office, 2006d). Agency status has already been achieved; the new Border and Immigration Agency was launched on 2 April 2007. On 29 March, the Prime Minister announced further restructuring, with the Home Office split into two parts. An expanded Department for Constitutional Affairs has been renamed the Ministry of Justice, while the 'new', streamlined Home Office has a revised remit that includes crime, terrorism, and immigration. The Home Office will also house a new Office for Security and Counter-Terrorism.

Thus, between 1997 and 2007 the delivery of migration policy underwent considerable change, ranging from managerial reforms and the implementation of new technologies to devolution and a diversification of delivery structure. The period can be aptly characterised by the overused epithet 'non-stop reform'.

Notes

[1] Somewhat oddly, the Social Policy Unit remained in IND and continues to focus on refugees.

[2] This should be put in the context of a series of IT project failures across government.

[3] The UK Borders Bill continues this trend.

SIX

A new direction

The Introduction drew attention to the preoccupations of different historical eras. It was argued that migration policy has its roots in laws enacted 200 years before 'modern controls', and such fundamental issues as the pros and cons of economic migration have been debated since the early eighteenth century. The second historical era (1905–1948) gave birth to a recognisable system of immigration control, which aimed to exclude certain groups of foreigners but was intricately bound up in empire. The third period (1948–1976) was crucial in that, after the dismemberment of empire, the dominant, *bifurcated* model – of 'zero-migration' and anti-discrimination laws – was established. The post-war policy response has thus shown 'a pronounced duality' where restriction on admissions has been combined with a process of managing 'race relations' (Zetter, 2002, p 42; see also Bhavnani et al, 2005). The fourth period, of mainly Conservative rule, was one of continuity (in an era of major economic and social policy change), where the most salient change was one of focus, where the target of policy changed to asylum seekers. Policy in this period can be seen in the light of pragmatic responses to new movements. Finally, the period between 1997 and 2007 can be characterised as one of managing migration in a globalising world.

Policy under Labour was described through an inductive analysis of five major policy themes. This analysis showed the direction of policy to be, on the one hand, a strong commitment to the management of migration for macro-economic gain, and on the other, the development of a tough security framework that combats unauthorised (or 'illegal') migration and reduces asylum seeking. The key question is what – if anything – has changed?

Anti-race discrimination measures have been reinforced and are central to equality. They are no longer simply a quid pro quo or one half of an immigration settlement. Anti-discrimination, race relations, community relations and community cohesion are difficult concepts to disentangle, but there has been a discernible move to mainstream race equality in acts of policy making under a banner of integration. The emphasis on integration marks a change from previous policy, but to suggest that this position has regressed to one of assimilation is an oversimplification. The references to adaptation on the part of host communities, typically characterised by the oft-used phrases 'a two-way street' or 'a two-way process', show this is not a simple case of 'old wine in new bottles'. Policy has moved away from its 'multicultural' pivot, but it is not clear to where it has moved.

Border control remains crucial but ministers have consistently refused to put a cap on the numbers entering the UK.[1] Security concerns have gained importance, although a securitisation of policy would appear an exaggeration, and the asylum system as a regime of protection has been eroded. Asylum policy has remained in a vicious circle of restrictionism, intended to reduce numbers, with new measures to separate asylum seekers by exporting borders, dispersing asylum seekers and reducing benefits; together with moves to harmonise procedures with other European countries. Furthermore, there has been a reorganisation of institutions and delivery mechanisms, together with a far from seamless incorporation of advanced technologies to improve efficiency and security.

However, the major change, plotted in the period 2001–03, is the concept of managing migration. This commitment to economic migration has been accepted across the political divide and consequently limitation and restriction on immigration is no longer a prerequisite for UK migration policy, ending the bifurcated model established in the period 1948–76. The injection of an economic element has therefore broken one half (the policy of limitation) of the immigration settlement of the last 40 years, 1962–2002 (Somerville, 2006a). Other changes have occurred, but they are not radical breaks with the previous policy direction.

Note

[1] For example, in an interview with Jeremy Paxman, David Blunkett refused to be drawn on numbers, BBC Newsnight, 12 November 2003.

Part Two
Influences on policy

SEVEN

The new global marketplace

Part Two explores the factors that have influenced migration policy development during the 10-year period from 1997 to 2007. The first three chapters focus on what interviewees described as major structural or 'global' forces that forced policy to develop in a particular way. The first of these forces was globalisation, the subject of this chapter. Specifically, interviewees referred to policy being forced to adapt to a new external environment of greater flows of labour, greater interconnectedness of knowledge and technology, and cheaper and faster travel and communication.

The argument presented below is that globalisation has had a two-fold effect: it influences the design of policy and sets the parameters of what policy measures can be considered.

The effects of globalisation

Globalisation is the phenomenon in which a set of processes increase the integration of the global market (see Held and McGrew, et al, 1999; 2003). Even those who take a sceptical view of globalisation concede that there has been greater economic integration in larger regional trading blocs, such as Europe, over recent decades (Hirst and Thompson, 1996). The literature exploring the juncture between globalisation and migration tends to focus on its effect in undermining state control over who is allowed to enter a country (Sassen, 1999b). Scholars have also argued that immigration has become one of the constitutive processes of globalisation (Sassen, 1999a; Castles and Miller, 2003).

The nexus between globalisation, migration and the economy is difficult to map empirically as there are many variables to consider. Nonetheless, the forces of globalisation have led to shifts in the UK economy and the evidence indicates that immigration flows have responded accordingly. One measure is the growth of immigration; migrants coming to the UK for more than a year increased significantly from the early 1990s, which coincided with an up-turn in the UK economy. The net immigration flow rose from 75,400 in 1995 to 138,800 in 1998, to 162,800 in 2000 and reached 222,600 by 2004: a tripling in 10 years (Home Office, 2006f, p 100). However, a better measure of the influence of globalisation than the net immigration flow is the net economic immigration flow (which excludes non-economic flows, such as asylum).

Between 1995 and 2005, the number of work permits tripled. Similarly, in 1995, the *net* work-related immigration flow was *negative*, totalling 26,300, whereas by 2005, it was *positive*, at 60,100 (Home Office, 2006f, p 96). This excludes other flows likely to be intrinsically linked to globalisation, such as student flows (the net inflow of students rose 64,300 between 1995 and 2005).

Not only has the absolute number of work permits increased, but the share of work permits has adjusted to reflect new economic realities: in 1995, most work permits were issued for administration, business and management services (16.7 per cent), financial services (13.2 per cent), and entertainment and leisure services (12.1 per cent). By 2005, the top three industries in which permits were issued were health and medical services (26.1 per cent), computer services (18.1 per cent), and administration, business and management services (11.8 per cent), reflecting changing economic pressures (Salt and Millar, 2006, p 345). Moreover, the fastest-increasing immigration flow, from Poland, is driven by the needs of the economy (ESRC, 2006a).

More importantly, there is evidence that migrants have responded more flexibly to job vacancies. Migrants are, for example, more likely to take jobs in sectors facing shortages (Loizillon, 2004, pp 120–1) and more likely to move to jobs. Third-country nationals in Europe are, for example, over 11 times more likely to move house than EU nationals.[1] Globalisation has therefore acted as an amplifier of existing supply and demand curves, intensifying their effects, and migration appears to have responded. Consequently, migration policy changes between 1997 and 2007 have taken account of the performance of the UK economy.

The UK economy has seen uninterrupted growth from the mid-1990s to the present, with GDP growth including no quarters of recession from 1997–2007. There has also been a net increase of jobs and a tighter labour market; the working-age employment rate rose to 74.5 per cent in 2006, up from 72.7 per cent in 1997 (HMT, 2006b, p 77), further increasing demand for new workers. A number of commentators have attributed the strength of the UK economy as the key variable in increased immigration (Layton-Henry, 2006).

This economic expansion cannot ignore the macro-economic policies enacted under Labour, such as independence for the Bank of England (HMT, 2006b, pp 13–20). The key 'take-away' point in discussing the UK economy and macro-economic policy framework is that globalisation has amplified existing economic trends. Whether or not globalisation as a set of processes would have had the same impact on migration policy making under different economic conditions is impossible to prove empirically in the absence of a counterfactual, but a hypothetical counterfactual (for example 40 quarters of recession) would – in all likelihood – have had a different impact on the labour migration patterns and hence on migration policy development.

Globalisation (through cheaper travel and improved communications) has also facilitated a huge increase in the net throughput of passengers to the UK, which has forced policy makers to rethink border infrastructure. Figure 7.1 shows that the number of international arrivals to the UK increased by 43.8 million over the 10-year period up to 2005. Furthermore, the increasing numbers of passenger flows have been matched by increasing trade flows. Freight traffic through Kent ports, for example, has increased at a rate of 6 per cent per year (Home Office 2007b, p 6).

Figure 7.1: Number of passengers arriving in the UK, 1995–2005

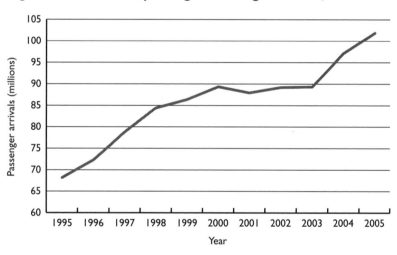

Source: Home Office (2006f) Control of Immigration Statistics

Policy makers' views on globalisation

Globalisation has therefore had some very real impacts on flows and the economy and thus on policy. However, globalisation also influences policy by 'setting the boundaries' of the policy conversation. Even if the assumption that globalisation results in inevitable global flows of labour is not entirely accurate, policy makers' perceptions of globalisation may be as important as the true effects of globalisation (Hay, 2002). Such perceptions may be heightened if politicians use it as a justification for a difficult-to-sell policy position (the 'we have no choice' argument). Perception is also important because it may help establish or cement particular interest groups or networks.

Labour has viewed globalisation as an inevitable force in policy formulation and has made the argument that globalisation is fundamental to the design of all social policies (HMT, 2006a, p 1). The Treasury, for instance, highlighted globalisation as one of the key long-term challenges facing the UK (HMT, 2006a). Such analysis has been applied specifically to migration policy. The 2002 White Paper dedicated 12 paragraphs to a discussion of global trends, for example, under the heading 'The challenge of globalisation' (Home Office, 2002a, pp 23–6). Globalisation is accepted as an inevitable trend: 'Globalisation also means that issues previously considered "domestic" are now increasingly international … Government policy making must respond, anticipate new challenges and be ready to capitalise on the benefits. Globalisation means that what happens in the UK must be considered in the wider European and international context' (Home Office, 2002a, paragraph 1.16). Similar paragraphs appear at the start of most migration strategies subsequently issued by Labour (see, for instance, Home Office, 2006d, p 6).

Policy makers therefore accept globalisation as a given, a position that is reinforced by three crucial calculations that policy makers have made: on demographics, on trade negotiations, and on attracting talent.

Demographic calculations

Migrants arriving in the UK are generally young: in 2004, there was a net gain of migrants aged 15–24 of 140,100 and a net loss of 19,100 migrants aged 49–64 (Home Office, 2006f, p 100). Flows to the UK therefore act as a partial corrective to the UK's ageing population. Indeed, net immigration is the most significant variable in making demographic predictions in the UK today.

The UK population is expected to grow by 7.2 million between 2004 and 2031, from 59.8 to 67 million, and net immigration, based on a net flow of 145,000 permanent migrants per year, is expected to account for 4.1 million, more than 50 per cent of this increase (GAD, 2007). Such predictions have an important bearing on savings and pensions policy as they change the dependency ratio (the ratio between the potential workforce (aged 20–64) and pensioners). In the UK, the dependency ratio is expected to rise from 27 per cent to 47 per cent by 2050 as a consequence of an ageing population.

Significant policy debate has consequently taken place over whether immigration can alleviate the consequences of an ageing population. For example, under a higher net immigration scenario (300,000 per year rather 145,000) the dependency ratio would drop, favourably, from 47 per cent to 42 per cent (Pensions Commission, 2004, p 8). However, many have opposed such a measure on demographic grounds, because, in short, migrants also age, and thus population growth would have to increase exponentially. Far less ink has been spilt over what would happen with a net emigration scenario, which would exacerbate the consequences of an ageing society.

General Agreement on Trade in Services

Policy makers have agreed to permanently open certain high-skilled labour flows (under limited conditions) as part of international trade negotiations. The General Agreement on Trade in Services (GATS), agreed in 1996, marked the first 'bridgehead' into global agreements that embedded the free movement of certain economic migrants. This was given further force by the EU, as it negotiated the agreement as a single bloc. The 1996 agreement included five groups of persons across all sectors: business visitors, natural persons involved in the establishment of a foreign branch, intra-corporate transferees, specialists, and contractual service suppliers. In addition there are sector-specific rules concerning construction, health and ICT services.

In the development of UK economic migration policy, GATS has been directly incorporated as a concessionary agreement within the work permit rules. As Sandra Lavenex (2004, p 45) notes, while in practice the treaty does not exceed national commitments of member states, it is the 'first multilateral treaty to include binding multilateral rules on migration' and, in addition, has a compliance mechanism through the World Trade Organisation.

In the current round of talks, European Commission negotiators have offered a more generous package. In February 2004, they offered a removal of the economic needs test, extension of stay, and new categories (such as graduate trainees). A revised offer in June 2005 included provisions for a 12-month exchange of management trainees and a six-month transfer scheme for skilled migrants in 21 sectors (European Union Committee, 2005, pp 13–14). Their offer, which would be legally binding, is thus committed to a liberalisation of rules towards high-skilled migrants.

Talent in the global marketplace

Globalisation has also made itself felt in firms' search for the 'brightest and the best' talents. This has come in two major forms: the search for individuals of 'outstanding achievement', who are uniquely talented or leaders in their field, and the selection of highly skilled individuals to expand the human-capital base of the country (Papademetriou and O'Neil, 2006, p 229).

The latter is well illustrated by the growing number of international students who have come to the UK to study in the last decade. The figures rose from 70,600 in 1997 to 117,200 in 2004 (Home Office, 2006f, p 96). Moreover, countries compete against each other for a larger proportion of the international student 'market'. The roots of the new initiatives and schemes discussed in Chapter 1 can be found in this assumption.

Policy makers have concluded that to respond to these three needs – demographics, global trade and human capital (the 'best and the brightest') – policy must accommodate, even facilitate, global movements.

Bringing the trends together

This chapter has highlighted that a set of trends associated with globalisation and a more interconnected world economy emerged in the early 1990s, including growth in the UK economy and a large increase in the numbers of travellers and permanent immigrants to the UK, particularly economic immigrants. Policy makers have been forced to come to an accommodation with these trends for the immigration system to function at all. Thus, policy makers have designed policies on the empirical facts of increasing numbers, rather than on perceptions or ideology.

However, by accepting the pro-market basis of globalisation, and by sharing in the goals of this philosophy, policy makers have set the essential boundaries of the policy conversation. This acceptance of globalisation has been reinforced by three important calculations: the off-setting of the ageing population and its public policy implications, the fact that human capital (migrants) has been brought into multilateral trade discussions (GATS), and a belief that to remain economically competitive, countries must facilitate the entry of the 'super-skilled'.

Consequently, while economic pressures and growing immigration flows meant that the immigration system was inevitably going to have to adapt, Labour was the first government to accept them as structural forces and to address them strategically. In other words, policy makers, from 2001, started to frame their policies *pro-actively* to meet the realities wrought by globalisation.

Note

[1] Personal calculation based on Family Panel Data.

EIGHT

The law and policy

This chapter addresses perhaps the most important debate in the literature: that the law, and in particular the development of human rights law and practice, has funnelled migration policy making in a particular direction. The argument proposed here is that there is a 'legal bottom line' and policy cannot circumvent it.

It also discusses the legal constraints on policy making, such as ensuring non-discrimination in policy delivery. In the UK, legal redress is possible if policies are implemented outside of the law, outside the powers of the public body, or are enacted unreasonably. The chief mechanism for this is judicial review, and its effect on migration policy is discussed more fully below.

International law

The general migration literature has long been cognisant of the importance of legal norms in circumscribing policy action (Guiraudon and Joppke, 2001). Yasmin Soysal has claimed that the development of international law has reached a point where policies must treat citizens and non-citizens in similar ways (as human beings). She argues that liberal democratic states are bound by 'post-national citizenship', which 'reflects a different logic ... what were previously defined as rights become entitlements legitimized on the basis of personhood' (Soysal, 1994, p 3). David Jacobson similarly argues that developments in human rights curtailed the ability of states to regulate citizenship and the rights of aliens. In his view, it is residence in a territory (as a human being) rather than membership of a national community (as a citizen) that affords rights (Jacobson, 1997).[1]

These claims, however, are muted when applied to the UK. The consensus view of the political science literature is that the (overly) powerful executive has generally ridden over the rights of migrants, a view completely at odds with the Soysalian proposition (see, for example, Joppke, 1999). This has been because the UK executive is particularly powerful (it lacks, for example, a written constitution) and has therefore been able to develop policy that treats migrants differently from citizens.

Unlike globalisation, there are few mentions of legal constraints in government documents on migration, whether they are White Papers or policy strategies, and Labour politicians have sometimes caricatured the legal establishment as an overly liberal bugbear, intent on slowing and blunting needed reforms. However, at the same time, Labour also claims that some of its biggest achievements have been in passing rights statutes.

The 'constraint' of human rights law

How far, then, has migration policy being circumscribed by the law and the legal establishment? The three case studies below have been chosen to illustrate the different ways human rights law has influenced policy.

Section 55

Section 55 refers to the relevant clause of the 2002 Nationality, Immigration and Asylum Act, which stated that unless in-country asylum seekers applied for asylum 'as soon as reasonably practical', state support could be withdrawn, leaving asylum seekers destitute. Human rights advocates and refugee organisations argued that section 55 contravened ECHR Article 3 and ICESCR[2] Article 11 (Archbishop's Council, 2005). The Joint Committee on Human Rights (JCHR) condemned it as 'in breach of human rights standards' (JCHR, 2004c, p 42). Two quantitative reports were commissioned specifically on section 55 to highlight its consequences of impoverishment and provide an evidence-based critique of the government stance (GLA, 2004; Refugee Council, 2004).

Labour remained unmoved, stating that there was widespread fraud in the system, with people making 'unfounded' asylum claims months or years after being in the UK, merely to be allowed to remain in the country. The government therefore continued to implement section 55.

A number of legal cases were consequently taken up. The case of Wayoka Limbuela, an Angolan national, reached the Court of Appeal in May 2004. Limbuela applied for asylum on the day of his arrival but his application was not deemed 'as soon as reasonably practical'. He subsequently spent two days without food, sleeping rough outside Croydon Police Station, where he was even refused a blanket. In the *Limbuela, Tesema and Adam* case,[3] the Court of Appeal found the government to be in breach of ECHR Article 3 (inhuman and degrading treatment). Section 55 was stopped pending a government appeal against the ruling. The Law Lords' final decision was delivered on 3 November 2005, unanimously upholding the verdict of the Court of Appeal.

The 2004 (Treatment of Claimants) Act and appeal rights

There has been a consistent thread through Labour's legislation to reduce asylum appeal rights. The 2004 (Treatment of Claimants) Act was particularly far-reaching in streamlining the appeals system into a single tier.

The 2004 legislation raised several human rights concerns, particularly on access to justice and the right of *non-refoulement*,[4] including potential conflict with ECHR Articles 3, 8 and 13 (House of Commons, 2003, p 60). The JCHR similarly raised concerns on the reduction of appeal rights in two reports (JCHR, 2004a, 2004b). Furthermore, the Constitutional Affairs Committee (2005) criticised the introduction of limits on public funding of asylum and immigration advice and representation, through retrospective funding and the 'merits test', as potentially disadvantaging legitimate appellants.

Despite such opposition, Labour successfully passed the legislation. But while the reforms were significant and led to the implementation of a streamlined system, they were quite different from what the government originally envisaged. The initial proposals made by the government in the 2004 (Treatment of Claimants) Bill included a streamlined, one-tier system, but also an ouster clause.

The ouster clause would have meant, in practice, that no judicial review could have been made of decisions by the Immigration and Asylum Tribunal. But the proposals were amended significantly during the various committee stages of the Bill. In particular, significant opposition to the clause emerged in the House of Lords, a broad coalition that included the former Lord Chancellor Derry Irvine. The upshot of such parliamentary intrigue was that the Act passed without the ouster clause.

Unaccompanied asylum seeking children (UASC)

The third example illustrates that the government's asylum legislation is not only contested under the ECHR but also under the Convention on the Rights of the Child (CRC), the international law on children's human rights to which the UK is a signatory.

The government has been criticised for potentially violating the CRC on a range of asylum child rights issues, including detaining children and disputing ages in asylum cases (Amnesty International, 1999; Refugee Council, 2002; BID, 2003; Rogers, 2004).

However, the contested government measures are made legally possible by the UK's reservation[5] to Article 22 (refugee children). The JCHR stated that the reservation is contrary to the object and purpose of the CRC (JCHR, 2005b, p 20), arguing that the UK cannot make such a reservation because it fundamentally changes the terms and conditions of the treaty. Nonetheless, these proposals and measures have been enacted.

The three examples provide several insights. The importance of the law in circumscribing policy is well illustrated by the first example – Section 55 – when the government was forced to withdraw a policy it had actually implemented. In contrast, the second and third examples show that legal standards are not insuperable.

The examples also show that, even on minimal criteria, the human rights of forced migrants have not always been met *and are not intended to be met*. This has led to friction as various policies targeting forced migrants have often been legally permissible measures, but against the spirit of international law treaties. The introduction of section 55, for example, provoked widespread opposition, but it was only revoked at the insistence of the Law Lords, the highest court of the land. Thus, laws have acted as a bulwark, obstructing policies rather than acting as their foundation.

This friction is neatly encapsulated by Labour's approach to the right of non-refoulement. On 25 July 2006, the Home Office explicitly stated that the government was seeking to overturn the legal judgment (the 1996 *Chahal* case) that introduced the right of non-refoulement. Overturning the judgment was a 'key challenge' (Home Office, 2006d, p 11) which would allow the Home Office to ignore non-refoulement obligations under international law. On the same day as the Home Office released its proposals (25 July 2006), the government also published a supportive review of the operation of the Human Rights Act (HRA), which suggested a 'dialogue' had been established between the European Court and English judges on human rights, and, moreover, that while they were seeking to intervene in the *Chahal* case, 'the Human Rights Act has not seriously impeded the achievement of the government's objectives on … immigration' (DCA, 2006b, p 4). Furthermore, legal observers have indicated that the *Chahal* judgment is highly unlikely to be overturned in the European Court of Human Rights. Thus, while the Home Office may see overturning the *Chahal* judgment as a key challenge, it is very unlikely to succeed.

Migration policy has therefore been circumscribed by the law, but to a limited degree. Judgement is complicated by the fact that the UK has incorporated into domestic legislation the ECHR, but not all human rights standards (for example, the Convention on the Elimination of Racial Discrimination), or has entered crucial reservations (for example, the Convention on the Rights of the Child). The speed at which legislation has been passed has also limited the number of legal cases. Nonetheless, while it is difficult to make the case that human rights law has funnelled policy, as many restrictive policies have been enacted, key human rights judgments reveal that the law has, on occasions, circumscribed policy.

Judicial review

The debate on whether human rights law has constrained national executives should not obscure the importance of other branches of law in influencing the development of migration policy. The most important tradition – other than human rights – has been administrative law, and particularly judicial review.

Judicial review applies to decisions and policies made or implemented unreasonably. In other words it operates as judicial scrutiny of the decision-making processes of the public body. The impact of judicial review has been underestimated in most accounts of UK migration policy making, where the focus has been on human rights.

Rawlings (2005, p 408) has argued convincingly that 'the powerful dynamics of asylum litigation have been rooted in the rapid development of a mass system of administrative justice'. More importantly, Rawlings views the vehicle of administrative justice as being effective in constraining the executive and ministers, reflecting the 'vibrancy of the common law tradition' (Rawlings, 2005, p 409).

Empirical evidence supports Rawlings' claim. Migration cases have driven the increase in the judicial review caseload over the last two decades, well before Labour was elected in 1997 (see, for example, Bridges et al, 1995). Significantly, however, the number of migration-related cases has increased under Labour.

Figures from the Lord Chancellor's Department and the Department for Constitutional Affairs show that over 50 per cent of applications for judicial review have typically been for immigration cases. In 2000, there were 2,120 immigration-related cases from a total of 4,247 (LCD, 2001, p 17) and in 2004, 2,221 out of 4,207 (DCA, 2005, p 23). In both 2002 and 2005, nearly 60 per cent of judicial review cases were 'immigration cases', accounting for 3,848 out of 5,949 (DCA, 2003, p 20) and 3,149 out of 5,381 (DCA, 2006a, p 23) respectively.

Summary: a line in the sand

Two important points emerged from the interviews. First, it was clear that policy makers and lawyers often lack a common language and understanding. For example, those who were policy makers typically displayed an ignorance of whether a particular policy was 'legally permissible' or not and rarely understood principles of proportionality and non-discrimination. Second, it is important not to lose sight of the fact that the 'law' is rarely neutral. Interviewees remarked, for instance, that the existence of the Convention on the Rights of the Child or the Convention on the Elimination of Racial Discrimination offers an advocacy 'template' for civil society. Legal practice must therefore be considered in terms broader than a simple credit and debit sheet of parliamentary measures passed or withdrawn, or court cases won or lost.

Nonetheless, given that many of the policies under Labour have been restrictive, one might be led to assume that an overweening executive renders the courts largely irrelevant. However, this chapter has shown that the legal framework in the UK – incorporating a mix of international human rights statutes signed into domestic legislation but also a strong tradition of administrative law in the form of judicial review – has ensured a minimum level of standards, despite the general tenor of policy and the intention of policy makers. In précis, there *is* a 'legal bottom line'.

Notes

[1] International law also states, unambiguously, that states have a right to control their borders (Rohl, 2005, p 7).

[2] International Convention on Economic, Social and Cultural Rights.

[3] *R (on the applications of Adam, Tesema, and Limbuela) v Secretary of State for the Home Department* [2004] EWCA 540, A [2004] All ER (D) 323, available at http://www.refugeelawreader.org/index.d2?target=open&id=73.

[4] The right of non-refoulement means a person cannot be returned – deported – to a country where they would face torture or inhuman and degrading treatment.

[5] A legal term meaning a legitimate limitation to the law.

NINE

The European Union

Commentators have differed over the degree to which the European Union (EU) has influenced UK policy making. Some have suggested the EU has had only a marginal impact on policy – Marsh et al (2000, pp 223, 230) record the EU's effect on the Home Office as 'minimal', for instance. The central question of this chapter is therefore: *to what extent* has the European Union influenced policy?

Asylum

Member States have agreed to create a Common European Asylum System by 2010. This is an area of 'binding' regulation, so Member States must implement the agreed measures into national law. As discussed in Chapter 4, the UK has opted into the asylum harmonisation process by signing various directives. However, it has done so reluctantly, neither obstructing nor leading the process of asylum harmonisation, but viewing it with ambivalence.

Interviewees described Labour's approach on European asylum policy as reticent. The UK was ambivalent at the most important summit on asylum harmonisation in Tampere (1999) during the Finnish Presidency of the EU, when the first programme to develop a common approach and increase joint working on asylum policy was agreed. Similarly, the UK stayed in the background at the Hague summit (2004), which included asylum but also other issues, such as a joint approach to integration policy and agreement on Common Basic Principles of integration. The UK nonetheless signed up to these measures, usually in return for diplomatic support for other measures. Thus, while the UK was never to the fore in agreeing such measures, it *did* agree them, despite the fact that they have occasionally gone against the national policy direction set by Labour (see for example European Directive 2003/9/EC on asylum seeker employment).

Economic migration

Seen through the lens of history, the EU was conceived, first and foremost, as an economic union (Hantrais, 2000), committed to facilitating freedom of movement (European Union Committee,

2005). However, the unrestricted European labour market is generally characterised by 'stickiness'. Europeans have the right to freedom of movement but, even after successive waves of enlargement, have not exercised it in significant numbers. The turning point for the UK was in May 2004: the 'big bang' enlargement that took in more states than ever before and when the potential of free movement turned to reality. The accession of eight Eastern European countries led to major flows of migrants to the UK.[1] While exact figures do not exist, applications for the Worker Registration Scheme (which requires A-8 nationals to register with the Department for Work and Pensions before taking up employment and is a decent proxy for the gross inflow), totalled 134,550 in 2004; 212,310 in 2005; and, in 2006, 232,050, with the cumulative total of applications reaching 579,000 in December 2006 (DWP, 2007, p 5). As these figures suggest, the increase in overall net immigration since 2004 has been attributed to enlargement (ESRC, 2006a).

Much has been made of the UK's support of EU enlargement and its decision not to impose labour market restrictions. But had it opposed such policies, it could only have blocked them temporarily under the European Commission's '2+3+2' formula. This stipulates that Member States can derogate from the provisions for an initial two years, subject to review. This can be extended to three years and then by a further two if required. Thus, more recent government restrictions on immigrants from Romania and Bulgaria, who joined in 2007, must eventually be lifted (in this case by the end of 2013).[2] The effect of EU enlargement and free movement policy has had other, direct effects on UK policy making, such as the policy goal of ending low-skill migration from *outside* Europe (Home Office, 2005a; see also Chapter 1).

In contrast, the EU has had less influence on economic migration policy pertaining to non-European migrants. In the main, this is because the EU's right, or 'competence', to act on legal migration, unlike asylum, is extremely restricted. The Council of Ministers only accepts changes to legal migration by unanimous vote, so any one country can veto a proposal.[3] Labour has been doggedly opposed to any EU measures on legal migration since 1997. For example, the debate in the second half of 2006 focused on taking the so-called 'passerelle' clause from the failed European Constitution, which would have allowed majority voting on legal migration, and implementing it as a stand-alone measure. Labour objected on principle and Home Secretary John Reid obstructed the move.

EU enlargement policy, combined with an ongoing commitment to free movement, has therefore acted as an accelerant to migration within Europe. By expanding the labour pool, it has allowed the forces of globalisation to have real 'bite', and this has influenced the UK's economic migration policy decisions. However, the European Union's effect on economic migration from outside the European Union has been negligible, largely because of a lack of competence on the issue.

Security and unauthorised migration

Since 2004, the European Commission has been responsible for proposing legislation in the area of unauthorised migration. While the laws relating to legal immigration must be agreed unanimously in the Council of Ministers, laws dealing with unauthorised migration are decided by Qualified Majority Voting in the Council and by the European Parliament, which has joint decision-making powers in this area.

As discussed in Chapter 2, Labour, and especially the Home Office, has enthusiastically supported cooperation with other Member States on unauthorised migration, particularly at the operational level (Home Office, 2007b, pp 14–15). This can be seen in the prominence of certain working groups, such as the Strategic Committee for Immigration, Frontiers, and Asylum (SCIFA) and the development of shared databases that hold information on migrants, including VIS (visas), SIS II (mark two of the Schengen Information System, which holds information on nationals refused entry to the EU, not yet in operation) and EURODAC (information on asylum seeker claims). The UK has also supported cooperation on border enforcement by showing its willingness to opt in to regulations on FRONTEX, the common border security agency (EU Council, 2006, para 24c).

The external dimension

Labour has also promoted a 'new' policy approach to countries along Europe's borders, particularly North Africa. This generally falls under the rubric of Europe's 'external dimension'. In return for development expertise, resources and 'mobility packages'[4] (easing visa restrictions and the potential for limited access to EU labour markets), countries on Europe's borders are expected to conclude readmission agreements and improve border management and security.

Labour has been at the forefront of such moves, particularly during Charles Clarke's time at the Home Office (Clarke, 2006). The 'global approach to migration', as it was named, was the flagship initiative on migration during the UK presidency of the EU in the second half of 2005. It was also successful: the European Council adopted the *Global approach to migration: Priority actions focusing on Africa and the Mediterranean* in its Conclusions of 16 December 2005.

European leaders discussed this 'global approach' in conferences in Rabat in July 2006 and Tripoli in November 2006 and gave it renewed impetus in the Finnish presidency conclusions of December 2006. Despite the fact that operational action remains in its infancy, Labour has been supportive of the approach because it fits well with the framework of reducing unauthorised migration (the measures have stressed control elements) while advancing international development goals.

Europe's many policy levers

The above analysis suggests the EU has had some distinct impacts on UK migration policy. However, the multi-layered governance that characterises European policy making makes for a more complicated picture.

The Council of Ministers, meeting at the Justice and Home Affairs Council, make the decisions on the majority of asylum and immigration policies. However, there are also inter-ministerial meetings and agreements outside of the Justice and Home Affairs Council. These are both formal and informal.

On a formal basis, states may agree certain treaties outside EU mechanisms that are incorporated into the European system at a later date, such as the 1985 Schengen Treaty or the Dublin Convention. To take the latter as an example, the Dublin Convention laid down the rules on determining which country must assess asylum claims (with the intention to prevent asylum being claimed in more than one country) and was agreed outside of EU mechanisms in 1990. Its successor, Dublin II, was negotiated inside the EU mechanisms and was strongly supported by Labour, led by Home Office minister Lord Filkin, in 2003.

On an informal basis, regular meetings occur at a national ministerial level. The most important for the UK have been the G6 meetings, typically held on a six-monthly basis between the Home Secretary and his equivalents in five other large EU countries (France, Germany, Italy, Poland and Spain). This initiative began in 2003 following a dialogue between David Blunkett and the then French Interior Minister, Nicolas Sarkozy (European Union Committee, 2006). The G6 meetings have helped steer policy on migration at the EU level, particularly with elements of security harmonisation. At the March 2006 meeting in Heiligendamm, Germany, for example, agreement was reached on new measures for combating illegal migration, expanding border and biometric controls, and sharing information (European Union Committee, 2006). The following meeting in Stratford-upon-Avon on 25–26 October 2006, chaired by John Reid, produced an agreement to exchange information on engagement with Muslim communities and on measures to disrupt organised immigration crime, and confirmed that the 'global approach' was the basis of future policy (European Union Committee, 2007, pp 15–18).

There are two other important EU institutions involved in EU asylum and immigration policy: the European Parliament and the European Commission. The European Parliament has power as a co-legislator in some areas of asylum and immigration policy, under the co-decision procedure. It is not only shared decision making that is important but also the fact that Members of the European Parliament are often elected from mainstream parties (including the Labour Party) and thus have a direct link to policy formulation in the EU.

The European Commission has a unique role because it can propose legislation in areas where it has competence to do so. The Commission has produced a range of policies on migration. In 2007, for example, the Commission plans to produce a framework directive on legal migration for the highly skilled, following the *Policy plan on legal migration* published in 2005. While the Commission is free to formulate and then propose policies, in practice its actions are limited by the priorities of the Member State that holds the six-month rotating EU presidency. It also needs to pass proposals through the European Parliament and, particularly, the Council of Ministers, who co-decide policy and can ultimately reject any proposals. Furthermore, when initiating a policy proposal, the European Commission must honour the principle of subsidiarity, where the EU only takes decisions and makes policy in areas where it has to. To put it more bluntly, the Commission cannot take decisions that should be left for the national level. As a result, it tends to be opportunistic, driven by the agenda of member states.

These decision-making processes and mechanisms, some formal and some informal, some made on an inter-governmental basis and some on a Community level, have meant that European directives and decisions are framed according to states' interests. Such interests have focused on the strengthening of control mechanisms, particularly regarding borders, and measures to reduce unauthorised migration. Geddes (2003, p 107) neatly describes the EU policy framework as centred 'on control and security dimensions'.

States in charge, but negotiating

The UK is known in EU policy circles for maintaining a strong national line on certain policies, which are determined in Whitehall. Keeping to a centrally determined line can often be difficult in the somewhat chaotic environment of the EU where there are (currently) 27 negotiating parties. Nonetheless, the UK has supported a number of measures, particularly on asylum and unauthorised migration, which it would have preferred not to. Much horse-trading takes place behind closed doors in the Council of Ministers and it is likely that when the UK signs up reluctantly to one directive, it is part of a deal brokered with one or several other EU member states to take the UK's line on another piece of legislation.

This suggests a process of negotiation. Clearly, nation states, especially the larger ones, who possess greater negotiating weight, are leading the way (as opposed to the European Commission). Yet negotiations are likely to be expedited by the EU's institutions, mechanisms, and fora for communication. On security issues, for example, the EU has hastened negotiated progress on policy and facilitated contact between officials in different states.

In addition to political cooperation, there has also been a strong legal input to UK migration policy through the jurisprudence of the European Court of Human Rights (as discussed in the previous chapter). Furthermore, the deepening relationship between the UK and the EU necessarily means that policy development is becoming increasingly interdependent.

Judging the influence of the European Union on policy making will never be clear-cut: there is no counterfactual – the European Union exists – but it seems unlikely that policy would have progressed in the same way without the EU in the period 1997–2007.

Notes

[1] Cyprus and Malta also joined on 1 May 2004.

[2] The UK has promised to review its restrictions in early 2008.

[3] There is one exception in regard to GATS, where the European Commission negotiates on behalf of the UK and other member states.

[4] The European Commission has rephrased this as 'mobility partnerships'.

TEN

Networks: the engine room of policy development

This chapter synthesises the key argument of this book: that a narrow interpretation of the Westminster model – of an overarching executive – is out of date and that migration policy change since 1997 has taken place in a more plural, fragmented environment. External actors, rather than an overarching executive, have had significant impact on certain dimensions of policy.

Such an argument is illustrated by adopting a specific model of interest group/government relations referred to as 'policy networks'. Policy networks are 'a means of categorising the relationships that exist between groups and the government' (Smith, 1993, p 56). This is different to the interest-group model, where the development of policy is seen in the context of competing interest groups. Instead, policy networks operate in a fragmented policy environment and are characterised by interdependence and constant 'manoeuvres' to gain resources (Evans, 1999). They are involved in a power relationship that may be a positive-sum gain, rather than the zero-sum gain of classic interest-group analysis.

Different types of policy network lie along a continuum (Marsh and Rhodes, 1992). Smith (1993), following Marsh and Rhodes, categorises the two extremes of the continuum as a 'policy community' and an 'issue network', which will be the terminology used in the analysis of two migration policy networks below. The literature on policy networks is significant and a certain familiarity with the conceptual model is assumed (Marsh et al, 2001; Marsh and Smith, 2000; for the model's most significant critique, see Dowding, 1995).

Economic migration: A policy community

The analysis of the economic migration network, with characteristics that correlate to a policy community, rests on five 'nodes' or groups of actors. Inevitably, in categorising any network, some voices are considered less important. For example, trade unions are not included, even though the TUC, UNISON and the TGWU (in particular) have participated in the economic migration network, because the trade unions were not core members of the policy network.

Employers

The first node is made up of employers who have pushed the government for a more liberal position on economic migration. Spencer (2002, 2003) confirms their importance in the development of Labour's migration policy, describing employers as forthright in pushing for policies to attract the 'brightest and best'. Employers who have lobbied for high-skilled labour migration include insurance companies, major oil and energy companies (such as BP and Shell), accountancy firms and financial companies working in the City of London financial markets. Low-cost airlines, major supermarket firms, recruitment agencies and hotel and catering industries have lobbied for more low-skill labour migration. One of the links between the business network discussed here and the macro-force of globalisation discussed in Chapter 7 is that many of the actors applying pressure for change are intrinsically *global* – such as the major high street banks, with outlets across the world. Typically, these disparate actors do not form a single bloc, but are brought together in associations. This first node therefore tends to coalesce around the major industry associations representing employers.

The major employers' associations have all been pro-immigration from 1997 to 2007. This is typified in the pro-labour market immigration stance adopted by the CBI, the major employers' association, but also by the Federation of Small Businesses (FSB) and the Institute of Directors. The CBI has softened its pro-immigration stance from around 2006 by supporting restrictions on Romania and Bulgaria (CBI, 2006), but the other associations have remained strongly pro-immigration, supporting free movement in the EU without restrictions (FSB, 2006; Institute of Directors, 2007).

Sector-specific industry associations, including the British Hospitality Association (hotels and catering), the Association of Labour Providers (gangmasters) and the National Farmers' Union (farming businesses), have also been pro-immigration and active in the debate, both formally, in terms of responses to consultations, and informally, with lobbying of civil servants and ministers.

Lawyers

The legal profession represents the second node in the economic migration policy community, because it channels the voices and interests of its clients (major businesses). Like the employer lobby, the legal profession has argued for a liberalisation of commercial immigration and is often represented by 'associations', most obviously by the Immigration Law Practitioners' Association's Business and Employment sub-committee, the pre-eminent legal voice in the economic migration policy community. Chaired by Phillip Trott of Bates, Wells & Braithwaite and including members from a series of leading law firms, such as Cameron McKenna, Fox Williams, Kingsley Napley, and Luqmani Thompson, the committee (and the legal profession it represents) is important in a number of ways.

First, government is reliant on cooperation with lawyers to deliver policy measures, reducing government 'control'. Second, lawyers are often practised in the legal procedures conducted within Parliament and understand the drafting of legislation and the codes used in its formulation. Third, lawyers are part of a largely cohesive profession. The legal profession has had input at the parliamentary stage, the drafting of programme stage, and in the implementation phase. For instance, lawyers had a hands-on role in the policy development of the original Highly Skilled Migrant Programme. When the programme was first conceived, policy makers envisaged a scheme where a high- skilled applicant would gain a certain number of points that would then allow him or her to come to the UK with up to 20 'unpointed' people (people who did not have to pass a points test). The idea was to attract small, high-value companies such as IT ventures. It was the legal profession that pointed out the inherent dangers of fraud and did much to outline and develop the system as it is now formulated.[1]

Lobbyists

The third node on the 'economic migration policy community' map is the member-only groups and committees that exist to lobby the government. These exist at both formal and informal levels. The formal level includes groups such as the Illegal Working Steering Group (IWSG). Originally set up by Beverly Hughes in November 2002, the IWSG is made up of major retailers, supermarkets, associations representing labour agencies and the hotel industry as well as invited members with relevant expertise. The IWSG advises on illegal working provisions but the agenda is wide ranging and allows important access, as it is chaired by the Minister of Immigration.

At a less formal level, PR companies have lobbied on promoting economic migration (particularly for high-skilled work permits) while business member-only organisations, such as the Westminster Forum, which exist to lobby government ministers on issues relevant to business, have held several sessions on migration policy.

Think tanks

The fourth key node is the influential coterie of think tanks and research organisations with links to the Labour government or 'progressive' centre-left politics. In particular, the Institute for Public Policy Research (ippr) has pushed the positives of labour immigration from the mid-1990s onwards and has been instrumental in both informing the evidence base and placing it on politically fertile ground (Corry, 1996; Spencer, 1994).

Other think tanks and research organisations in the UK, notably MigrationWatch, Civitas and the Optimum Population Trust, have opposed large immigration flows. Their analysis has highlighted the limitations of certain policy approaches. For example, the demographic argument that migration is the solution to an ageing population was made strongly from the late 1990s (UNDP, 2000). This has been significantly undermined by think tanks such as MigrationWatch, who point out that net immigration would have to rise exponentially to meet demographic deficits. Similarly, the think tank Civitas made several interventions in the debate in early 2003, with the general policy position that immigration should be reduced (Browne, 2002; Harris, 2003). However, while these think tanks have made waves in the press (MigrationWatch stands out in this regard), they have been largely excluded from the economic migration policy community, probably a result of almost Malthusian policy recommendations (placing them outside the ideological status quo) and because of politics (while think tanks generally have charitable status, they are strongly orientated to certain political positions). Thus, they are not represented on advisory bodies or generally consulted by civil servants developing policy. Their outlets tend to be opposition (Conservative) MPs and media outlets such as the *Daily Mail, Daily Express*, and the *Daily Telegraph*: 'classic outsider group strategy' (Marsh et al, 2001, p 184).

Government

The final and most important node is the government. Crucially, in the 'economic migration policy community', government is not confined to just the Home Office but includes the Treasury, the Department for Work and Pensions (DWP), and the Department of Trade and Industry, together with the Bank of England.[2] Other departments also have a stake in economic migration policy. For example, the Department for Education and Skills has an interest in the impact on skill levels and the Department of Health has an interest in foreign labour.

However, the Treasury is by far the most powerful of these players and, under Labour, has had a strong political influence over particular departments, such as DWP. The Treasury recognised the economic benefits of migration to the macro-economy early, and especially the clear fiscal gain (migration was good for the coffers). While there was no 'battle', the government – as the key player in any network – was not restricted to a single department (the Home Office) but in a set of departments, one of which was the all-powerful Treasury, which helped ensure the Home Office moved policy in a liberal direction.

Policy network theory dictates that to be consistent with a strong 'policy community', all the above players must share the same ideology. The economic migration network is characterised by support for a liberal ideology, open trade and globalisation (see Chapter 7). There have been three mutually reinforcing effects on this ideology.

First, New Labour ideology strongly supports policies that are pro-market, provided they are coupled with 'social justice' (Ellison and Pierson, 2003). Thus New Labour's belief in the global 'knowledge economy' (Timmins, 2001) is in line with a liberalisation of the economic migration system.

Second, the government-funded research agenda on migration, which began in earnest from around 1999, prioritised the 'economics' of migration, along with asylum and illegal immigration. The findings of this research have strongly supported the theoretical supposition that migration brings economic benefits, creating an empirical justification for the policy. Two streams of work, jointly conducted by the Cabinet Office and the Home Office, deserve particular mention as a number of their recommendations contributed directly to policy development. The first stream of work produced a series of publications (for example, Gott and Johnson, 2002) and was brought together in the joint Home Office/Cabinet Office publication *Migration: An economic and social analysis* (Glover et al, 2001). The second stream of work also led to a

number of publications (for example, Mitchell and Pain, 2003).[3] DWP
has also conducted a number of studies on economic migration. The joint
approach to research and strategy has broadened the economic migration
policy network. The personnel have also overlapped. For example, the
team that produced the 2001 report was led by Jonathan Portes in the
Cabinet Office, who went on to become Chief Economist at DWP.

Third, the ideology is one shared by other developed countries.
Theories of international policy transfer have not traditionally been
seen as important in migration policy development (Dolowitz, 1997;
Dolowitz and Marsh, 1996). This is perhaps either because transfer has not
happened or because the major international organisations (as the agents
of transfer) are not considered players in the domestic debates. However,
in the case of economic migration policy, there are unambiguous debts to
US, Canadian, New Zealand and Australian migration policies. UK policy
makers have consulted various supra-national organisations (such as the
OECD) and think tanks have acted as agents in policy transfer (Stone,
2001). This was well illustrated by the Home Office's official consultation
on the points system, which was hosted by ippr and attended by Australian
and Canadian experts. There is tangible evidence of policy transfer, most
obviously the creation of the UK points-based programme (the Highly
Skilled Migrant Programme), which closely resembles Canadian and
Australian models (Geddes, 2005, p 727).

The combination of a limited number of actors, external players
with resources and a shared ideology suggests the economic migration
network closely resembles a policy community, especially when policy
was liberalised in 2001–02.

Asylum policy: an issue network

Members of the network that deals with asylum policy lack resources,
are less stable and, most importantly of all, do not share the same
ideological worldview. Asylum policy has been subjected to a valuable
network analysis (Statham and Geddes, 2006). Statham and Geddes'
description refers to immigration politics and is somewhat flawed in that
nearly all the actors they describe are asylum (rather than immigration)
groups. However, their analysis is particularly useful for mapping the
four nodes of the asylum policy network.

Government

The most important node in the asylum policy network is the
disproportionately powerful Home Office. Unlike the economic

migration network, the only other government department outside of the Home Office with a concrete interest in asylum policy is the Department for Constitutional Affairs, which is dwarfed in size, budget and political influence by the Home Office. The recent creation of the Ministry of Justice may change this balance, but it is too early to judge at present. Statham and Geddes (2006, p 265) confirm that the state dominates a weak pro-migrant sector. The power of the Home Office as the major resource in the 'asylum policy' network is unrivalled, which contrasts with the 'economic migration' network, in which actors have greater resources.

The Prime Minister's private office has, however, played an energetic role in developing asylum policy (far more than is usual for the Prime Minister's Office). An announcement by the Prime Minister (particularly if it is made to a public audience) essentially 'bounces' the Home Secretary into action. Political advisers in the Prime Minister's private office therefore input ideas into the Home Office policy making apparatus and help steer the overall direction of policy.

Other players

There are three other nodes in the network, which feature a range of scattered actors. The first is the refugee charity sector, typically represented by organisations such as the Refugee Council, Refugee Action and Amnesty International. The second is the legal profession, with actors such as the Refugee Legal Centre, the Immigration Law Practitioners' Association's asylum sub-committee, and the Joint Council for the Welfare of Immigrants. The third is the children's charities, which include all the major charities, often grouped under the auspices of the Refugee Children's Consortia.

All three nodes are well versed in campaigning (behind-the-scenes lobbying, public campaigning and litigation strategies). They also work together effectively, for example in cooperating over responses to legislative Bills or through umbrella bodies such as the Asylum Rights Campaign. Furthermore, they have established formal networks with government, such as the stakeholder group on asylum policy that meets with senior civil servants in IND.

These three nodes have some influence, which contrasts with the majority of those with a stake in the development of asylum policy. Most actors are on the periphery, occasionally 'flitting' into the orbit of asylum policy but rarely staying. Even the groups in the three well-organised nodes have been under pressure in recent years. The legal profession, in particular, has suffered from reductions in public funding of asylum cases and administrative squeezes.

One of the main reasons why asylum policy forms an issue network rather than a policy community is that there is no agreed worldview. There is a genuine ideological divide between the government and the NGO sector on the causes of asylum seeking, the 'pull' and 'push' factors, and whether asylum claims are genuine or not.

This ideological gulf is played out in the debates over 'evidence' in policy making. The evidence used to develop asylum policy is deeply contested. Certain questions are given inadequate attention, even fundamental questions such as the drivers of asylum seeking. The Home Office has often been accused of narrowing the scope of research, delaying publications, or releasing only executive summary findings. For researchers and NGOs, salt is rubbed into the wounds when policy then ignores even these limited findings.

Unlike economic migration, where the evidence comes from different sources, such as in the Economics and Resource Analysis Unit of the Home Office, or other departments, such as DWP and the Cabinet Office, the evidence base on asylum is commissioned exclusively from Immigration Research and Statistics Service. IND must also approve all projects, so researchers' independence is likely to face constraints.

To complicate matters further, the NGO sector is also fractured ideologically. Some NGOs have presented measures that are in tune with Labour's view of asylum. The think tank Demos, for instance, has followed Labour thinking on extra-territorial processing, for example, in its publication *People flow* (Demos, 2003).

The exception that proves the rule is Labour's approach to refugee integration (which some readers may consider to be outside asylum policy). The government has a coherent vision and strategy on refugee integration, largely accepted by the voluntary sector. For example, NGOs have supported the government-sponsored National Refugee Integration Forum (NRIF). This has led to tangible progress, such as with the SUNRISE case-worker programme. However, the disproportionate power of the Home Office is ever present: in October 2006, the NRIF was abolished without warning.

The Home Office: where policy is made?

The two policy networks outlined above, and the importance attached to them in influencing policy, go against the grain of mainstream migration analysis by placing less weight on the executive for certain dimensions of migration policy, namely economic migration. However, this does not mean that state institutions are irrelevant. Theorists have long asserted that institutions are actors in the policy process, shaping values, behaviours and identities (Hall and Taylor, 1996; Smith, 1988). Institutions are generally perceived as stabilising forces in policy development. When radical changes in policy do occur, theorists have suggested they are the result of sudden performance crises or external interventions at critical junctures (Krasner, 1988; March and Olsen, 1989).

The following will argue that the Home Office, as the most important institution, where migration policy is most embedded, has had varying degrees of influence on policy making. It should not be assumed that the Home Office (and more broadly the executive) is central to a convincing narrative of policy development since 1997.

The Home Office is one of the largest and most traditional of Whitehall departments, with the reputation of having an entrenched 'view' (Richards and Smith, 2002). Marsh et al's (2001) analysis of modern Home Secretaries' tenures indicates that it requires concerted efforts to change Home Office culture, often by heavyweight politicians. This would imply that a strong Home Office culture exists which has shaped migration policy. There are certainly specific examples of what might be termed the 'Home Office Memory Bank'.

Policy measures introduced or proposed prior to 1997 have re-emerged in only slightly altered forms under the Labour government. For example, the so-called 'white list' was dropped when Labour first came to power but then re-introduced as policy makers tried to reduce asylum claims. Similarly, an existing law before 1997, never implemented, restricted refugees' 'leave to remain' (residence) to five years. Labour legislated to ensure refugees were given Indefinite Leave to Remain (permanent residence), before performing a volte-face and reintroducing the temporary leave prior to the 2005 election. The temporary leave – restricted to five years – was implemented in August 2005.

There have also been examples of adapting previous policy measures, such as the proposals for financial securities for migrant workers (which would require migrants to pay a deposit before coming to the UK, which would be returned on their departure). Originally introduced as 'bonds' for visitors in the 1999 Act, they were shelved following a consultation. However, in 2005 the Home Office made clear that the powers enacted by the 1999 Act would be used as the legislative basis for bonds for migrant workers coming to the UK. The Home Office, despite widespread opposition to such an initiative, announced it would rename bonds 'financial securities' and introduce them 'in due course' (Home Office, 2006a, p 21).

However, these are rather isolated examples of institutions (in this case the Home Office) 'stabilising' policy development. Much of this book makes the point that there have been significant, even radical, policy changes. How, then, can these be explained? One explanation lies in the external 'shocks' of 2001.

2001: events that changed the course of policy?

In 2001, three major events occurred in quick succession that, taken together, constituted a febrile moment in policy making. The three crises were the riots in Bradford, Burnley and Oldham; the Sangatte issue; and, most importantly, the 11 September 2001 terrorist attacks. David Blunkett was Home Secretary during this period and his biographer, Pollard, suggests that Blunkett made it clear to senior Home Office staff that his agenda – and the world – had changed overnight (Pollard, 2005).

Blunkett initiated a policy review on 12 September and, in a meeting on 14 September, discussed with senior Home Office management the content of a new terrorism Bill, how asylum and immigration concerns would be included, and – apparently for the first time – identity cards (Pollard, 2005, pp 242–4). The events literally piled on top of each other. The date 12 September, when the policy review was initiated, had originally been scheduled for a key meeting to resolve the Sangatte 'crisis'. Perhaps as importantly, the speed and strength of policy change may have been reinforced by Blunkett's chairmanship of key Cabinet committees, including DOP (IT) T (terrorism) and DOP (IT) R (resilience).

The reaction to these external events undoubtedly shook up the policy making firmament and accounted for many policy changes. For example, the US demand that microchips containing individual biometric data be implanted in the passports of visa-waiver countries (which include Britain) partly accounts for the acceleration of new technologies in border controls. But they are less convincing for policy changes that may be considered 'pro-active', such as those made to the economic migration system.

Summary: networks, not the executive by itself, are central to policy development

This chapter has argued that the 'engine room' of policy development is made up of professions, agencies, departments, think tanks and interest groups of the modern polity, and a single, overweening executive is an outdated starting point for analysis. The examination of migration policy development through the lens of network analysis and the detailed discussion of the two policy networks above reveals a more fragmented policy-making environment, less beholden to the all-powerful executive of many previous analyses (for example, Hansen, 2000; Joppke, 1999). The policy network model of interest group/government relations also reveals the importance of disaggregating migration policy into its component parts.

The different dimensions of migration policy correspond to different types of networks along the policy network continuum. Asylum has always been an 'issue network', dominated by the executive (a combination of the Home Office with directional input from the Prime Minister's Office). The examples of the 'Home Office Memory Bank' and the fact that the change of government in 1997 did not hugely affect a trajectory of tougher measures against asylum seekers indicate that the Home Office has had a role in 'stabilising' policy development, a fact that goes with the grain of general analysis of how migration policy has been developed.

In contrast, the economic migration policy network, comprising government departments but also a number of powerful external actors, equates to a strong 'policy community', especially around the years 2001–02, and was instrumental to developing policy.

Notes

[1] The changes in November 2006 to the HSMP went against the wishes of the network and caused friction, including threats of judicial review. This illustrates how networks change over time.

[2] The Bank of England's goal of low inflation has made it a strong supporter of migration.

[3] It should be noted that before 1997, policy was based on very little evidence.

ELEVEN

Politicians and parties

This book has not referred to politics in any meaningful way so far. In part this has been deliberate, to avoid the heuristically convenient yet real-life illusion that policy stages exist, from elections decided on party manifestos to policies subsequently enacted by elected representatives. However, the impression that policy is made in a vacuum is wrong: politics matters. This chapter seeks to examine some of the key events, the most important political players and how the two main parties have locked horns on the issue of migration. The subsequent chapters consider how politicians and parties have responded to electoral attitudes, and how far the media has affected policy.

There are many *political* accounts of immigration policy development (for example: Layton-Henry, 1984, pp 30–43; Saggar, 1992, 1998), some of which have focused on influential politicians, such as Margaret Thatcher (Messina, 1989) or Enoch Powell (Foot, 1969). This is unsurprising as the political decision makers have long been considered important in the policy process (Lasswell, 1948; Parsons, 1995). In fact, Marsh et al (2000) argue that Cabinet ministers have taken on an *increasingly* significant policy-making role over the last decade. Commentators have also suggested that special advisers under New Labour have increased their leverage in pushing through ministerial directives and have a greater role in advising ministers about feasible policy options (Dorey, 2005, p 8). The four Home Secretaries in this study have all employed special advisers with expertise in immigration policy.

Furthermore, interviewees *all* referred to at least one senior politician as having an impact on migration policy. Interviewees generally saw actions taken by politicians as having a direct, causal impact on policy, although this may reflect the complexity of the policy process, even for those intimately involved in it.

'Trigger' events

Senior politicians must be well attuned to changes in society to exercise leadership effectively and last in their positions. The events of 2001 were discussed in the previous chapter (in terms of the impact on the Home Office agenda), but a larger number of events was picked up in the interviews. Interviewees commonly cited the Sangatte 'crisis'; 9/11; the 2001 riots; the accession of 10 countries to the European Union in May 2004; the terrorist attacks of 7 July 2005 (and the two subsequent bomb plots – a month later and then a year later, in August 2006); and finally the Birmingham riots that occurred simultaneously with the unrelated riots in Paris in October 2005.

Unsurprisingly, interviewees cited events and politicians according to their respective areas of expertise. Those concerned with asylum often discussed Sangatte, while those concerned with integration policy often mentioned the northern riots and the London bombings (see Chapter 3). In general, interviewees spoke of particular events as a catalyst for politicians to make certain policy decisions. They can therefore be seen as 'triggers' for aspects of policy change.

Politicians

The most commonly cited politician (in the interviews) was the Prime Minister, Tony Blair, followed by David Blunkett. This section examines these two leaders in more detail, before examining other relevant politicians.

Tony Blair

Tony Blair has held a strong interest in various aspects of immigration, including asylum, security and integration. He has shown particular interest in 'the asylum issue', especially since the start of his second term, when he made it a crucial aspect of his domestic political agenda. A memo from Blair written in the summer of 2002, for example, listed asylum as one of the two key domestic issues (Seldon, 2004, p 681). The reason behind Tony Blair's interest in asylum is, of course, a source of conjecture. One of his biographers, Anthony Seldon, attributes Blair's interest to his 'political antennae', which told him that people felt the asylum system was being exploited. Blair himself felt the asylum system was 'perverse' (Seldon, 2004, pp 635–6). Another plausible explanation was voiced by one interviewee, who pointed towards Blair's desire to develop narratives on issues that 'the Left' had previously ignored. The failure to deliver a viable approach to issues such as immigration meant parties of the Left were not perceived as the natural parties of government. This view was apparently triggered by the failure of the Labour Party in Australia, who lost consecutive elections over the issues of crime and immigration.

Tony Blair grappled with asylum from 2000 onwards and many of the ideas he promoted found their way into the policy process around this time. Gripped by the idea of extra-territorial processing of asylum seekers, his interest is imprinted on policy proposals launched at the national level (Home Office, 2003a) and at the European level (for example at the 2002 Seville summit). Blair's interest in asylum peaked in September 2004, when he first laid down what was to become a crucial asylum target: 'By the end of 2005, and for the first time in Britain, we will remove more each month than apply and so restore faith in a system we know has been abused' (Blair, 2004b). The so-called 'tipping point target' has had a major role in changing the direction of asylum policy and realigning resources (see Chapter 4).

Tony Blair's second interest was in security, and he personally prompted certain measures (see Chapter 2). For example, after the resignation of Minister for Immigration Beverly Hughes, Blair ordered a 'one day summit' on asylum and immigration at Number 10. The attendees included David Blunkett, Jack Straw, Lord Falconer, Lord Goldsmith and Des Browne (then the new Minister for Immigration) and members of the security services. At the summit a range of immigration issues was discussed, with a particular focus on control (BBC Politics, 2004).

Finally, Tony Blair's interest in various integration initiatives has made the subject an important part of his 'policy legacy' in his last year in office. In a major speech on multiculturalism in 2006, he proposed a new measure linking the funding of community organisations to integration (Blair, 2006b).

Tony Blair's interest in different aspects of migration policy has led him to take 'personal charge' of delivery. He has kept a firm grip on aspects of migration policy through the coordinating mechanisms of government. For example, he set up the Cabinet committee MISC20 in 2002, which expanded the focus of its predecessor, MISC16, from examining 'illegal working and managed migration policy' to the 'social and economic aspects of migration' (*Hansard*, 24 June 2002, col 721W). He also chaired the successor to MISC20, the Asylum and Migration Cabinet committee, the terms of reference of which are 'to consider the impacts of migration; and coordinate and oversee delivery of the government's policies on asylum and immigration' (Cabinet Office, 2007).

By taking a public role, the Prime Minister can 'bounce' his Home Secretary into action, but it is through his private office that much of the pressure on the Home Office is applied. The rise of special advisers has facilitated this aspect of policy making.

David Blunkett

David Blunkett became Home Secretary after Labour's second election victory in 2001. Within a week of assuming the role of Home Secretary, he laid down a very public manifesto in an article for *The Sunday Times*, published on 10 June 2001, In it, he said there would be a need to connect 'the work permit system with the needs of the economy', to fill skill shortages and undermine illegal immigration. He therefore took a close interest in economic migration from the start of his tenure at the Home Office (so much so that he 'brought' Workpermits (UK) with him (Chapter 5).

However, most interviewees associated David Blunkett with integration. He took a personal interest in a range of integration measures, perhaps inspired by a belief in communitarianism.[1] In particular, he developed the community cohesion agenda and active citizenship policies and appointed one of his mentors, Bernard Crick, to the task force designed to prepare the ground for the new language and citizenship tests.

The final area of migration policy in which Blunkett took a strong interest was asylum, not least prompted by the Sangatte 'crisis'. Blunkett believed that Labour had to 'get a grip' of the immigration machinery and demonstrate toughness in order to be taken seriously on the issue (Pollard, 2005, p 219). Asylum was the 'hot potato' political issue of the time, and he emphasised the need to instil order.

Politicians in arms

Tony Blair and David Blunkett did not operate in isolation. Their importance in influencing the policy process rests in part on their making migration policy a priority while *both* were at the zenith of their power and influence, at the beginning of the second term of the Labour government. At precisely the same time (2001–03), the two men enjoyed a strong personal and political relationship where their political stars were aligned, and they worked closely together (Seldon, 2004).

The strength of this alignment can be shown in Blunkett's success in his battle with the then Lord Chancellor, Derry Irvine. Irvine was the Lord Chancellor during most of Blunkett's period in the Home Office and clashed with Blunkett privately and publicly (Pollard, 2005, pp 270–1), mostly on the direction of asylum reform. While David Blunkett was approaching the apogee of his influence, Derry Irvine was still a major legal figure, and former pupil master to Tony Blair.

In essence, they clashed over the legal protections accorded to (among others) asylum seekers, and, following an unwise and unscheduled BBC Radio 4 Today programme interview where Derry Irvine criticised Blunkett's approach, he was pushed out. The impolitic Radio 4 interview spelled the end for Irvine, but it was Blunkett who had successfully isolated him politically.

Other Labour politicians

Blair and Blunkett are not the only Labour politicians who have had an impact on policy formulation. New Labour is often cast as the creature of two politicians: Tony Blair and Gordon Brown. Gordon Brown is often seen at the crux of domestic policy formulation, so to suggest he has had little influence may strike readers as unusual. But in regard to migration policy, this appears to be the case, barring three aspects of policy (Somerville, 2007).

First, he has consistently recognised the macro-economic benefits of migration and has generally supported liberalisation measures. This has allowed others the freedom to manoeuvre. For example, the development of economic migration policy in the first Labour term was, in effect, sanctioned by the Treasury.

Second, the Scottish Gordon Brown has made several speeches on 'Britishness' and citizenship that have given a particular gloss to 'integration' policy. For example, he contributed to a Smith Institute pamphlet in 1999, and made a major speech to the Fabian Society in 2005 in which he floated the idea of a 'national day' to celebrate Britishness. A public relations offensive in June 2007 by Liam Byrne, Minister for Immigration, and Ruth Kelly, Secretary of State for DCLG, together with a Fabian Pamphlet – entitled *A Common Place* – they co-authored, suggests a more substantial citizenship programme, including a citizenship day, may be in the offing. Such policy proposals clearly take their lead from Gordon Brown.

Third, he was chiefly responsible for freezing spending for the first two years of the Labour government, from 1997–99. There seems little doubt that this had a major effect on the ability of the immigration machinery to cope with the increasing volume of migrants and the escalation of asylum claims.

These three influences are, compared to Brown's impact on other policy areas, relatively insignificant. It also appears that Brown has been generally supportive of Labour's migration policy. The obvious exception to this was a documented spat over the prominence of asylum policy in Labour's second term of government. Seldon (2004) suggests that Gordon Brown believed Tony Blair's focus on asylum to be deeply misguided. However, this was apparently less to do with the *content* or *direction* of policy on asylum and more to do with placing too high a priority on asylum as a political issue.

It is important not to ignore other Labour politicians. They include the other Home Secretaries, Jack Straw, Charles Clarke and John Reid, and a spectrum of other ministers. Different politicians stand out as important for different policy themes. Barbara Roche (as Minister for Immigration) and Alan Johnson (as Minister for Competitiveness) stand out as strongly supportive of a liberal immigration regime. Together with Margaret Hodge, they were influential in the birth of Labour's managed migration policy.

Jack Straw stands out for trying to incorporate human rights and race statutes into immigration policy. His tacit support for economic migration, while Home Secretary, ensured that, when David Blunkett arrived at the Home Office, the ground had been prepared for major policy change. Beverly Hughes was instrumental to many of the reforms conducted during 2001 and 2002, including some of the integration reforms (on citizenship and refugee integration) as well as pushing through a stronger response to unauthorised immigration. Des Browne was effective in driving through reforms to the asylum system and in taking a more restrictive line toward unaccompanied asylum-seeking children, while his successor, Tony McNulty, proved less able to deliver policy reform but more capable of successfully passing legislation.

More recently, John Reid and Liam Byrne have been associated with institutional reform of the immigration system (such as the Home Office split and the Border and Immigration Agency) and in prioritising policy on unauthorised migration and border control.

The Conservative politicians

The leaders of the Conservative party since 1997, William Hague, Iain Duncan Smith, Michael Howard and David Cameron, have all – to some degree or another – influenced the UK immigration system. Of these, Michael Howard emerges as having had the most impact on the process as he made immigration a centrepiece of his 2005 election campaign, discussed more fully below.

The other key figure in the Conservative Party who must be mentioned is David Davis, the long-serving Shadow Home Secretary. He has proved himself to be a master at uncovering inefficiency in the Home Office and using it for political gain (or pain) in Parliament.

David Cameron may, in the future, prove to be the most influential of all Conservative leaders in this period, as he represents a change in Conservative Party thinking on immigration. While the substance of this change is unclear, the tenor of debate is important and the period of his leadership may come to be viewed as a rapprochement of party positions that could entrench a new 'immigration settlement'. The period immediately after the Conservatives' election loss in 2005 provided space for a more balanced debate, particularly because migration proposals had played such a prominent role in the 2005 election campaign. Prominent Conservatives with either strong 'social conservatism' or 'free-market' orientations pushed a new policy direction. For example, during the fencing for leadership, John Bercow, MP for Buckingham, put forward proposals on how Conservative policies should be developed (Bercow, 2005) that were moderate in comparison to *all* parties.

More important are the changes that David Cameron has made since becoming leader. The most obvious is the frequency (or more aptly, infrequency) of statements on immigration. He has deliberately avoided the issue. More concretely, he has commissioned a policy review on migration, the content of which is not known at the time of writing, but its chair, the Shadow Immigration Minister, is Damien Green, MP for Ashford, known as a social or 'one nation' Conservative. He is vice-president of the Tory Reform Group (its president is Ken Clarke) and chair of Parliamentary Mainstream (the parliamentary arm of Conservative Mainstream), whose aims are 'to be open-minded and generous in social policy'.

There are some indications of what migration policy may resemble under Conservative rule, and they are significantly different from those adopted by the Conservatives under Michael Howard. A 2006 pamphlet by Damien Green and David Davis acknowledged the benefits of an economic migration system, and suggested that the system should work to select the most valuable migrants and encourage temporary migrants, while also ensuring services are not overburdened and community tensions are reduced (Davis and Green, 2006). The Conservatives have also proposed some measures. On 3 January 2007, David Davis announced their support for the European Convention on Action Against Trafficking in Human Beings, a law that guarantees minimum protection for the victims of trafficking. In effect, this support outflanked Labour on the left. On 22 January 2007, Tony Blair announced that the UK would sign the Convention.

Liberal Democrat politicians

The third major party, the Liberal Democrat Party, has generally focused on maintaining rights for migrants and adopting a line far more 'progressive' than either Labour or the Conservatives. Despite its success in the House of Lords, where many Liberal Democrat peers have amended Bills and either slowed or blocked House of Commons legislation, the impact of the Liberal Democrat Pary has been limited.

Parties

Migration is unusual in that it cuts across traditional 'left' and 'right' politics and may internally divide particular political parties (see, for example, Layton-Henry, 1992). In addition to inter- and intra-party differences, there may also be differences according to the regions or territories of the UK, which have different demographic and political calculations to make. The Labour Party in Scotland is a good example of this. While migration policy is a 'reserved matter' (decided only in Westminster), the reality of devolution has led to differences. For example, the suspension of family deportations of failed asylum seekers in Scotland followed a significant campaign from pressure groups, with substantial support inside the Scottish Parliament.

Any discussion of politics and immigration cannot ignore how the far or radical right – in the UK, this refers to the National Front and, particularly, the British National Party (BNP) – has influenced policy development (see, for example, Schain, 2006).

Mainstream political parties do not seem to have 'co-opted' the positions of the BNP, in an attempt to squeeze them further to the margins. In examining policy trends, while there have been restrictive asylum measures, a tougher line on unauthorised migrants and a vigorous assertion of values – which could be at least a partial response to the threat of the BNP – managed migration policy appears unaffected and even elements of the 'affected' themes are not a *direct* response. For example, there has been no capping of numbers, and asylum dispersal was hardly a policy designed to undermine the BNP. However, while policy may not have been dramatically altered, the BNP may reconfigure the terms of engagement between parties as issues such as integration or the volume of immigration flows remain high on the agenda, at local and national levels. Furthermore, in specific cases, such as Barking and Dagenham in London, the BNP is Labour's main challenger, and requires normal electoral engagement, rather than the 'politics of isolation'.

The three elections

The remainder of this chapter is devoted to an analysis of the three general elections and how the parties campaigned on immigration policy. Elections rarely turn on single issues and parties may define themselves differently at different points in the electoral cycle. Parties may also have different packages of policies on show to different audiences. For example, in October 2005 Labour published a list of its top 50 achievements for its members (Labour Party, 2005b), but none related to asylum seekers, refugees or migrants specifically. The only two that could be considered relevant are number 42 (the Human Rights Act) and number 49 (the Race Relations (Amendment) Act), both of which were first-term achievements and unrepresentative of the direction of migration policy. In contrast, prior to the May 2006 local elections, Labour campaign organisers gave advice on five key local messages for campaigners to use on the doorstep. One of them (the fourth message) was relevant: a statement that Labour had successfully halved asylum applications. This vignette of political marketing illustrates an ambivalent party position towards a liberal party audience on one the hand and a tough and restrictive message for certain local electorates on the other. Nonetheless, examining party positions at elections provides a useful sketch of how parties have approached immigration.

The 1997 and 2001 elections

The 1997 and 2001 election manifestos are marked largely by the *absence* of migration policy measures, although the temperature was rising by 2001, particularly on asylum issues. However, the political configuration of New Labour has meant that it is important for the party to arrest a traditional gap in electoral perception that it is 'soft' on immigration. (It may not be entirely coincidental that immigration is often associated with crime in Labour policy categories, as they are both considered 'weak spots' in the electoral armour.) However, at both the 1997 and 2001 elections there was no politicisation of major immigration changes. All major parties were virtually silent on immigration.

Labour's 1997 manifesto made reference to strict rules, dropping the primary purpose rules and streamlining visa appeals. It also referred to asylum, mainly in terms of speeding up decisions and ensuring a 'crackdown' on fraudulent [immigration] advisers and certification (Labour Party, 1997). On the subject of integration, Labour promised a new law criminalising racial harassment. The Conservative Party was even less voluble – giving over only two short sentences to the subject – and promising 'firm, but fair immigration controls' and asylum seekers treated sympathetically if they were genuine (Conservative Party, 1997). On 'integration', it referred to legislation on protection from harassment.

Labour's 2001 manifesto contains only one paragraph on immigration and three on asylum (Labour Party, 2001, p 34). On economic immigration, Labour only briefly mentioned skill shortages. On asylum, Labour acknowledged that it was important to provide a home to those fleeing persecution and to integrate refugees, but also a restatement that asylum was not an alternative immigration route and tougher measures were needed. (The manifesto included the target to deport 30,000 people.) On integration, there was a general commitment to diversity and to common values in a multiracial society, but concrete measures focused on implementing the remaining recommendations of the Stephen Lawrence inquiry (and pointing to their achievement in passing of the 2000 Race Relations Amendment Act). The Conservatives' 2001 manifesto commitments were entirely focused on asylum. Under the heading 'A safe haven, not a soft touch, on asylum', the manifesto criticised backlogs, costs, the 'chaos' in the system and proposed that all asylum seekers would be secured in reception centres (Conservative Party, 2001, p 31). Neither economic immigration nor integration was mentioned, aside from a fleeting mention about building a stronger society of all races.

The 2005 election

In contrast, immigration was at the centre of debates during the 2005 election. The Conservative Party made an early, powerful intervention in the immigration debate with an advert in *The Sunday Times* on 23 January 2005, laying out proposals for a new immigration policy. This was followed by a speech by Michael Howard the following day, when he advocated some *extremely* restrictive measures, including withdrawing from the 1951 Refugee Convention and imposing an annual quota. The measures were perhaps even more far-reaching than the Conservatives themselves realised, as they would have involved a renegotiation of the UK's relationship with the European Union, a fact that had appeared to escape the notice of those responsible for drawing up the ideas. They were nonetheless included in the Conservative manifesto (Conservative Party, 2005, p 19). Equally as important as the restrictive policy prescriptions was the tone used by the Conservatives. For instance, one of their political campaign adverts read: 'It is not racist to impose limits on immigration'. The Conservative intervention was thus not simply one of individual policy measures but one of direction, appealing to anti-immigrant feeling.

Labour did not sit idle while the Conservatives set the agenda. In an obviously political calculation in advance of the May general election, Labour released a five-year plan on asylum and immigration, *Controlling our borders: Making migration work for Britain*, in February 2005. Labour chose to publicise many of the restrictive measures but also to defend the Refugee Convention (Home Office, 2005a, p 17). The five-year plan was a clear response to the Conservative proposals, especially given the fact that a first-term Labour government had publicly floated ideas of renegotiating the said Convention.

This was made explicit in Labour's 2005 manifesto, which pointed to Conservative proposals as 'savage' and its asylum policies as 'fantasy island' (Labour Party, 2005a, p 54). The manifesto reiterated the plans for a points system (Labour Party, 2005a, p 52), but the majority of commitments were restrictive. The proposals fell under the chapter 'Crime and Security' and, unsurprisingly, were largely punitive, such as fines for employers of illegal immigrants, fast-tracking, and removals of failed asylum seekers. Such commitments were presented in the manifesto next to 'tough action to combat international terrorism' (Labour Party, 2005a, p 53).

Examining the three elections, one clearly sees that the parties have reacted to one another's proposals and in certain policy areas – notably asylum – there is evidence of a 'race to the bottom', overlaid with a discourse on security. The absence of other policies, such as economic migration, signifies a more general acceptance of the policy across the political spectrum.

Note

[1] Communitarianism favours community politics as a response to the atomistic consequences of liberal politics, and David Blunkett certainly met (or rather shared an evening meal) with the leading communitarian thinker Amitai Etzioni during his time at the Home Office. Tony Blair is also said to have been influenced by the communitarianism of John MacMurray (see for example, Rentoul, 1995; for a thoroughly opposite view, Hale, 2002).

TWELVE

Public attitudes

This chapter examines how public attitudes influence UK migration policy. A key line of thinking in the literature, drawing on political science, posits that the attitudes of the public are reflected in policy as government reacts to voters' intentions, as one would expect in a liberal democratic society (Hansen, 2000). However, there is a second, more traditional line of thinking that draws on sociology. This explains UK migration policy change as paternalistic and elite driven. The 'elite' were of their time, and worked in a framework of empire and commonwealth that was prejudiced against non-white immigration (Paul, 1997; Spencer, 1997). Such attitudes were widespread in British society, which was overwhelmingly hostile towards non-white immigrants: in other words British society was (and may remain) socialised against non-white immigration.

These two arguments tend to have one particular feature in common. To differing degrees, they assume that public attitudes have influenced migration policy to restrict entrants to the UK, with the aim of a 'zero-migration' settlement; and that from the 1970s this has more or less been successfully achieved. However, earlier chapters have shown that 'zero-migration' no longer exists in practice or intention, which in turn demands a rethink.

This chapter takes its cue from such debates and is based on two questions. What are public attitudes to immigration? And have such attitudes impacted on political calculations?

Public attitudes: are they negative?

The growing evidence base on public attitudes towards immigration (for example, ICAR, 2005a; Coe et al, 2004; Crawley, 2005; Saggar and Drean, 2001) clearly shows that there is widespread resentment of immigrants in the UK, particularly of asylum seekers and illegal immigrants (Halman, 2001; McLaren and Johnson, 2004; Lewis, 2005). The most conclusive evidence on UK attitudes comes from the *British social attitudes survey*, which has tracked public attitudes since 1983. The trend over the course of Labour's administration is one of rising resentment: in 1995 approximately two-thirds of the population believed the numbers of immigrants should be reduced, a proportion that rose to three-quarters by 2003 (McLaren and Johnson, 2004, p 172).

The fact that measures of public attitudes indicate hostility towards immigrants is unlikely to be a revelation to readers. Significantly though, public attitudes are not homogenous, differing by gender, race, geography, wealth, education, values and other variables. In discussing attitudes, commentators have generally not paid enough attention to the *segmentation* of attitudes, such as differences according to ethnicity, with minority groups less likely to be concerned about 'cultural' issues but more concerned over economic competition (COI Communications, 2004; Lewis, 2005). Thus, while the overall, broad-brush picture is one of hostility, with the public generally convinced that there are too many migrants and the country is in an 'immigration mess', the fine-grain picture is rather more complicated.[1]

The question underlying such findings is 'what informs policy?'. In particular, have restrictive immigration and integration measures been predicated on prejudice against non-white immigrants (Spencer, 1997)? Prejudice has different guises (Jackson and Penrose, 1993), and racism based on colour in the 1960s and 1970s (against Asian and Caribbean immigrants) may have changed or merged with the issue of asylum from the late 1980s (Hassan, 2000); and perhaps may now include a religious dimension, as resentment towards Muslims. The 'other' is a crucial concept to understanding how prejudice and negative attitudes are formed and is particularly pertinent to immigration, as immigration and immigrants are at the 'frontier of identity', where British identity is decided (Cohen, 1994).

However, studies suggest that a range of factors, beyond prejudice, contribute to negative attitudes towards immigrants. Chief among these are concerns over employment and welfare competition. Duffy's (2004) survey found high levels of resentment and mistrust towards others regarding the use of public services and benefits, with most suspicion expressed towards asylum seekers and recent migrants, and little towards minorities. Concerns over competition for jobs and other employment concerns have been shown as contributing to negative attitudes (Lewis, 2005). Further, McLaren and Johnson (2004) find evidence that *perceived* social consequences are related to anti-immigrant hostility.

Halman (2001) suggests British attitudes towards immigrants are more negative than the EU average but more positive on the issue of racial diversity, indicating that racism is not the most important factor relative to other countries. In contrast, Dustmann and Preston's work on the causes of negative public attitudes posit three variables of welfare concerns, economic competition and race. They assign race as the key determinant, especially among lower socio-economic groups (Dustmann and Preston, 2003). Other work has confirmed that the degree of racism should not be underestimated (Lewis, 2005).

Furthermore, a binary debate – between race and resource competition – on what forms attitudes may miss a range of other factors, from the media to community interaction. Two factors are particularly relevant to policy: regulation and leadership. Attitudes are influenced by regulation and legislation (Coe et al, 2004), where 'tough legislation' may breed 'tough behaviour'. Bauer et al (2001) find that immigration policy alters 'native sentiments'. They find that countries with strong labour migration policies are more likely to believe migration (and hence immigrants) is good for the economy. They find that countries with strong political migration policies (by which they mean asylum policy) are more likely to believe that immigrants push up crime rates. They conclude that there are 'indications that immigration policies affect natives' sentiments of immigrants' (Bauer et al, 2001, p 24).

The second, more significant, factor is how government responds to negative attitudes. Labour has made clear that the public concern about immigration is valid and policy must respond accordingly. Charles Clarke put major political capital on restoring faith in the immigration system. In his foreword to the five-year plan on immigration he stated, 'When I became Home Secretary I said that my top priority is public confidence in the immigration system' (Home Office, 2005a, p 7).

Flynn (2003) sums up Labour's approach by saying that public statements by senior politicians and government departments often refer to public concern as 'legitimate'. The government approach of 'restoring confidence' in the immigration system is one of responding to concerns rather than challenging them. The experience of Scotland, where more positive attitudes to immigrants exist, and where a strong, positive political message has been given repeated emphasis, indicates that leadership can modify attitudes.

Have public attitudes influenced political calculations?

This brings us to whether Labour has responded – as other political parties would do in a liberal democratic polity – to public attitudes. Here, the work of Anthony Downs (1957) provides a useful purchase on the debate. Downsian theory would predict that Labour would respond to voter preferences by moving to the centre point of the ideological continuum – to the median voter.[2] Together with the fact that Labour has long been sensitive to public opinion (Norris, 2001), it would seem almost inevitable that Labour would chase the median voter.

The MORI polls show that voters consider immigration to be 'important' (MORI, 2007). However, as noted above, it would be facile to suggest that voter preferences are homogenous. In fact, a sizeable minority can now loosely be called pro-immigration (RSA Migration Commission, 2005). Nonetheless, the median voter would like to see less immigration and more restriction. Downsian theory would predict that migration policy would become more restrictive, given the restrictive attitudes of the public. Chapter 4 showed that asylum policy became more restrictive, and the move away from multiculturalism towards integration is one that chimes with a public concerned about losing 'British culture', both of which suggest that policy has responded to the concerns of the median voter. On the other hand, some policies do not conform to the Downsian thesis. Labour has not restricted the volume of immigration or pursued a 'zero-migration' policy, as one would expect. (There may be a significant group that favours an economic migration dimension to policy, but it is not the median voter.) It is also anomalous that government was restrictive towards asylum seekers before 1999, when the public emphasis on race/immigration was slight.

Prejudice against immigrants is widespread in the UK and attitudes have undoubtedly had a bearing on policy. However, the segmentation of attitudes indicates that there is no easy causal leap from prejudice to policy, and negative attitudes do not correlate with the development of all policies. There is a paradox if we consider migration policy as a whole, which might suggest that attitudes are not affecting policy or that opinion polls are unhelpful in explaining attitudes. If we consider the impact on individual policy themes (such as asylum, integration and economic migration) we find a more helpful, albeit incomplete, explanation. Labour's introduction of restrictive asylum policy measures is consistent with 'chasing the median voter', for instance, but its liberal economic migration policy measures are not.

Notes

[1] The trend over time is crucial: the new, politically significant, pro-immigrant group did not exist in the 1960s (RSA Migration Commission, 2005).

[2] This is more likely in a two-party political system (Congleton, 2002).

THIRTEEN

The media: policy in the furnace

This chapter explores the media's influence on migration policy. The UK press regularly reports on the subject of migration. While *The Financial Times*, the *Economist*, and *The Times* (Duvell and Jordan, 2003, p 319) strongly support economic migration, the majority of migration coverage is negative, often connoted with crime, security and social welfare benefits (ICAR, 2005b). This has led some commentators to suggest the media is a malign influence on migration policy development (ICAR, 2005b). Stanley Cohen (2002a) goes further, stating that the coverage of asylum resembles a 'moral panic', with one differentiating factor – the asylum moral panic is *ongoing* (his definition of moral panics are that they are temporal spasms).

The policy makers interviewed for this book, especially politicians and those representing politicians, decried the influence of tabloid newspapers, such as the *Sun* and particularly the *Daily Mail* and the *Daily Express*. Politicians stated that they had no room to manoeuvre or that if they were to take a particular policy line, they would have the proverbial *Mail* reader on their backs. The media itself claims it has a direct effect on policy. Editors of newspapers have, for example, trumpeted success in changing immigration policy – the 'Sun Wot Won It' claim.

In much of the literature on media and policy, it is difficult to determine whether the media directly affects policy or reinforces negative attitudes towards immigrants that subsequently influence policy. The media may 'frame' issues, set the agenda (McCombs, 1994), or cement stereotypes, possibly racist ones (Hall, 1981). The interplay between government image management (spin) and the media makes it difficult to assess the influence of the latter on policy development. However, the effect of the media, in certain instances, is undeniable. Several examples could be used to illustrate a direct media effect on policy. The following examines the Worker Registration Scheme.

A case study of the media having a direct effect

The Worker Registration Scheme (WRS), designed and implemented in 2004, requires nationals of eight of the countries who joined the EU in May 2004 (referred to as the A-8) to register in order to work.

After one year of employment, A-8 nationals are allowed to claim unemployment benefits, but only if they are registered. In essence, the WRS was set up to prevent welfare 'scrounging'.

The decision to offer A-8 nationals unrestricted access to the UK labour market was formally announced in December 2002, and was based on evidence that indicated there would be significant economic benefits, with few welfare claimants. Given such evidence, it may seem odd that the WRS was created and implemented in the space of two months in 2004 in the lead-up to EU enlargement, over a year after the original decision to open labour markets had been taken. There are three further reasons why the creation of the WRS is puzzling. First, employers (quietly) opposed the scheme. Second, it was legally suspect in the context of reciprocal European social security agreements. Third, there were significant gaps in coverage – the self-employed did not have to register, for example.

The only plausible explanation for the creation of the WRS is that it was a knee-jerk reaction to tabloid pressure. From January 2004, the prospect of EU enlargement and unrestricted labour market access provoked a media frenzy. *The Sunday Times* ran a story on 18 January 2004 of 100,000 migrants waiting to come to Britain and raised concerns over welfare benefits; the *Sun* ran a front-page story the following day: 'See you in May: Thousands of gipsies head for Britain' (19 January 2004); followed by the *Daily Express* (20 January 2004), where the front page read '1.6 million gipsies ready to flood in'. Coverage peaked in February 2004, when the *Sun* published 45 articles on immigration, 25 of which were dedicated to accession (Kalia, 2004).

The media was thus instrumental to the creation of the WRS, but other factors also contributed to its conception. For example, Conservative leader Michael Howard ensured the A-8 migration debate reached the Commons, asking three consecutive questions at Prime Minister's Question Time. This inevitably turned a media debate into a political question (*Hansard*, 4 February 2004, col 753).

Notwithstanding the difficulties of isolating examples where the media has direct effects on policy, it is also important to acknowledge the fact that the media may also have indirect effects. For instance, the discussion of the media must take account of the role of 'presentation' in policy development.

Who leads whom?

Does the media lead the agenda, to which the government responds, or vice versa? To some extent, this question is of the chicken-and-egg variety. Government policy makers on the receiving end of media coverage, however, are certainly aware of it. Marsh et al (2001) document, for example, that officials can be affected by media pressure and as a result formulate ill-conceived policy measures.

The existence of a powerful tabloid media (that typically sets the media agenda) has thus changed the way policy is formulated. Policy now anticipates, or at least considers, how the media will respond. The extent of how far policy develops with the media in mind is a matter of debate. Franklin (2004) suggests that New Labour was the first government to go beyond political marketing to consider which policy options lend themselves well to the public and the media. He quotes Peter Mandelson, speaking on 16 September 1997, as saying: 'if a government policy cannot be presented in a simple and attractive way it is more likely than not to contain fundamental flaws and prove to be the wrong policy' (Franklin, 2004, p 74).

The suggestion is that Labour has elevated presentation to a greater significance within policy making than was previously the case. Policy measures are not only a reactive response to media pressure but also designed with the media in mind. If correct, this is likely to affect immigration policy making more than other social policies, as immigration policy attracts so many headlines. Marsh et al (2001, p 206) confirm that the 'Home Office is particularly affected' by the media and that policy makers are increasingly concerned by how a new policy will play in the media. The restrictive policy measures in the five-year plan were reinforced by internal Labour Party polling and by focus-group research commissioned by the Home Office (COI Communications, 2004) that emphasised the need for a tough response to assuage public concerns. The 'floating' of proposals in the weekend media may also be seen in this bracket.

Interestingly, the debates over the accession of Romania and Bulgaria on 1 January 2007 followed a similar pattern, except the media influence went alongside an unlikely coalition of think tanks (such as MigrationWatch) and senior opinion formers (such as Digby Jones, former director of the CBI, and Labour backbencher Frank Field). The government was also hamstrung by its earlier prediction of low numbers of migrants and the lack of fervour among former advocates of enlargement. The CBI, rather surprisingly, greeted the decision to impose restrictions with equanimity, even approval (CBI, 2006).

In the case of immigration from Romania and Bulgaria, restrictions on the labour market have been introduced, but the government introduced a 'compromise' where the Seasonal Agricultural Workers Scheme (SAWS) was ring-fenced exclusively for the use of Romanians and Bulgarians. But again, this was a short-notice policy change, much like the introduction of the WRS, and implementation was ham-fisted enough to prompt a judicial review case. The judicial review case was brought by farming interests, as the new rules on SAWS constituted the second major change to SAWS in less than a year. Six months before John Reid announced the new rules concerning Romanians and Bulgarians on 24 October 2006 (*Hansard*, 24 October 2006, cols 82–84WS), the government had decided that the SAWS scheme would be phased out (*Hansard*, 7 March 2006, col 55WS). Farming interests had lobbied successfully to win a partial reprieve on this decision that would keep SAWS operating until 2010 and had barely finished celebrating the fact when the new rules were announced.

However, as the discussion in the preceding chapter concerning public attitudes showed, political leadership is an important factor in how public attitudes are formed, and consequently what the media reports, and how it reports it. More specifically, the media may take its line from senior politicians. In understanding indirect media effects, what emerges is the existence of a feedback loop composed of the media, the public and senior opinion formers, in which each actor influences the others.

FOURTEEN

Officials: policy at the frontline

This chapter explores the influence of civil servants on migration policy making. In general, such 'street level bureaucrats' (Lipsky, 1979) are employed in the Immigration and Nationality Directorate (IND, since 2 April 2007 known as the Border and Immigration Agency). Successful policy requires the support of such civil servants. Indeed, their importance to successful policy implementation is likely to grow as the Civil Service shifts from policy advice to service delivery (Dorey, 2005), a trend accelerated by the decision to give IND agency status.

In spite of the fact that the UK government spends over £1.5bn on immigration services (Cabinet Office, 2006, p 8) and the Immigration and Nationality Directorate numbers 16,000 employees, officials delivering migration policy have not been the subject of much academic research. There is one striking exception: a study by Duvell and Jordan (2003). In it, they examine parts of the immigration machinery, where major differences were noted between departments or units, most notably between economic migration, Work Permits (UK), and enforcement, then called the Immigration Service Enforcement Directorate (ISED). The study drew a distinction between a business-friendly, customer-focused unit on one hand, Work Permits (UK), and a more chaotic system in ISED, with anomalies and an inward-looking culture or 'siege mentality' (Duvell and Jordan, 2003, p 315).

There is even less academic research on how migration policy is implemented outside of IND, such as by education or health officials. Earlier research carried out by the author suggests such officials have concerns over enforcement action, but also that reluctance to engage with Home Office civil servants is due to a lack of understanding about how immigration policy interacts with their own policy and legal duties and responsibilities. In other words, ignorance may be veiled by a philosophical objection to immigration controls.

While there is a paucity of academic literature, there are many official government and non-governmental submissions and documents (for example, Home Affairs Select Committee, 2006b; Home Office, 2006b; National Audit Office, 2004a; Sutton, 2004). The general consensus of both official government documentation and NGO sources is that the culture of IND is closed and inward looking (Home Affairs Select Committee, 2006b).

This 'defensive' culture applies both to IND and to entry clearance operations abroad. For example, in oral evidence given to the Home Affairs Select Committee (2006b), critical voices vent spleen. Dr Ann Barker, chair of the IND Complaints Audit Committee, noted that 'officials are defensive' (Q14); Fiona Lindsley, Independent Monitor into Entry Clearance Refusals without the right of appeal, stated that 'there is a culture of attitudes which differentially impacts on some communities' (Q84); Chris Randall, chair of the Immigration Law Practitioners' Association, stated that the '[entry clearance operation has a] much more negative culture than Work Permits UK' (Q303); and Keith Best, chief executive of the Immigration Advisory Service, suggested that a culture of disbelief is 'concentrated in … particular posts where … it seems to become self-fulfilling' (Q204).

These voices – all independent of government – might be expected to be critical. However, voices criticising IND culture (and performance) have also come from within. Within a month of taking the post, Home Secretary John Reid infamously stated to the Home Affairs Select Committee that his department was 'not fit for purpose', in full view of (or perhaps for) the press (Home Affairs Select Committee, 2006b). However, a reading of government documentation shows that this 'official' view of an inadequate system had been evolving for some time. Importantly, it was shared by a number of officials, and not simply senior politicians.

In 2005, the Partial Regulatory Impact Assessment on the Points-Based System gave a surprisingly forthright view of the immigration system. The criticisms ran from difficulties in managing the system – 'it is not easy to administer … there is scope for inconsistency and incorrect decisions' (Home Office, 2006b, p 1) – to operational inadequacies – 'the system can be inefficient' (Home Office, 2006b, p 2). In 2006, the Cabinet Secretary, Britain's most senior civil servant, conducted a series of capability reviews. The review of the Home Office was critical: two of its key findings were that the 'Home Office does not yet have the overall capability and the corporate services to meet the scale of the changes it faces' and 'governance needs to be strengthened to enable the Home Office to operate as a single entity with a specific culture' (Cabinet Office, 2006, p 15).

Overall, the main conclusion from government reviews and documentation is that some parts of the immigration service have defensive cultures, whereas other parts are responsive and efficient. This suggests that there are particular 'hot spots' where practice differs extensively from elsewhere, and where policy implementation – if at odds with such cultures – is likely to be particularly difficult.

The impact of officials on policy

The question of how far the culture (or cultures) of immigration officials has affected the delivery of policy can be answered in a general sense by evaluating whether policy aims set at a strategic level have been achieved on the ground (the purpose of Part 3). But some aims may not be fixed and officials may still have a major influence. For example, the Independent Race Monitor, Mary Coussey, has made the point that the 'negative atmosphere can affect decision-making on individual cases, as it makes caution and suspicion more likely' (Coussey, 2004, p 28). This type of influence may not be picked up in an evaluation of goals and aims.

There are, though, specific examples where officials have had a direct impact on the development of migration policy. This is best shown through the discussion of two detailed 'case studies': the operational breakdown of the visa system in Bulgaria and Romania in 2003 and changes made to the Working Holidaymaker Visa.

The affair in Sofia and Bucharest

On 1 April 2004, Beverly Hughes, Minister for Immigration and Citizenship, resigned after she 'unwittingly' misled Parliament over the operation of visas in Bulgaria and Romania. A summary of the affair is that the entry clearance operations in Sofia and Bucharest were at odds with the Home Office over the criteria for entry to the UK of certain Romanian and Bulgarian nationals. In essence, the Home Office was more expansive in its interpretation.

There is clear evidence that the 'front-line', in this case entry clearance officers in Sofia and Bucharest, differed in their interpretation of policy from the centre (IND in Croydon). The differences were significant enough to alter the approach. The Home Office view, which should have been decisive, was not accepted internally by staff in Sofia and Bucharest. The discontent reached a climax when the FCO consul in Romania, Mr James Cameron, passed details of the conflict to the Conservative opposition in Parliament. This led to questions where Beverly Hughes was revealed to have misled Parliament, and subsequently resigned.

The major report into the fiasco was written by a serving civil servant, Ken Sutton. His report and other evidence indicates that there was a great deal of communication between the Home Office and the entry clearance operation in Sofia and Bucharest (for example, correspondence and visits by staff in March and August 2003) but the conflict of approaches remained (National Audit Office, 2004a; Sutton, 2004). Ken Sutton's second finding is worth relaying in full:

> The second key finding is that officials handling ECAA applications have been sharply divided in their view of the relevant law.... Entry clearance staff in Sofia and Bucharest favoured an approach which, if adopted, would have meant that the majority of applicants would have been refused. Home Office staff in IND thought that refusals on that basis would be unsustainable in law and took an approach under which the majority of applicants were granted. The Home Office view prevailed – but the tension between the approaches continued and remains to be resolved (Sutton, 2004, p 6).

The National Audit Office also investigated the issue and similarly concluded that there was a 'lack of common understanding' based on differing interpretations of the law (National Audit Office, 2004a, Appendix 7). The Public Accounts Select Committee report into the affair also concluded that the two departments (the FCO and the Home Office) were divided in their approach (see for example, Public Accounts Select Committee, 2005, p 3 and Questions 45–61). The report places the blame on the Home Office for the conflict in approach. The Committee recommended that the Home Office should try and track down visas issued to Romanian and Bulgarian business people to ensure they were valid (Public Accounts Select Committee, 2005, Recommendation 10, p 5).[1]

The above evidence clearly indicates a difference of opinion on the frontline that had a major effect on policy making in the centre. The validity of those concerns and opinions is an open question. Clearly the Public Accounts Select Committee report and the resignation of Beverly Hughes would indicate that policy was not valid and weaknesses were simply exposed. The account of the affair in a pamphlet by the Conservative politicians David Davis and Damien Green also indicates that the minister knew more about fast-tracking and backlog clearing exercises than she let on, and the tone is overtly critical of Labour's management of the crisis (Davis and Green, 2006, pp 10–12). However, evidence from interviewees and from the key report suggests otherwise. First, the Home Office's view was based on an interpretation of the law it believed to be correct. Second, given EU accession of these two countries and the importance placed on business, this was strategically defensible. In other words, this was not simply a case of 'uncovering fraud' or exposing weaknesses. This was about street-level bureaucrats changing the delivery of policy laid down from above because they disagreed with it.

The curious case of the ever-changing visa

The account above, of a visa scandal, provides a very political example of fallout, but one that ultimately did not lead to major deviations in policy. However, changes to the Working Holidaymaker Visa provide an example of the successful frustration of policy objectives by IND officials.

The Working Holidaymaker Visa was designed as a long-term tourist visa for young Commonwealth persons (typically from Australia, Canada, New Zealand and South Africa). The visa was for 24 months, but allowed 12 months' work incidental to the 'holiday'. This work was, however, restricted (you could not 'pursue a career' or work in 'business'). In other words, it was aimed at young people, working in low-skill, often seasonal work, and travelling around the UK and Europe on the proceeds. In 2005, it attracted 56,560 people (Salt and Millar, 2006, p 350).

In 2002, policy set out to reconfigure the Working Holidaymaker Visa as an economic migration route. The Home Office consultation paper on the scheme asked, 'What is the most efficient and cost effective way to provide information about sectors of employment with recruitment difficulties to working holidaymakers?'. This signalled the government's 'intention to end the "tourist" status of this scheme, and to transform it into a mainstream labour migration channel' (Flynn, 2005b, footnote 12, p 488). The policy objective had an additional, pragmatic bonus. The Working Holidaymaker Visa was considered by immigration experts among the most abused of all visas, with visa-holders *routinely* working for the full 24 months and not the 12 months required under the terms of the visa.

The new rules entered into force from August 2003. The changes were significant. First, full work and residence for 24 months were permitted (with an assumption that those working for 24 months would switch to work permits after the first year). Second, the upper age limit for applications was raised from 27 to 30. Third, the type of work a person could undertake was derestricted (so Working Holidaymakers could, for example, undertake work in professions and high-skilled work). Finally, the new rules were intended to encourage all Commonwealth citizens to apply for a Working Holidaymaker Visa, as opposed to those from the (mainly white) Old Commonwealth countries. These changes were also mutually reinforcing. For example, by removing employment restrictions, members of New Commonwealth countries could prove more easily that they were able to support themselves in the UK without recourse to public funds (by working).

Beverly Hughes, the minister at the time, summarised the changes in a statement on the 20 June 2003: 'the main aims behind the review [of the visa] were to make the scheme more inclusive of the whole Commonwealth, to remove unnecessary employment restrictions and to reduce abuse of the scheme' (*Hansard*, 20 June 2003, col 22WS).

The aims of the review were clear, as were the policy changes needed to bring them into effect. However, the implementation of the policy proved problematic. The first sign of difficulties was in visa sections in various High Commissions in the New Commonwealth countries. It became clear that officials were reluctant to grant Working Holidaymaker Visas (RSA Migration Commission, 2005, p 37). Applicants were told in certain missions that it did not cover people who had not been to the UK before (patently incorrect) and entry clearance officers in visa sections in Africa and Asia asked for detailed itineraries of holidays, with hesitant or incomplete response being treated as evidence of a suspicious application. In effect, 'officials in missions in African and Asian Commonwealth countries were approaching interviews and evidence ... differently from their counterparts' (RSA Migration Commission, 2005, Annex 1, pp 37–8).

As a result of these difficulties, the new rules were soon under review. By February 2004, Baroness Scotland of Asthal told Parliament that the 'government are reviewing the impact of the changes to the scheme' (*Hansard*, 12 February 2004, col WA176). By 2005, the reforms were dead in the water. From 8 February 2005, Working Holidaymaker Visas reverted to 12 months' employment incidental to holiday.[2] Some of the vestiges of the economic migration approach remained, for example the ability to 'switch' to certain economic migration categories (Somerville, 2006b, pp 49–50). Des Browne, who took over from Beverly Hughes, made a statement on 7 February 2005 revealing how far policy had returned to its original formulation (and how little the previous, comprehensive consultation had meant): 'the main change for applicants is that we are strengthening the requirement that the work be done in support of holiday and travel intentions. It is anomalous that as a holiday and cultural exchange route it should not have attached to it any conditions that prevent migration based on long-term employment and other economic motives' (*Hansard*, 7 February 2005, cols 70WS-71WS).

The scheme was also changed at the same time, so it is now administered on a bilateral basis, with broad powers to restrict applications. Des Browne stated to Parliament that 'in the future it will operate on the basis of country-by-country bilateral arrangements. This means that we will be able to vary the arrangements with individual countries in the light of such things as degree of cooperation with our own immigration control and the capacity of our posts overseas to handle large numbers of applications' (*Hansard*, 7 February 2005, col 71WS).

The changes provoked significant irritation from the NGO sector, which had invested time and effort in developing the original proposals. The changes were, for example, described as 'racist in effect if not in intent' (Churches' Commission for Racial Justice, 2005).

The case of the Working Holidaymaker Visa is a bona fide example of officials frustrating implementation. It is made more interesting because the policy objectives were not only frustrated but redrawn in order to accommodate officials' concerns. For example, the new bilateral powers are broad, and, more importantly, are completely within the gift of officials (who decide on which missions have 'backlogs', for instance).

On 2 April 2005, eight weeks after the new rules were announced, the visa sections in Colombo, Kuala Lumpur, Gaborone and Windhoek halted all applications for six months because of a backlog. There are currently a number of restrictions that are ongoing in certain countries, mostly to do with backlogs. The proportion of visas awarded has changed, but the most salient fact remains: in 2000, 69.2 per cent of visas were awarded to nationals of Australia and South Africa; the most recent figures, from 2005, show that nationals from these two countries account for 69.5 per cent. The Old Commonwealth has retained its monopoly.

These two case studies have shown that officials, on certain defined occasions, have slowed the pace of reform and made it more difficult, as well as 'tilting' policy to suit their own aims. But there are also implementation issues that have little to do with the values and work of 'street-level bureaucrats'. The most obvious of these refers to technology. The problems with new technologies in IND remain among the most important of all implementation issues, as they absorb significant resources and are intimately tied to management objectives. It is also important to consider the work of officials outside of particular examples of failure. For example, as Chapters 2 and 4 illustrated, officials in various EU countries have developed a series of initiatives on asylum and security. This is evaluated more fully in Part Three.

Notes

[1] Given that the entry of Romania and Bulgaria to the EU had been agreed for either 1 January 2007 or 1 January 2008 (it turned out to be the former), this was not a particularly useful recommendation, in view of the cost implications.

[2] Statement of change HC302, laid before Parliament on 7 February 2005 under section 3(2) of the 1971 Immigration Act.

FIFTEEN

A fresh perspective on policy change

The political science literature is extremely limited in explaining the influences on UK migration policy making. An important exception is the work of Hansen (2000). Hansen draws on the theory of 'path dependency', where policy changes must be seen in the context of previous policy decisions, to explain change over the last half century. He explains policy development from the 1948 British Nationality Act, which drew the boundaries of entry and citizenship widely and set a crucial direction (or 'path') that subsequent policy grappled with (in trying to rein in the boundaries). After 1962, he sees the source of restrictionism in British institutions and in particular in two aspects of the Westminster model: a weak legislature and the lack of a Bill of Rights. Britain's government, free from legislative and judicial checks, thus had a freer hand and imposed greater restrictionism from the 1960s onwards (Hansen, 2000, pp 240–3). However, given that Hansen (2000) is explaining a situation of 'zero-migration', his explanation for immigration policy change under Labour is unconvincing.[1]

Part Two aimed to provide a fuller account of the influences, inputs and transformational processes that have operated upon the construction of UK migration policy. Influences have included the processes and perceptions of globalisation; the UK legal framework; the impact of the European Union and its powers; the attitudes of the public towards immigrants; the role of the media, particularly the tabloid press; the array of interest groups, government departments, NGOs and think tanks; senior Labour politicians, political parties, and the impact of major events; as well as officials themselves. In order to make sense of these numerous influences, the conclusions presented below are simplified into three tiers: macro, meso and micro. This does not seek to privilege one over another, but may contribute to analytical clarity (Hudson and Lowe, 2004).

On a macro level, three major influences emerge. The first is the series of processes that can be loosely described as 'globalisation'. Prior to 1997, policy did not grapple with globalisation and the economic trends it serves to magnify and expose. Policy development after 1997 has taken account of global labour flows, adapting to the major numerical increases in passenger numbers and immigrant flows resulting form globalisation. Furthermore, globalisation has an ideological dimension in helping set the 'rules of the game'.

The second influence has been international and national law. The legal framework, and how it interacts with executive power, does not necessarily fit easily under the 'macro' heading because it is national, and bounded by territory. But some of the key legal norms under consideration (such as human rights) cascade down from international law and practice. There have been two conflicting trends in migrants' rights. There have been some advances but the countercurrent has been much stronger, and a number of measures have served to undermine migrants' rights.

Nonetheless, the two fundamental, internationally accepted legal rights, the right to seek asylum and the principle of non-refoulement, have been incorporated into UK law and policy. These minimum standards have been maintained, indicating a constraint on UK policy making. In short, there *is* a bottom line and it has been repeatedly emphasised by the courts.

The third macro force is that of the European Union (EU), the major source of binding supranational regulations. While the Home Office initially resisted interference from the EU, there has been an increasing 'give and take' since 1997. This has come in two forms. The 'economic' side of Europe has promoted globalisation and free markets. The commitment to enlargement and free movement has had a major effect on economic migration policy, especially in ensuring global market forces are felt more fully in the UK. The 'political–legal' side of Europe has contributed to changes to asylum and security policy, for example in regard to the reception of asylum seekers.

In discussing globalisation, law and Europe, three points stand out. First, all three matter; this undermines some of the state-centred comparative analysis of political scientists (see, for example, Joppke, 1999). The idea that EU directives on asylum reception or EU enlargement have not had a significant impact on policy is untenable, for example. Having said that they are significant, they are not fundamental. Policy success in reducing the numbers of asylum seekers shows the power of the nation-state, for instance. This undermines the arguments of globalisation and international law theorists (Sassen, 1999a; Soysal, 1994).

Second, the EU has given *substance* to the forces of globalisation and to law; the EU has been crucial in putting 'flesh on the theoretical bones' through the creation of both a single market and institutions that affect government policy. While the EU has always been an economic area that prescribed free movement (anachronistic in the context of restrictive immigration policies from 1976 to 1997), it is only recently that the leap has been made from theory to reality. EU enlargement in 2004 expanded the labour pool in the UK and resulted in a major inflow. The EU has also given substance to law. The European Convention on Human Rights is binding on member states, as are EU directives. For example, the European Court of Human Rights has been brought into the EU mechanisms and ensures that duties under Article 3 are honoured by Member States.

Third, these three influences are not of equal importance on each dimension of migration policy. In particular, globalisation – and the perception and justification of pro-market ideology – has been important in the development of economic migration policy. The same cannot be said for asylum policy, despite the fact that a more interconnected world has contributed to increased numbers of asylum seekers. In the case of asylum policy, the legal framework, particularly human rights norms of non-refoulement and the right to seek asylum, has been important.

Globalisation, the law, and Europe have therefore all been important in setting the boundaries for the development of migration policy making. They are used as touchstones by all the actors in the policy process and ensure there are certain *policy parameters*.

On a meso level, the importance of networks emerges strongly. A policy network perspective reveals that there has been insufficient academic attention paid to changes to the Westminster model of government over the last two decades towards a more plural system of governance. Such an argument stands in opposition to the narrative developed by Hansen (2000). Policy networks are particularly helpful in explaining the dynamics of change in liberalising economic migration policy in the period 2001–02.

The negative attitudes of the public and a broadly hostile media have often been labelled explanatory variables for change. The picture is complex, but likely to include political agenda setting as much as the media or public opinion (Kaye, 1998). Public attitudes are segmented and a homogenous anti-immigrant public is an unsatisfactory basis for analysis. Equally, the media frames issues and changes priorities, as well as impacting directly on policy in certain circumstances. Thus a nuanced understanding would include 'feedback loops', made up of the media, but also senior politicians and opinion formers, and finally the public. In terms of the most-affected dimensions of policy making, asylum policy stands out. The media and public attitudes influence asylum policy more than any other theme of migration policy.

Issues of politics and personality draw on important strands of thinking in policy analysis. Labour politicians, notably Blair and Blunkett, have had a major impact on policy. Equally, inter-party (Conservative and Labour) conflict has led to the development of a restrictive policy on certain themes, notably on asylum and security. The political rhetoric on security can be seen to have legitimised and expanded restrictions on asylum and on unauthorised migrants, but has had little effect on economic (managed) migration.

If the macro level indicates some of the broader structural forces and is critical to understanding the boundaries or parameters of migration policy, the meso-level analysis accounts for the development of *policy content* over the last decade.

On the micro level, the role of policy implementation emerges as important, particularly at certain junctures. A key strand of public administration analysis is that of implementation. Limited attention has been paid to the role of officials in the literature, yet decision makers on the front-line have significant input into delivery, both causing delivery difficulties and tilting policy away from its original intentions. The micro level inputs and influences move from *policy content* to the reality on the ground and how policy is actually delivered and implemented.

Part Two may not have produced neat answers, but the exploration of the key influences on the policy-making process may allow us to identify some of the 'missing' pieces. By accepting that UK governance is more diffuse, the role of networks and globalisation, in the development of economic migration in particular, becomes clearer. Similarly, the role of parties and politicians, together with the media, comes to the fore for asylum policy. Finally, across the all migration policies, it is clear that there is a legal bottom line.

Note

[1] Hansen (2000) also places the executive as extremely powerful in comparison to the courts in the UK. The role of the courts in setting parameters is understated. Later work acknowledges change, placing market forces as the explanatory variable (Hansen, 2004). However, this later work is not extensive.

Part Three
Evaluating Labour's record

SIXTEEN

Evaluating immigration policy making

Labour's transformation of immigration policy has been intense and innovative. The final part of this book provides a template to evaluate the government's reforms. Part Three is divided into six chapters, the first of which discusses what the aims of policy are, how progress towards them can be measured, and the pros and cons of such an approach. The remaining chapters echo the policy themes used throughout this book. Chapter 18 focuses on asylum and unauthorised migration, where there are *precise* objectives. Chapters 19 and 20 focus on integration and delivery, where there are *less precise* objectives. Chapters 21 and 22 focus on *imprecise* objectives, on economic migration and international development.

Evaluating policy

The evaluation framework used here takes its inspiration from two main sources. First, it employs an approach, similar to programme budgeting,[1] where outcomes and performance measures are analysed. Objectives and measures are largely drawn from the Public Sector Agreement (PSA) regime, with some additional objectives and measures drawn from other government documents. Public Sector Agreements are measured by Key Performance Indicators (KPIs), which act as the main performance measures in this evaluation.[2]

The PSA regime was an innovation of the Labour government, but can be seen in the context of ongoing change to public sector management, pioneered under Thatcher and often termed 'New Public Management' (Osborne and Gaebler, 1992; for a critique of managerial approaches to policy, see Minogue, 1983). Ed Balls, architect of PSAs as Economic Adviser to the Treasury in 1997–98, described the rationale as one where government could 'set out the key outcomes it expected investment and reform to deliver' (Balls, 2006). The PSA regime was designed to move government spending away from 'inputs' and towards 'outcomes'. James (2004) suggests it has had some, albeit incomplete, success in doing so by producing (weak) incentive effects and starting to link expenditure to priorities. The value of the PSA regime is not only that it concentrates on outcomes and is supported by some performance measures, but that it was also designed, in part, to monitor the performance of departments (James, 2004, pp 406–8). Together with the fact that the PSA regime has now been in operation for a decade and is currently being reframed for the next three-year period, it is the best available yardstick for evaluating migration policy. (It is worth reiterating that these goals are, at the time of writing, coming to the end of their cycle. The 2007 Comprehensive Spending Review is not considered here.)

The UK government generally evaluates all policies through versions of a cost–benefit analysis (CBA). This might be a technical CBA, typically using the template set by the Treasury Green Book; a best-value audit; or the now mandatory Regulatory Impact Assessments (RIA) that must be made of all new policies and which again draw on the Green Book (HMT, 2003). It could be argued that an evaluation approach based on the PSA regime is in fact a narrow version of a CBA. The Green Book, for instance, proposes four techniques – one of which is the analysis of performance measures (HMT, 2003, p 48) – to evaluate policy. There are three main reasons why this evaluation does not employ a CBA. Not all the information is available (such an approach requires financial information that is difficult to unearth); it is too prescribed (there is a strong emphasis on costs in the Green Book); and it necessarily comes with a certain worldview.

To illustrate this with an example: there have been a series of RIAs on migration policies, including on the Points-based System (Home Office, 2006b). The RIA on the Points-based System noted that a precise analysis of costs and benefits is not possible. However, it did assert that the overall costs are likely to be lower, before going on to list a series of cost reductions and benefits (Home Office, 2006b, pp 17–20). These costs and benefits betray a certain worldview and smack of justifying the proposals. For instance, on describing new sponsorship requirements, the RIA expects that an employer will inform the Home Office if a migrant worker does not appear for work. In the same paragraph, the RIA states this will not be an 'onerous burden' because this 'expectation already exists' (Home Office, 2006b, p 19), which is simply incorrect. The 'expectation' that an employer will inform the Home Office if someone does not come to work is not shared by anyone outside the Home Office.

The second main source for the evaluation framework is five key policy questions (adapted from Hills and Stewart, 2005).

1. Have problems and issues been recognised and analysed?

2. Have targets and objectives been set, and are the targets and objectives appropriate?
3. What specific policy changes were made?
4. What evidence is there of impacts from evaluations and other assessments?
5. What are the problems and gaps in the policy mix?

Labour aims on migration policy

There is no complete statement of Labour's migration policy objectives, underpinned by detailed measures. However, a set of abstract aims can be derived from the Public Sector Agreement (PSA) regime.[3] There have been two rounds of PSA target setting – from the Spending Review 2002 (SR2002) and the Spending Review 2004 (SR2004). In each PSA round, aims (or objectives) are set for departments. Underneath each aim, targets are agreed, which are intended to measure performance.

The Spending Review 2002 referred to a general aim on migration. Home Office PSA Aim 6 (SR2002) read:

> To regulate entry to and settlement in the United Kingdom effectively in the interests of sustainable growth and social inclusion. To provide an efficient and effective work permit system to meet economic and skills requirements, and fair, fast and effective programmes for dealing with visitors, citizenship and long term immigration applications and those seeking refuge and asylum. To facilitate travel by UK citizens.

The Spending Review 2004 also had an aim on migration, albeit one that was shorter. Home Office PSA Aim 4 read:

> Migration is managed to benefit the UK while preventing abuse of the immigration laws and of the asylum system.

Furthermore, departmental objectives are aligned with the PSA regime, which provides additional technical measures. The Home Office PSA target thus gives 'expression' to the Home Office departmental objective (Home Affairs Select Committee, 2005, p 6).

There are also alternative statements of aims, often overlapping, made in press statements,[4] speeches and in White Papers.[5] These are less useful as they are not supported by technical performance measures, but they do offer aims and goals where the PSA regime is 'silent'. Thus, while PSA targets are set at a relatively high level of abstraction and are not supported by a *complete* set of indicators or performance measures against which policy can be measured, real and implied targets do exist and offer an evaluation framework.

Problems with evaluating from the PSA regime

There are at least five problems with using the PSA regime as a basis for evaluation. First, policy has to be built on a cogent programme of desired outcomes and measures of progress. However, different groups may want different outcomes: politicians may desire an outcome of minimal political and media 'fire'; voluntary groups may want greater protection of rights; civil servants may have to make efficiency gains and so on.

Evaluating from PSA targets runs the risk that the targets set down in the PSA regime are understood to be the *only* goals and targets. This changes one's view of success: after all, and broadly speaking, while Labour may not have achieved all its targets, there has been progress towards them and by the time the next cycle of PSA targets is completed, it would be surprising if the majority of goals had not been achieved. By stating alternatives, the point is made that, fundamentally, there are alternative discourses and understandings of the purpose and objectives of migration policy, even though government may view them as illegitimate. This evaluation framework seeks in part to overcome this problem by setting out goals, but also acknowledging different discourses and understandings.

Second, the policy goals do not all cascade down to neat operational targets or KPIs, making evaluation problematic. Procedural performance measures exist in some areas (discussed fully in the next chapter), such as the numbers of unfounded asylum applications in a particular period, but even here, interpretation is important: community organisations may not interpret fast-track processing efficiency as 'fair', for example.

Third, the objectives distilled from the PSA targets in both the 2002 and 2004 Spending Reviews do not translate into the government's only objectives: there are 'hidden aims' (Castles, 2004). For example, the tenor and direction of questions in Labour's Big Conversation (which were designed to inform the 2005 New Labour manifesto) do not fit easily into the aims outlined above, instead emphasising enforcement, security and eliminating 'fraud' and 'illegal immigration'.[6]

Fourth, the PSA target regime has been critiqued for its lack of connection to agency targets. Furthermore, management culture has been criticised for failing to translate PSA aims into clear strategic direction (Cabinet Office, 2002; Public Administration Select Committee, 2003). The Home Office objectives may be especially confusing and vague. Parliamentary scrutiny has revealed inconsistency between PSA targets and Home Office objectives and a lack of transparency on KPIs (Home Affairs Select Committee, 2005). As with other government departments, PSA targets also overlap. For example, Home Office staff in the year 2005–06 worked to *two* 'migration' PSA targets (PSA Aim 6, Target 7 from SR2002 and PSA Aim 4, Target 5 from SR2004). This was in addition to departmental objectives and targets set by the Prime Minister.

Finally, basing evaluation on PSAs has meant some valid aims have received no references. Examples might include relevant economic issues, such as the importance of migrants to the UK tourism industry, the contribution of overseas students to UK universities, or the increasing acceptance of migration's role in reducing inflation at a macro-economic level (Bank of England, 2004, p 6; Treasury Committee, 2005). Similarly, they may include social issues, such as the promotion of human rights.

Of course, the lack of a complete set of specific targets may make assessing success and failure impossible. In some cases this appears to be the case, as policy is applauded and condemned at the same time. For example, progressive commentators have called UK policy (specifically on asylum) both 'sensible' (Toynbee, 2002) and 'shameful' (Lister, 2001).

Policy and its effect on migration

Notwithstanding such problems, an evaluation template based on a PSA regime remains the best available set of goals against which to judge policy. But before evaluating policy, one fundamental question remains: does policy have an impact on flows and types of migration? There are profoundly different answers to this question. On the one hand, many political statements often suggest the state has full and complete control over immigration. On the other, there is research evidence to suggest that factors *outside* state control most affect migration. In reality, the impact of migration policy on migration is unclear. There are two main reasons for this: there is no counterfactual (of what migration would be like without state involvement) and because the full set of policy aims has not been elucidated (either deliberately for political reasons or because they are too numerous to catalogue).

Evidence of policy impact or lack of impact is often made on prima facie grounds or based on weak correlations masquerading as causation.

For example, if we choose 'zero-migration' as a policy aim behind the reforms of 1962, there are regular references to policy failure in 'closing the door' to Indians, Pakistanis and Bangladeshis (Herlitz, 2005), suggesting a lack of impact of policy. More recently, Mitchell and Pain (2003) provided an econometric study that showed entry and exit policy changes have statistically insignificant effects on the numbers of immigrants. On the other hand, Weil (1995) argues that border controls are extremely effective and if we choose the 1971 Act as a policy, most commentators argue that primary migration was ended as a result (Hansen, 2000), suggesting significant policy impact towards a goal of 'zero-migration'. There is also evidence that migration policies have not achieved their intended outcome or aim (Castles, 2004), but this does not mean that they have not had an impact, especially if we take time-lag effects into account.

Empirically, assessment is difficult, given the confusion over theoretical models of migration and therefore what the dependent and independent variables are. There are competing theoretical 'models' of the causes of migration (Massey, 1999). Most writings on causes of migration can be found in the economics literature (for example: Arrango, 2000; Green, 2002), but at least three broad sets of causes can be identified (Hollifield, 2000): push and pull factors, typically found in the economics literature; global transnationalism, mainly in the legal and sociology literature; and nation-states, in the political science literature. Studies of UK policy have found a variety of factors behind migration (ippr, 2003; Mitchell and Pain, 2003).

In general, there are some prima facie policy successes and failures (having an impact or not) but no incontrovertible evidence of causality. Clearly, the underlying causes of migration are crucial to this discussion, as policy may complement underlying trends,[7] impact on particular migration routes, or impact on certain (more vulnerable) groups. Overall, it is difficult to contend that policy has not had *some* impact – but the *extent* and *effect* of the policy impact on flows and types of migration remain unclear.

Notes

[1] Budgets are agreed with defined outcomes.

[2] Prior to 2004, the government used the terminology of Service Delivery Agreements (SDA) rather than Key Performance Indicators.

[3] Despite the high level of abstraction, this represents a step forward as there were no aims or objectives before Labour was elected in 1997.

[4] The government recognises at least three broad aims: preventing asylum abuse, opening up managed migration routes and promoting refugee integration (Home Office Press Release, 2003c).

[5] The most important of these was the 2002 White Paper, which included the following objectives: 'We will develop our citizenship and nationality policy to create a supportive, safe and cohesive community. We will manage flows through legitimate entry routes, developing managed migration policies to attract the people we need to compete and prosper in the global economy in a manner consistent with our international commitment to eliminate world poverty and domestic commitment to achieve employment opportunities for all. We will develop our methods to counteract organised immigration crime and illegal working and crack down on those who undermine and abuse our system. And fundamental to our moral and humanitarian objectives we will develop a seamless asylum process which is clear from induction to integration or return' (Home Office, 2002a, p 20).

[6] For example, question two from the Big Conversation website concerning asylum and immigration was: 'Do we need to work with the international community to update the UN Convention so that it focuses assistance on those countries where there is a genuine refugee problem rather than giving people from every country a right of asylum if they make it to our shores?'

[7] One may argue that Labour's success in reducing asylum claims has benefited from a drop in asylum applications worldwide, for example.

SEVENTEEN

Targets of restriction: asylum (and security)

This chapter covers the *precise* targets, which are mostly associated with asylum, and, to some extent, the theme of security. Such measures are generally restrictive. As discussed in the previous chapter, while the overall Public Sector Agreement (PSA) aims on migration are quite broad, in both Spending Reviews (2002 and 2004), when examining the PSA targets attached to these aims, there is a palpable sense of 'narrowing'. It should also be emphasised that the Home Office has chosen (or at least negotiated) such a set of PSA targets.

The Asylum PSA targets

PSA Target 7 (SR 2002; linked to Home Office Aim 6) is to:

> focus the asylum system on those genuinely fleeing persecution by taking speedy, high quality decisions and reducing significantly unfounded asylum claims, including by: fast turn-around of manifestly unfounded cases; ensuring by 2004 that 75 per cent of substantive asylum applications are decided within two months; and that a proportion (to be determined) including final appeal, to be decided within six months; enforce the immigration laws more effectively by removing a greater proportion of failed asylum-seekers. (Home Office, 2005e, p 116)

PSA Target 5 (SR 2004; linked to Home Office Aim 4) is to:

> reduce unfounded asylum claims as part of a broader strategy to tackle abuse of the immigration laws and promote controlled legal migration.

The measurement is focused on 'unfounded' asylum claims, which includes both failed asylum claims and cases where persons are not granted refugee status but granted temporary leave. The baseline period is the year 2002/03 and the target will have been achieved if the number of unfounded asylum claims in the year 2007/08 is less than in the baseline year.[1]

These two targets are very clearly focused on asylum and are the *only* performance measures linked to the broader 'migration' PSA Aim.

Other restrictive targets

In addition to the targets on asylum set out above, the only other precise measurable targets refer to unauthorised migrants. Labour has set two quantitative targets, both for deportations. The first deportation target was to remove 30,000 failed asylum seekers per year in 2001/02. The second, known as the 'tipping point' target, was introduced in an article in *The Times* penned by the Prime Minister, in which he presented a target of deporting more failed applicants per month than those who made unfounded applications by December 2005.[2]

It is clear, from the target on halving unfounded asylum claims, that aims on *asylum* and aims on *unauthorised migration* are deliberately confused. This is repeated across Home Office target setting. For example in the 2004 Home Office Annual Report, under 'reducing illegal inflows', policy is 'continuing to secure borders and press down on monthly asylum intake' (Home Office, 2004c, p 117). Another illustration is the numbers of asylum seekers in detention, with 76 per cent of the immigration detention estate made up of failed asylum seekers (Home Office, 2005f). There are also other targets that are not within the official PSA regime. For example, Tony Blair announced in 2004 that there would be an extra 1,000 detention spaces (*Times*, 2004).

Have these targets been met?

The indicators in PSA Target 7 (SR2002) were largely met. First, on 'reducing unfounded asylum claims', the numbers were more than halved. The figure from March 2005 was 2,165 applications, down from 8,770 applications in October 2002. Second, the indicator on the 'quality of asylum decisions' was also met (81 per cent on a target of 80 per cent). Third, the number of 'substantive asylum applications decided within two months' for 2003/04 was 82 per cent, which exceeded the indicator of 75 per cent (Home Office, 2005e). Three key indicators were therefore met or exceeded.

Ministers have widely publicised 'achievements' in reaching goals (Home Office Press Release, 2005c), and 'building on successes' (Home Office Press Release, 2006a). Furthermore, this success (in meeting asylum policy indicators) is attributed directly to measures introduced by the government (Home Office Press Release, 2005a).

The government has also consistently indicated that the removal policy is working well. For example, in 2005 the Home Office stated that 'the continuing rise in the number of failed asylum seekers removed shows the success of government policies' (Home Office Press Release, 2005b).

On detention, Labour has significantly expanded the immigration detention estate. The number of those detained has increased significantly. In 1998, there were 741 detainees. In December 2005, there were 1,950 people in detention, with a peak of 2,220 in the third quarter (Home Office, 2005f). The fact that more people have been detained could be construed as a basic indicator of success, especially as the targets on deportations may be helped by the increased numbers in detention.

However, a broader view of the evidence indicates that success is not as clear cut as might be implied from government statements. As discussed above, the Home Office target on quality was met, but at the same time was criticised by independent observers as being of poor quality. In 2004, for instance, 20 per cent of appeals against initial decisions were accepted (National Audit Office, 2004b).

There has also been slippage on some of the performance targets. For example, on the indicator of 65 per cent of 'final appeals being decided more quickly', the results of 60 per cent of final appeals for the first half of 2004/05 was actually a 4 per cent reduction from 2003/04, suggesting performance had deteriorated (Home Office, 2005e, p 13). More recent evidence has revised this total upwards, to 67 per cent, which has meant that the target is back 'on course' (Home Office, 2006h, p 100). However, the aim of 75 per cent decided by 2005/06 remains ambitious.

Furthermore, some indicators have been manipulated. For example, the indicator on 'turnaround of manifestly unfounded decisions' was 'under review' for some time, so this measure cannot be assessed (Home Office, 2005e). It was eventually decided (in July 2005) that the target was 'to remove 75 per cent of detained non-suspensive appeal cases, certified as clearly unfounded and detained throughout the process, within 28 days' but there has been slippage on this target – the latest figures indicate that only 70 per cent has been achieved (Home Office, 2006h, p 100).

The existence of a performance measure and the fact that it is met should not automatically mean that performance is excellent or the policy itself is good. Factors external to government policy may account for the decrease in asylum claims. Furthermore, as voluntary sector advocates have argued, Home Office indicators have been narrowly interpreted from the broader objectives, to mean reducing asylum numbers and speeding up claims through the system. There has also been deep disquiet over what (lack of) evidence constitutes an 'unfounded' claim. As a result, there is a less than complete understanding between government and stakeholders of how to measure 'fair, fast, and effective' processes (Williams, 2004).

To more fully evaluate these claims it is worth recalling the detail of the measures used by Labour on asylum discussed in Chapter 4, such as visa regimes. The wording used in the Home Office's own annual report perhaps reveals a certain official ambivalence as to just how 'unfounded' the asylum claims were:

> Almost all the rise in applications in 2002 can be accounted for by increases in claims made by Iraqis and Zimbabweans. Nonetheless, our strategy is focused on reducing unfounded asylum claims. During 2002–03 we have begun implementing a strategy that addresses the key inflow at source and at main points of entry through juxtaposed controls, new detection technology and the implementation of visa regimes where appropriate. (Home Office, 2003d, p 93)

In fact, claiming asylum after having arrived legally in the UK is now impossible.[3] The critique of whether this is a 'fair' system is clearly a valid one.

Similarly, the targets on removals have either not been reached or have been reached only with qualifications. The first target (to remove 30,000 per year) was dropped after concern over its appropriateness and massive failure to meet the figure – the Home Office deported 11,515 in 2001/02 (Home Affairs Select Committee, Question 30, 2002). The second target was met, but not within the original time limit (Home Office, 2005e, p 13), and in the context of a steep fall in asylum claims. The most recent evidence available at the time of writing indicates that this target was missed by 10 per cent for the last quarter of 2006, with 4,085 asylum seekers and dependants removed, compared to 4,560 who applied (Home Office, 2007c).

There have also been negative consequences of increasing the numbers in detention. A series of critical reports has documented inadequate welfare safeguards, evidence of discrimination, evidence of violence and abuse, issues of access to justice, and evidence of inadequate provision for children and those with health needs (Amnesty International, 2005; BID, 2005; Children's Commissioner, 2005; HM Chief Inspector of Prisons, 2004; HM Chief Inspector of Prisons,

2006a; HM Chief Inspector of Prisons, 2006b; Prisons and Probation Ombudsman for England and Wales, 2005). Evidence also shows that detention causes mental health problems, particularly for families and for torture survivors, and that detention policy has corrosive effects on vulnerable groups (Fazel and Stein, 2004; Fazel and Silove, 2006; McCleish et al, 2002; Salinsky and Dell, 2001).

Furthermore, on practical implementation, the National Audit Office has pointed to problems of a lack of management information and separation of application, support and enforcement systems (National Audit Office, 2005a, 2005b).

The Home Office has suggested the New Asylum Model (NAM) may answer some of these concerns. NAM has, however, had a mixed reception. The single case-worker approach is likely to lead to better decision making, and has been given a guarded welcome by NGOs, but there have been concerns over the time-scales to process claims in the streams and the intention behind them. The labelling of one NAM stream as 'late and opportunistic' caused particular irritation, for example (Refugee Council, 2005, p 4). There have also been concerns over the speed of implementation. NAM is being rolled out faster than the National Asylum Support Service (NASS), for instance, while the Immigration and Nationality Directorate – now the Border and Immigration Agency – is settling into its new agency status.

Many of the concerns on asylum policy cannot be reduced to a single policy 'complaint'. For example, the detained fast-track appeal rates are high, a likely result of both the time-scale and reduced legal aid.

Policy problems with precise targets

The following six problems can be identified with PSA Target 7 (on asylum):

1. The 'type' of performance measures is problematic. Barnow (1992) identifies measures from gross outcomes (outcomes at a particular date) to net outputs (value-added measures). Propper and Wilson (2003) survey the evidence and conclude that gross outcomes do not provide a sufficiently accurate portrayal of performance. The asylum and unauthorised migrant targets are based on gross outcomes, so are unlikely to be as effective as value-added measures.
2. There is evidence that performance measures have a selection effect – often known as 'cream skimming'. If we consider the implications for asylum and unauthorised ('illegal') working performance measures, we might expect results that are not necessarily the object

of policy. For example, 'cream skimming' in terms of the removals target could translate into authorities deporting the most visible and the 'easiest' targets (Lewis, 2007, p 50). This may include those supported by the state, those whose children are in education, those who report most regularly to the immigration authorities, those with dependants (more numbers in a single 'hit') and those who will offer least resistance, rather than people who have 'disappeared'. In fact, 'cream skimming' of families (who easily meet the above criteria) is already happening.[4]

3. There is evidence that performance measures create perverse incentives as bureaucrats 'game' the system to make it easier to reach targets. For example in July 2005 PSA target 5 (SR2004) (to 'reduce unfounded asylum claims as part of a broader strategy to tackle abuse of the immigration laws and promote controlled legal migration') was changed so 'unfounded asylum claims' was defined as 'those not granted full refugee status (Indefinite Leave to Remain) … i.e. failed asylum seekers (applicants refused refugee status at the initial decision stage for which no appeal has been received, and applicants whose appeal rights are exhausted)' (Home Office, 2005f, p 10). The baseline is set for the year 2002/03 and is in absolute terms (including dependants). The measure is problematic because it does not take account of those granted either Humanitarian Protection or Discretionary Leave. Moreover, a policy measure introduced in August 2005 has meant that refugees are also no longer granted Indefinite Leave to Remain (the stipulation in the PSA). More significantly, the use of a baseline from 2002/03 is unlikely to be strenuous, given that this was the year when 'unfounded asylum claims' reached record levels. If performance were measured at any time since that year, the Home Office would pass with flying colours. It is difficult to see how the Home Office could fail this test.

4. There is likely to be conflict between performance measures. Home Office operational targets are focused almost entirely on asylum and 'illegal' entry. For example, Home Office Aim 6 (SR2002) translates into targets that all relate specifically to asylum. This is not to suggest that no operational action is taken on other aims. For example, the Home Office records other initiatives under its PSA Target 7, such as the introduction of citizenship ceremonies (Home Office, 2004c, pp 118–19, col 3). However, the government has placed asylum and unauthorised ('illegal') entry at the top of its agenda to the detriment of other aims. In practical terms, this means that other aims do not receive sufficient attention or priority. This may impact on performance, as suggested by the report into the Romanian and

Bulgarian visa affair, where the focus on asylum meant neglecting other areas (Sutton, 2004, pp 32–3).

5. The connection between deportations and asylum numbers is problematic on the grounds of principle. It undermines the concept of asylum because, in practice, it means the target can be met by weighting the other arm of the scales. If incoming asylum numbers are depressed to zero, then no deportations need take place. This undermines the essential meaning of seeking asylum, where countries are obligated (an obligation enshrined in international law) to offer sanctuary from persecution for all those who enter its territory. The fact that this target refers only to the deportation of failed asylum seekers, one category of unauthorised migrants, is symptomatic of the policy focus, which is on asylum, not unauthorised migration.

6. There is an unrealistic assumption underlying policy: that failed asylum seekers and other unauthorised migrants will be deported. The deportation of all unauthorised migrants will be impossible to implement. Official figures estimate the number of undocumented migrants at 430,000 and National Audit Office figures show deportation can cost up to £11,000 per removal when detention costs are included (Woodbridge, 2005; National Audit Office, 2005a, p 4). This is exacerbated by the fact that the definition of unauthorised or 'illegal' migrants includes a spectrum of statuses and types of work. Furthermore, definitions of illegal migrants are subject to administrative change, suggesting policy failure is inevitable, as migrants can move in and out of legality on administrative decisions.

Some of these policy problems have been acknowledged by the Home Affairs Select Committee in its 2006 report. The Committee pointed to unintended impacts on other parts of the immigration system, due to major political targets on asylum sidelining or manipulating other work; targets being set for one part of a system without consideration of the effect elsewhere; targets on speed having a negative impact on quality; and targets being met without having any impact on the underlying objective (Home Affairs Select Committee, 2006b, p 134; see also Somerville, 2006a).

Policy failure: conflict between goals

There are three instances where the targets on asylum have led to conflict with other goals that have resulted in policy failure. First, asylum policy, like any other government policy, is subject to the best-value (auditing) regime and to stringent financial controls. However, the stress on certain targets led to cost-*in*effectiveness. In 2002, IND redeployed resources to 'removals', a decision that led to fewer initial decisions on asylum claims and cost the taxpayer £200m (National Audit Office, 2004b). Similarly, NASS has been criticised for lacking financial controls (National Audit Office, 2005b) and its management, operation and performance have been the focus of independent criticism (Noble et al, 2004).

Second, asylum policy has been criticised for causing integration or community cohesion problems. In particular, 'dispersal' has attracted criticism for its negative impact on community relations in various parts of the UK unused to new migrant flows (Carter and El-Hassan, 2003; Temple et al, 2005).

Finally, asylum policy has been critiqued for *causing* rather than combating social exclusion (Burchardt, 2005; JCHR, 2007). One policy measure that attracted particular attention was the decision in July 2002 to remove asylum seekers' right to work in the UK labour market. (The logic behind this was to remove any incentive for people who might be economic migrants to claim asylum and it was justified by the fact that asylum decisions would be made within six months.) This change has been questioned on a number of grounds, including: theoretically – asylum seekers' decisions are not based on labour market imperatives (Gilbert and Koser, 2003); on grounds of burdening the public purse (CTBI, 2003); undermining integration; encouraging unauthorised work;[5] operationally – with only 63 per cent of applications decided within six months (National Audit Office, 2004b); and on the grounds that if one accepts the logic that paid work is the route out of poverty and exclusion, one must also accept that removing the right to work ensures poverty and exclusion.

Policy gaps

There are two major policy gaps, one related to what is not measured, and the other to possible solutions. The first is a policy gap that reoccurs throughout this evaluation: a lack of appropriate measures. There is an absence of policy measures on unauthorised migration, anti-terrorism and exploitation. For example, employment verification legislation has been strengthened and Labour has introduced identity cards but there are no specific performance measures. One could proclaim the 'success' of intelligence-led enforcement operations or the 'failure' of the minuscule number of prosecutions for illegal working (Home Office, 2003c); but without agreement on what is being evaluated, there is little prospect of progress. Equally, there is evidence in certain sectors in which undocumented migrant workers are concentrated that suggests that there are frequent breaches of employment and tax law by employers, covering such areas as the basic minimum wage, health and safety regulation, and VAT returns (Anderson and Rogaly, 2004; CAB, 2004; Lawrence, 2004, 2006). How can this be evaluated in the absence of any indicators?

The second policy gap refers to the fact that certain policy solutions, most obviously regularisation, are not seriously considered within government, despite the opportunity costs of not bringing undocumented migrants into the mainstream. Such opportunity costs include a lack of integration, loss of tax revenue and a larger informal economy, public health risks, and health and safety considerations.

Notes

[1] It is worth noting that asylum applications peaked in 2002 and that 2002/03 has been chosen as the baseline, with the numbers in absolute terms. It is also worth noting that the definition of 'unfounded' claims includes those given leave on human rights grounds.

[2] 'Building on our success in reducing applications, we now want a step change in the number of failed applicants who leave this country. By the end of the next year, we want the monthly rate of removals to exceed the number of unfounded applications so that we start making increasing inroads into the backlog.'

[3] This was illustrated very clearly in an exchange in the House of Lords on 23 January 2002 (*Hansard*, 2002, col 1462):

Lord Dholakia: My Lords, can the Minister explain whether there are any legal means by which an individual can enter this country and claim asylum?

Lord Rooker: My Lords, I think that the short answer to the noble Lord's question is no.

[4] In addition to anecdotal evidence, a Home Affairs Select Committee (26 October 2005) took evidence from IND officials and Sir John Grieve, then Permanent Secretary to the Home Office, where it was acknowledged that resources are deployed to where they have the most impact. The same session revealed that the Home Office knows the location of over 50 per cent of failed asylum seekers with families but only 25 per cent of the location of the

total number of failed asylum seekers. This implies that asylum seekers with families are proportionately more likely to be deported.

[5] For example, Green (2005, p 19, fn 48) suggests that asylum seekers are likely to work in unregulated and exploitative sections of the London economy as illegal workers.

EIGHTEEN

Integration: a consistent record of failure?

The Home Office PSA Aim 5 (SR2002) and the Foreign and Commonwealth Office (PSA Aim 6, SR2002 and Aim 9, SR2004) share the same objective that policy must be in the 'interests of ... social inclusion', which might be considered a proxy for 'integration'. However, neither PSA Aim is supported by specific integration measures.

Nonetheless, there are *less precise* targets that can be used to come to some judgements, the best of which can be found in PSA Aims that are *not* overtly connected with migration, in particular Home Office PSA Aim 5 (SR2004), which reads: 'citizens, communities and the voluntary sector are more fully engaged in tackling social problems and there is more equality of opportunity and respect for people of all races and religions', an aim – in essence – about race relations and community cohesion, that can be considered here as the best proxy for 'integration'.

The relevant target under Home Office PSA Aim 5 (SR2004) is Target 7: to 'reduce race inequalities and build community cohesion'.[1] For the purpose of measuring performance, the two elements in PSA Aim 5, Target 7 (SR2004) are disaggregated. The 'race' element is measured by 'a decrease in the number of people from Black and Minority Ethnic communities who perceive that they would be treated worse than people of other races by one or more key public services and in the labour market, as measured through the Home Office Citizenship Survey' (with baselines of 2001 and 2003) and the 'community cohesion' element by 'an increase in perceptions of community cohesion, as measured through the Citizenship Survey Local Area Boost' (baseline 2005). Both elements therefore use surveys as measures.

PSA Aim 5 (SR2004) forms part of the government-wide race equality and community cohesion strategy, known as *Improving opportunity, strengthening society* (Home Office, 2005b), described in Chapter 3. Two other Public Sector Agreements (PSAs) are closely linked to this strategy, one on reducing 'the difference between the employment rates of the disadvantaged groups [which includes Black and Minority Ethnic Groups] and the overall rate' (DWP PSA 4) and one on promoting 'ethnic diversity' (DTI PSA 10). In addition, there are six other PSAs where departments monitor progress in tackling race inequalities.

In addition to the PSAs, there are two other relevant sets of integration indicators. First, indicators for community cohesion developed elsewhere – for example the Commission for Racial Equality's 'good race relations' guidance or the Quality of Life Best Value Indicators used by the Audit Commission. Second, there are also relevant 'social exclusion' indicators. Labour sets out its aims, measures and progress on social exclusion through its annual *Opportunity for all* reports. The seventh annual report makes clear that the aim is to create 'safer and stronger communities' and that 'all of us ... have a role ... in helping Britain move towards an inclusive society based on mutual respect, an outcome that benefits the whole of society'. The report then states the three ways success will be measured: 'We have a target to reduce race inequality and improve community cohesion ...; we will publish an annual review of progress against the commitments in the *Improving opportunity, strengthening society* strategy; and, thirdly, you will judge our success by the difference in all our lives – stronger communities in a more inclusive society' (DWP, 2005a, p 65).

Have these aims been realised for migrants?

The only target that can be assessed, Home Office Aim 5, PSA Target 7, on community cohesion, cannot be assessed with confidence, but, according to the Home Office, it has 'probably' been met (Home Office, 2006h, p 102). However, the reliance on survey data and polling does not provide a particularly useful evidence base. Such a narrow view does not even begin to do justice to the complexity of trying to work out whether aims on social inclusion, community cohesion and so on have been met for migrants.

The majority of evidence indicates that these aims have *not* been realised. This will be illustrated through two examples: employment and combating social exclusion.

Domestic employment and migrants

Labour has consistently underlined work as the key route out of poverty and social exclusion (Finn, 2003; Powell, 2002). Given 8.3 per cent of the UK population is foreign born, migrants should form an important consideration in employment policy, but they are not disaggregated for performance management purposes. In other words, there are no migrant-specific performance indicators; consequently, data and evidence to evaluate policy relies on independent research.

Such research has shown that the employment rate among migrants is around 64 per cent, compared to around 75 per cent for the UK born (Kempton, 2002). The gap is larger for 'new' migrants than 'settled' migrants (Kyambi, 2005), although this still compares favourably to rates experienced by ethnic minorities in the UK (Strategy Unit, 2003).

However, the aggregate employment level of migrants hides huge disparities. There are major differences by nationality, with Bangladeshi and Pakistani migrants having particularly poor outcomes (Kyambi, 2005; Ognjenovic and Somerville, 2004).[2] In London, recent data suggests Somali, Congolese, Rwandan and Afghani migrants have particularly high levels of unemployment (GLA, 2005a). The existing evidence suggests that refugees in particular have high unemployment and underemployment relative to other migrant groups and minorities (Bloch, 2000, 2004; Somerville, 2006c). The evidence on migrant earnings also suggests disparities among nationalities. Migrants working in low-skill sectors may have extremely low wages, with consequent in-work poverty (Evans et al, 2005). Furthermore, migrants may work in a different labour market from UK-born workers, in the forms of both low-wage legal employment and unauthorised employment.

The causes of high unemployment, underemployment and low wages among certain migrant groups are difficult to establish and are likely to include a range of factors (Kempton, 2002). While there is insufficient space to discuss all the causes of disparities in employment rates, it is important to assess the impacts of migration policy on employment, as interventions that affect migrants' ability to enter the labour market are clearly relevant to the success and failure of domestic employment policy.

There are several such impacts. First, policy may directly restrict employment. Some migrants are precluded by their immigration status from undertaking any employment (asylum seekers); some from working in particular kinds of employment; some for working beyond a maximum number of hours (students can work for a maximum of 20 hours per week in term time); and some from shifting to jobs that pay more or offer enhanced opportunities (seasonal workers) (Somerville, 2006b).

Second, policy may inhibit advancement. While policy makers acknowledge that sufficient English is crucial to securing a job or progressing in the labour market, English for speakers of other languages (ESOL) provision is beset by over-demand, together with coordination and funding problems (Griffiths, 2001). Recent cuts in ESOL provision, together with increasing obligations to speak English to secure permanent residency and citizenship, have exacerbated problems with provision. Furthermore, migrants on short-term visas may not invest in their own human capital. The lack of an effective system for recognising foreign qualifications also falls within the policy framework and may hinder migrants' access and progress within the labour market.

Third, research has identified discrimination specific to migrants, based not on ethnicity but on status, and employer discrimination due to mistaken fear of prosecution (see case studies in TUC, 2002; Employability Forum, 2003). Lack of documentation or long delays in securing documentation have also been factors in preventing employment (NACAB, 2000).

Fourth, policy may undermine social security incentives. Currently, there is a complex interaction between the social security system and migration status (CPAG, 2002; Somerville, 2006b). This means that for some statuses, entitlement is heavily restricted. The government has imposed strict conditionality requirements through legislation (to stop 'benefits tourism'). The number of immigration statuses and the hugely complicated social security caveats attached to each status, especially for the means-tested benefits, mean there is a widespread lack of understanding. They also undermine incentives: migrants, for example, cannot generally claim tax credits (Somerville, 2004a, p 312).

There is a further angle to the discussion on social security and work. Policy is currently driven by an assumption that conditionality is required so as to reduce incentives to come to the UK. Research shows that this is a false assumption: migration is not driven by benefit rules and 'benefits tourism' is not widespread (Robinson and Segrott, 2002). This is particularly true for asylum seekers, where the belief that the asylum system is used as a route to UK benefits is a key policy building block, but is undermined by the evidence (Gilbert and Koser, 2003).

Finally, exploitation in a wide range of sectors is likely to be extensive. Evidence suggests exploitation takes the form of extremely long hours, low gross rates of pay, substandard accommodation, excessive deductions from pay for utilities, transport and accommodation, failure to provide a contract of employment, failure to pay the National Minimum Wage, summary dismissal and denial of basic employment rights such as paid holidays and maternity leave (Anderson et al, 2006; Anderson and Rogaly, 2004; CAB, 2004; Lawrence, 2006). The reality of exploitation has also been attested in the print media (*Guardian*, 2005) and driven home by the Morecambe Bay tragedy of February 2004.

Combating social exclusion

There are again no specific performance measures pertaining to migrants in the social exclusion policy framework. It is possible that 'migrants' do not fit within definitions or even concepts of social exclusion. For example, if we apply to asylum seekers the four indicators – consumption, production, political and social engagement – used by the independent Centre for the Analysis of Social Exclusion, we find that they fail on all four: they are not allowed to work, live on 70 per cent of benefit levels with no assets, are forcibly dispersed and cannot vote.

For an analysis of how far migrant groups are vulnerable to social exclusion, we must again turn to independent research. Such research reveals incontrovertible evidence that certain groups of migrants, both children and adults, are vulnerable to social exclusion.

The evidence for children indicates that asylum-seeking children are particularly at risk from exclusion (Children's Commissioner, 2005; Fitzpatrick, 2005; Nandy, 2005). However, migration policies may interfere with government aims on child poverty for all migrant groups (Rutter, 2003) and may also conflict with child welfare (Jones, 1998). For example, not all migrant groups can claim benefits or tax credits, removing the key plank of Labour's strategy to eliminate child poverty by 2020 for such groups. A range of reports has also shown that migration policies may cause or exacerbate adult poverty and exclusion (GLA, 2004; Joseph Rowntree Foundation, 2005; Penrose, 2002; Refugee Survival Trust, 2005; Robinson and Reeve, 2006, pp 21–2). Particular groups may suffer more than other groups. For one group in particular – asylum seekers – poverty levels and social exclusion are particularly high (Refugee Media Action Group, 2006).

The key point is that policy worsens such poverty. As Tania Burchardt (2005, p 210) bluntly, and correctly, puts it, 'policy has had the effect of generating social exclusion, rather than preventing or ameliorating it'.

These two extended examples – of policy on domestic employment and combating social exclusion – reveal their goals to be undermined by migration policy. Moreover, these examples are not unique – they are reflective of the extensive literature on failure to reach such aims for migrant communities. If we examine housing, for example, we find that it is inappropriate to migrants' needs (Robinson and Reeve, 2006; Shelter, 2004), particularly for asylum seekers and refugees (Buck, 2001; Kelly and Joly, 1999; Wilson, 2001), and again policy bears much of the blame. For example, asylum dispersal policy has had a negative impact on communities and housing (Cole and Robinson, 2003; Office of the Deputy Prime Minister: Housing, Planning, Local Government and the Regions Committee, 2004). Similar arguments can be made for other social policy areas, such as health.

However, while the literature indicates that the 'integration' of migrants has been undermined by policy and goals have not been met, the lack of agreement on measures renders the government unaccountable. For instance, one could argue that increasing the numbers of those granted citizenship is a measure of integration. Such grants have doubled between 1999 and 2003 alone (Dudley and Woollacot, 2004) and more than one million foreign nationals have become British citizens since Blair took office, indicating 'success', if that is the measure.

Policy gaps

There are two major gaps. The clearest policy gap is the lack of specific measures. In the overlapping framework of integration aims, measures and indicators, there is little room for migrants, who are an invisible group, appearing only in relation to other groups (settled minorities or race, for example).

This is best illustrated by examining government strategies. The strategy to increase race equality and community cohesion, *Improving opportunity, strengthening society*, dedicates little space to discussing migrants (Home Office, 2005b). Despite the intention of the strategy to cut across government, the focus on migration is limited to 'integration' provisions in the form of citizenship ceremonies and new help for refugees, and is covered on a single page (Home Office, 2005b, p 45).

The best assessment of policy over time is the eight *Opportunity for all* reports, the yearly reports to monitor progress towards a fairer, 'more inclusive society' (DWP, 2003c, foreword). There are perhaps three major conclusions that can be drawn from a reading of the eight reports.

First, ethnic minorities receive consistent attention as a policy goal. There are initiatives, strategies and resources for various needs (housing, advice, education), in addition to work on increasing the employment rates of ethnic minorities. The reports – in general – make much of initiatives and resources (such as new funds) but refer less to anti-discrimination laws and how effective policy has been. For example, the fifth annual report includes an analysis and audit of action on minorities, but little on the effectiveness of measures (DWP, 2003c, pp 128–45).

Second, it is clear that new migrants receive virtually no attention. For example, the third and fourth annual reports do not have a single reference to asylum seekers, refugees or migrants (DWP, 2001; 2002). References to migrants appear in relation to legal aid (DWP, 2004b, p 79), or Europe, or the occasional scattered mention concerning documentation or language training. For example, the description of migrants as a 'group' requiring intervention occurs in only one of the eight annual reports, and this in the context of EU policy (DWP, 2005a, p 114). While many new migrants are ethnic minorities, this is not a mutually inclusive group. There are no specific migrant measures or goals.

Third, in respect to asylum seekers and refugees, the reports appear to go in phases: the first phase (reports 1999–2000) see asylum seekers and refugees as a small, interrelated issue and are concerned with 'improving outcomes' for this group (DSS, 2000, paragraph 68, p 103); the second phase (reports 2000–2001) completely ignores the issue, despite the fact that asylum seekers and refugees were a major policy concern during this period; and the third phase (reports 2002–2005) is a growing policy response to recognised refugees only, with asylum seekers excised from the debate. For example, the eighth report provides a short summary of the various initiatives undertaken to help integrate refugees, which appears under the heading 'community cohesion' (DWP, 2006, pp 9, 23–4; see also the fifth report: DWP, 2003c, p 19).

This first policy gap (a lack of measures) means that issues such as the exclusion of migrants from certain discrimination laws, or their treatment in detention, are not addressed (Coussey, 2004, p 3). There is a clear exception to this, with a focused debate on goals and indicators for *refugees*, set out in the government strategy, *Integration matters* (Home Office, 2005c). However, the rhetoric does not resemble reality. No specific measures on employment or on language have been set for refugees (which are the only two targets in the strategy). Furthermore, an analysis of resource allocation – to 'reveal the preferences' – shows funding for refugee integration as a proportion of spending on refugee and asylum accounts for less than 1 per cent (Dunn and Somerville, 2004). Also, measures of the impact of migration are absent. McGhee (2006) argues, for instance, that too little attention is given to the host community. In effect, the government is 'managing migration' but not 'managing settlement'. Thus there is also a gap regarding 'host communities', with no measures on communicating with settled groups to address the concerns they have.

The second major gap is in relation to public services. The provision and resource use of public services is essential to community relations and inclusion, but is only recorded as part of a survey measure on whether ethnic minorities feel they have been treated as well as other groups. This again does not come close to realising the complexity of the connection. There are no measures for migrants, such as access to services or whether services meet migrants' needs – this despite policy interventions potentially worsening such essential inclusion goals. For example, increasing conditionality has undermined migrant access to services, and the fact that some migrant groups pay full (income) tax but are not necessarily eligible for (negative income) tax in the form of tax credits or for social security benefits may undermine inclusion.

The impact of services on inclusion is similarly excluded from the discussion, despite evidence that establishes a direct link between migration and community relations (over the use of shared resources) (Craig at al, 2004). Services are also developing practice in regard to certain groups of migrants, as they are obliged to do by the 2000 Race Relations (Amendment) Act, but again, specific measures are absent.

The gap lies not only in the impact of public services but in how migrants and public services are interdependent. For instance, the data for foreign-born employees show there are over 0.25m workers in the health sector alone (Salt, 2001). In fact, 26.8 per cent of health professionals and 9.2 per cent of teaching professionals are foreign born. There is also change over time in migrant labour supply. Between 1992 and 2000, the stock of foreign-born doctors rose by over 40 per cent, suggesting that public services are becoming more, not less, reliant on migrant labour. This has implications for policy.

In short, there are serious gaps regarding specificity (no measures for migrants) or services (outside of the discussion).

Notes

[1] The SR2002 PSA included Home Office Aim 6: 'support strong and active communities in which people of all races and backgrounds are valued and participate on equal terms', which linked to Target 9 to 'bring about measurable improvements in race equality and community cohesion across a range of performance indicators, as part of the government's objectives on equality and social inclusion'.

[2] This also applies to ethnic minorities in the UK labour market (Strategy Unit, 2003).

NINETEEN

Delivery

The theme of delivery, like integration in the previous chapter, can only be evaluated with *less precise* measures. Like integration, there are relevant Public Sector Agreements (PSAs) outside of the specific 'migration' PSA Aim. The most relevant refer to 'entry clearance' and are held by the Foreign and Commonwealth Office (FCO).

However, the 'delivery' of migration policy is wider than the entry visa system. There is a spectrum of other measures that can be used to evaluate the operation of the immigration system. For instance, in 2002 the Prime Minister set a target for all government services to be 100 per cent online by 2005 (Cabinet Office PSA 3, SR 2002), which the Immigration and Nationality Directorate achieved within the necessary reporting time frame.[1] Three further measures with particular relevance are discussed in this chapter. First, measures of efficiency (savings targets); second, drawing on the discussion of the White Paper *Modernising government* (Cabinet Office, 1999) in Chapter 5, there is an analysis of joined-up government; and finally, individual project delivery is assessed.

The operation of the immigration system

In the space provided, the best target to evaluate the overall operation of the immigration system is the PSA on visas, set for the FCO (shared with UKvisas). Helpfully, the PSA Aim has been the same over both Spending Reviews (PSA Aim 6, SR 2002 and PSA Aim 9, SR 2004): 'High quality consular services to British nationals abroad. Effective regulation of entry to, and settlement in, the UK in the interests of sustainable growth and social inclusion.' However, the underlying targets are slightly different between the two. The first set of PSA targets (SR 2002) was (Target 1) 90 per cent of straightforward non-residence visa applications to be decided within 24 hours; (Target 2) 90 per cent of posts to make a decision within 10 working days on non-settlement applications requiring an interview; (Target 3) 90 per cent of posts to meet target times for settlement interviews; and (Target 4) 0.04 per cent of visa holders whose leave to enter the UK is cancelled on arrival at a UK port. In the PSA targets (SR 2004), Target 2 has been lengthened to 15 working days and Target 3 has a time limit of 12 weeks. Target 4, on visa holders, has been discontinued and replaced with: '60 per cent of visa applications to be processed by posts with Risk Assessment Units or visa assessment teams in 2005–06, rising to 70 per cent in 2006–07 and 75 per cent in 2007–08.'

Have operational targets been reached?

The underlying operational performance has been close to, or exceeded, stated objectives. By 2004, Targets 1 and 3 were achieved with 92.1 per cent and 98.3 per cent; Targets 2 and 4 were narrowly missed with 88.8 per cent and 0.047 per cent respectively (UKvisas, 2004). By the end of the reporting period, all four of the original targets were met and only the new target recorded slippage – to 55.7 per cent on a target of 60 per cent (FCO, 2006b, pp 123, 151). The success or near-success of meeting such targets also indicates effective delivery. More importantly, we should view this in the context of a 'challenging external environment' – a fast-rising volume of applications. For example, visa applications have increased by 55 per cent over the four years 2001/2 to 2005/6 (Home Office, 2006k, p 13).

However, the success of UKvisas in nearly meeting its targets should be put in context. For example, the success in meeting entry clearance targets included the year when there was a major debacle in Bulgaria and Romania (see Chapter 14). Furthermore, more than 50 per cent of visa appeals by visiting families were successful, with a lack of robust decision making being at least partially responsible (National Audit Office, 2004a, paragraph 19).

Savings targets

The other obvious measure for the overall operation of the immigration system can be found in the two government reviews that focused on improving efficiency across government, the so-called Gershon review and Lyons inquiry. These introduced certain targets for the Home Office, including the Gershon efficiency savings target, which set a target of saving £1,970m by March 2008 and the Lyons inquiry headcount reduction target of 2,700 by March 2008 and a relocation target of 2,200 by 2010.

The Home Office had delivered £1.6bn in savings by March 2006, £0.2bn ahead of the target set by the Gershon review (Cabinet Office, 2006, p 10). The Home Office had also made progress against its Lyons inquiry targets: by March 2006, headcount had been reduced by 1,089 (behind forecast of 1,933) but had relocated 497 posts (ahead of the 434 forecast).

This picture of success in making efficiency gains and reaching savings targets is painted differently by those representing migrants. For example, the reforms to the legal system (reducing the costs of legal aid) have been widely criticised as denying justice to, especially, asylum seekers (BID and Asylum Aid, 2005; GLA, 2005b). There have also been criticisms of financial management. For example, as the earlier discussion of asylum showed, auditors have indicated that losses of £200m were avoidable (National Audit Office, 2004b).

Joined-up government

Labour has viewed joined-up government (JUG) as crucial to the delivery of all social policies, as encapsulated in the *Modernising government* White Paper, and this has included migration policy, particularly in Labour's first term, where it was a major feature of the 1998 White Paper (Flynn, 2005b).

In passing, JUG should be distinguished from performance management. Indeed, JUG may undermine performance management targets as individual departments and agencies prioritise their targets rather than cross-cutting policies. Pollitt (2003) offers three models for assessing the success of JUG. The first is to examine 'best practice'; the second is to try and identify the outcomes of JUG; and the third is to seek the views of stakeholders. This analysis draws on the last model, using the expert interviews carried out for this book to evaluate JUG.

Of the 22 interviewees, seven indicated that policy was joined up. There is evidence to support their claim. For example, the Department for Constitutional Affairs (now Ministry of Justice) has a joint PSA with the Home Office on the numbers of asylum seekers and a joint budget (the Single Asylum Budget); the Foreign and Commonwealth Office has a joint PSA with the Home Office on entry visas. At a supranational level, the government has signed up to moves to harmonise reception procedures in Europe.

However, the majority of interviewees suggested JUG was a chimera. Their claim is also supported by evidence. For example, the Home Office PSA target on migration is generally focused on asylum, with no performance measures on areas such as legal migration. Similarly, the infrastructure and resources that deliver migration policy are clustered around the Home Office (Somerville, 2006a, p 59). This contrasts with other countries, where responsibilities are more diffuse (Van Selm, 2005).

Several interviewees noted there was little joining up of integration policies. The cross-cutting strategy on race equality and cohesion is backed up by a board consisting of senior civil servants and public figures drawn from across government but the omission of migrants from the strategy has meant a lack of institutional coordination. The agendas are owned by different departments (CLG, DWP and the Home Office at a minimum) and are also disconnected internally. For example, the units responsible for the inclusion of migrants, including the Active Citizenship Unit, the Civil Renewal Unit, the Cohesion and Faiths Unit, the Race Equality Unit and the Social Policy Unit, do *not* join up thinking in regard to migration policies.

In reality, both claims are correct. The distinction is that joined-up government exists but only in the asylum–security nexus. The momentum and pressure to 'join up' policies is restricted to these areas.

Project delivery

The majority of 'migration' projects have been associated with upgrading systems and upgrading technology. (While the rationale for such projects or 'pilots' has often been efficiency, there are few figures on individual cost savings.) There has also been consistent investment in cutting-edge technologies for external functions, particularly at border controls. However, there has also been a series of well-documented failures, indicating poor delivery. The most visible failures have been around recording, counting and upgrading processing systems, as noted in Chapter 5. In addition, the Home Office has been criticised for having poor project management and an over-reliance on external consultants (Cabinet Office, 2006, p 15).

The interviews with experts revealed four key factors in poor delivery. The first was that the initial squeeze on funding, when the Labour government continued with the Conservative spending restrictions for the first two years of office, led to a situation of diminishing resources during a period of escalating need. This contributed to later chaos. Second, a lack of independent monitoring of enforcement and external accountability has led to poor practice. The announcement of a new accountability mechanism in December 2006 by Liam Byrne, Minister of State, showed Labour responding to this issue. Third, the 'fragmentation' of resources and 'lack of communication', particularly of management, within the Immigration and Nationality Directorate undermined delivery (for example, Home Affairs Select Committee 2006b, p 7). Finally, there have been key technology failures. Ongoing problems with processing and technology have impeded performance; the 2006 IND review correctly described the systems as 'outmoded' (Home Office, 2006d, p 4).

Note

[1] Services were 100 per cent online by April 2006; personal communication with Cabinet Office.

TWENTY

Economic migration: has the vision been realised?

In this and the following chapter on international development, there are no specific PSA target measures to evaluate policy, despite the fact that there are recurrent allusions to both in government aims. Both PSA aims since 2001 refer to economic (managed) migration in some form. Home Office Aim 6 (SR2002) refers to an 'efficient and effective work permit system to meet economic and skills requirements' and Home Office Aim 4 (SR2004) is that 'migration is managed to benefit the UK'. This is backed up by other aims: for example the 2002 White Paper refers to 'prospering in the global economy'.

The lack of targets makes evaluation problematic; nonetheless there are some *imprecise* measures from which some partial judgements can be made. For example, Work Permits (UK) has a target to decide 90 per cent of complete applications within one day and 90 per cent of all applications within one week. This has been achieved. Work Permits (UK) provides 'an excellent service to employers, turning around 90 per cent of work permit applications within a day' (Home Office Press Release, 2003a; see also Home Office, 2005e).

While such a proxy measure is important, it is narrow. This chapter tries to capture the 'vision' of managed migration, which is taken to mean extracting the maximum amount of 'economic value' from migration. This 'economic value' is defined here as (a) the balance between immigration flows of workers and non-workers, what might be termed the 'migration mix' – and (b) the macro-economic benefits (or not) accrued from migration.

Has the vision been realised?

A. Figure 1.1 in Chapter 1 shows the number of approved work permits and first permissions from 1995 to 2005, which have more than tripled, with the steepest rises taking place under the Labour government. Policy has successfully changed the 'migration mix', towards a net inflow that favours skilled workers and students. In effect, the system has been remoulded around economic migration (although it should be noted that causation is difficult to attribute, and factors beyond government policy must be considered).

The proportion of incoming migrants coming to the UK for work, alongside the other main categories, is detailed in Figure 20.1. The trend is clearly one of more work-related migration, from 18.2 per cent in 1995 to 24.7 per cent in 2004. If we include the numbers coming to study (from 20 per cent in 1995 to 23.4 per cent in 2004) and the fact that certain streams (such as the Working Holidaymaker Visa) are included under 'Other', we must conclude that there has been a significant change in the 'migration mix', which has attracted more workers and students, thus extracting greater 'value'.

This is supported by the literature. Findlay et al (2003, p 4) summarise this when they say the recent trend is one that favours 'the net immigration of skilled people. This has come about not only because of the strong economic performance of the UK economy, but because of significant changes to the regime governing UK migration policy.'

Figure 20.1: Main reasons for migration to the UK, 1994–2004

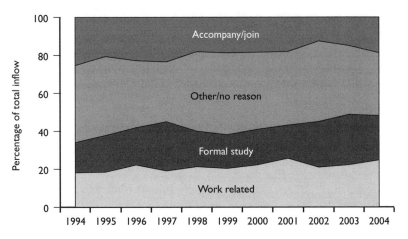

B. The quantitative evidence on economic migration is, in broad terms, positive, indicating considerable policy success (Kempton, 2002). Migration to the UK has had a negligible effect on employment levels and a small positive impact on wage levels (Haque, 2002). The macro-economic gains include greater labour market flexibility, fewer skill shortages, and lower inflation. For example, migrants are more likely to be employed in sectors of the economy with skill shortages (Loizillon, 2004). There has also been a clear fiscal gain, estimated in the region of

£2.5bn (Home Office 2002b), or as high as £5.4bn by the Centre for Economic and Business Research. A more complete analysis indicates that from 1999 to 2004 the foreign born contributed more than the UK born (Sriskandarajah et al, 2005, see especially pp 10–11). Finally, the impact of the Eastern European accession states has been viewed as particularly positive (Ernst and Young, 2006; Portes and French, 2006).

However, there are likely to be negative as well as positive effects. Little account has been taken of distributional impacts, and the impact of migration on maintaining the positive wage and employment effects depends at least in part on the substitutability of migrant workers. This may have particular consequences for low-skill workers. Furthermore, it will have implications for the current reforms to the immigration system.[1]

Policy problems

The main policy problems with the managed migration system are the ever-present issues of complexity and bureaucracy. In terms of complexity, from 1997 to 2006 there were more than 22 schemes covering different aspects of economic migration, with the result that neither practitioners nor those subject to immigration control had a clear understanding of the system. Labour's reforms sought to address some of the difficulties identified as a result of its growing complexity (Home Office, 2005a, p 7; 2005d), proposing the scheme be simplified by amalgamating all managed migration categories into a unified 'points-based scheme', albeit one consisting of five separate tiers (Home Office, 2005d).

However, in many ways this simply 'scoops' the existing schemes into five new boxes. This complexity is reflected in the objectives of the system, which include economic and international competitiveness, control, students, responsibility and 'other' (Home Office, 2005d, p 19, para 5.2). The system should also satisfy a number of 'tests'[2] which include operability, robustness, objectivity, flexibility, cost-effectiveness, transparency, usability and legislative compatibility (Home Office, 2005d, p 19). The trade-offs between such objectives are not acknowledged. For example, any test of 'objectivity' will require increased guidance materials, which, together with the new sponsorship requirements, is likely to conflict with the test of 'flexibility'.

The new system will be more bureaucratic as changes from 2005 have made the system less employer led. The 'tiers' seem to be based on absorbing the existing schemes rather than on a clear rationale of who constitutes an 'economic migrant'.

Policy gaps

The main policy gap, and one shared with policy on migration development, is that there are no agreed measures of success for economic migration. It is notable that PSA Target 5 (SR2004) does not have a measure of 'legal migration'. The *Selective admission* proposals contained objectives, but again without any detail on performance measures (Home Office, 2005d). Even the Work Permits (UK) indicator is not a 'formal' performance measure and is not included within the PSA regime.[3]

Notes

[1] For example, the proposals may change the balance between how far the immigration system is a demand-driven or a supply-driven system.

[2] The tests might more usefully be considered as principles.

[3] The introduction of an indicator has been under discussion from 2004 but is likely to be overtaken by events as the proposed 2006 reforms will integrate work permit and visa decisions.

TWENTY-ONE

Outside of the circle: international development

The previous chapter noted that no PSA targets pertained to the nexus between migration and international development, but, like economic migration, migration development goals are mentioned in several documents. The Home Office five-year plan, for instance, states that 'we also have a responsibility to ensure that our migration policies do not compromise the economic well being of poor countries' (Home Office, 2005a, p 18) and refers to putting migration at the centre of relationships with other countries. The 2002 White Paper refers to the objective of attracting migrants 'in a manner consistent with our international commitment to eliminate world poverty' (Home Office, 2002a, p 20).

However, no PSA has underlying indicators that refer to migration development goals. The closest expression is probably the Department for International Development's (DFID) target to 'increase the impact of the international system in reducing poverty, preventing conflict and responding effectively to conflict and humanitarian crises', but this does not mention migrants, migration, refugee or displacement issues specifically.[1] DFID has recently released a policy plan on migration, noting that it is a new area of activity, and setting out areas where migration will be incorporated into policy (DFID, 2007, especially pp 37–40). However, while evaluation is promised (in 2010), there are no targets.

An absence of measurable targets does not mean there has been no policy action, though it has been limited. For example, policy guidelines have been laid down to ensure that recruitment to UK public services does not lead to 'brain drain' in the developing world, an innovative measure in the international context. DFID has also funded a website on providing information on remittances and has developed remittance 'partnerships' with Nigeria, Ghana and Bangladesh (DFID, 2007, p 17).

The research on the effects of the (limited) policy measures that have been introduced reveals little success. For example, there has been no independent evaluation of whether the guidelines to ensure ethical recruitment in the NHS are effective, but the evidence that does exist suggests the voluntary guidelines may not be enforced (House of Commons, 2004). Furthermore, the assumption behind the policy may be wrong; active opportunities to emigrate may encourage human capital accumulation and indeed may already be part of policy (for example in the Philippines). Similarly, online tools to facilitate remittances and building partnerships are important steps, but remain policy tools in their infancy, especially given the fact that remittances exceed the global aid budget.

References to migration development goals do not cascade down to measurable targets, but they also refer to few policies. A more honest acceptance of government goals was provided by the *Selective admission* consultation (Home Office, 2005d) which presented one of its goals as 'international competitiveness' but ignored development goals. The notion of 'migration partnerships', of placing migration at the heart of relationships with other countries, is less about development and more about ensuring that 'returns' to source countries are managed effectively.

Policy gaps and problems

The gaps in the policy framework run from imprecise measures and incorrect assumptions behind policy, to a simple lack of policy tools and development. While Chapter 18 made the point that migrants are often excluded, contributing to national inequality, international migration undoubtedly reduces *global* inequality. Consequently, international migration may be a crucial global anti-poverty tool (Galbraith, 1979, p 7) and contribute to DFID's targets on eliminating world poverty. At present, however, there is no stomach for using migration policy to do so.

Note

[1] The PSA (SR2004) was to: 'Eliminate poverty in poorer countries in particular through achievement by 2015 of the Millennium Development Goals.'

TWENTY-TWO

Conclusion

This book has described the themes of immigration policy under Labour, a perspective that has shown there have been continuities but also radical policy changes since 1997. The post-war settlement of restriction and integration has been recast around a work-focused system, ending the bifurcated policy that lasted 40 years and, in particular, the policy of limitation. The analysis of five different dimensions, themes or domains of migration policy showed that there was no 'single' policy with its own internal dynamic of change, but instead a number of interdependent 'layers', that often only make sense when analysed individually (for more detail, see Chapter 6).

This book has also offered an original examination of the forces and influences that have led to such a new policy direction. A range of inputs accounts for change, from setting parameters and developing content, to implementation; and categorising the inputs at macro, meso and micro level provides a more complete picture of why policy has changed. The three macro-level influences (globalisation, domestic and international law, and Europe) emerge as boundary setters, with Europe providing the infrastructure and space for the first two forces to have real impact. At a meso level, network theory supplements our understanding of policy change in the period 1997–2007, explaining how – in a globalising world – economic migration policy was shaped to meet the new reality. The chapters on politics, attitudes and the media showed that politics has shaped the content of policy; politicians, the media and attitudes, particularly on asylum and security issues, were interdependent, part of feedback loops that bounced off one another. Officials emerge as important in policy implementation, but less important as explanatory variables for policy change.

Furthermore, by disaggregating to the level of policy theme, some influences stand out strongly. Managed migration has been strongly influenced by globalisation and a strong network or 'policy community', while asylum has been dominated by public attitudes, the media and the politics of electoral calculation (for a thorough summary, see Chapter 15).

Finally, the last part of this book presented an evaluation of policy, using the aims and targets laid down in the Public Sector Agreement (PSA) regime, to provide insights into whether Labour's migration policy objectives have been achieved. There are caveats to the evaluation framework: PSAs may not fully reflect all or even the 'right' aims and may not provide benchmarks and measures.

Precise targets exist for asylum and are largely based on restricting numbers by speeding up and reducing applications. Labour has succeeded in making the asylum process more end-to-end and has increased the speed of asylum processing. However, it has a mixed record of achievement on its own performance measures: some targets have been met, others not. Measures on 'security' are largely to reduce the unauthorised population through deportation. Existing evidence suggests success and failure in meeting targets, with some negative consequences for migrant communities. The picture is deliberately confused, as policy has blurred the distinction between asylum seekers and unauthorised migrants.

Less precise targets exist for integration and delivery. Coherent measures on integration can be found elsewhere in the PSA regime through the relevant race and cohesion targets and a number of 'social inclusion' targets. The evidence base indicates clear policy failure, with certain groups of migrants exhibiting *higher* levels of exclusion and a lack of integration in a context of *decreasing* social exclusion for other groups (Hills and Stewart, 2005). Moreover, policy has a demonstrable (negative) impact for some vulnerable migrant groups. Migration policy is therefore not consistent with Labour's general approach to social exclusion as policy interventions work against the grain: migrants are largely excised from inclusion policies, entrenching 'a stratified system' (Morris, 2002, p 413).

The policy aims to improve delivery have not been reached: joined-up government and project delivery, especially where new technologies have been applied to internal systems, have been poor. Nonetheless, it is difficult to conclude that delivery has been a complete failure, given the challenging external factors and operational successes in reaching certain targets, such as visa processing.

The targets for economic migration and international development are *imprecise* as there are no reasonable proxy measures. The aim of policy on managed migration was interpreted broadly, to liberalise routes and extract greater value from this migration stream for macro-economic benefit. The evidence on outcomes appears to be consistent with the policy aims (especially if we include students as part of managed migration), albeit with a number of inconsistencies and contradictions (often the result of the system's complexity) that will increasingly create challenges in the future.

The evidence on international development is unclear, largely because there are no targets and thus a lack of precision. However, the fact that there is *no* explicit mention of migration development goals, that potential policies are either nascent or not on the agenda, and that the limited available evidence points towards the exclusion of development concerns, suggests that migration policy is *not* 'consistent with world poverty objectives'.

Labour's resources have been skewed towards asylum–security, whereas for migrant integration policy in particular there has been less resource allocation, and inconsistencies and contradictions within the system. The concentration of resources around the Home Office does not allow resolution of the inevitable conflicts – or potential trade-offs – within policy. The asylum–security aims clearly take precedence over integration policy aims (especially social inclusion), for example. Of course, it is quite possible that all the aims expressed by the Home Office may not be logically compatible with each other, but there are currently no mechanisms to allow for practical trade-offs to balance policy.

In bringing this book to a close, it is worth remembering there is a growing consensus that migration is here to stay. Based on predictions, there will be net gain of four million permanent migrants in less than a generation.[1] The importance of migration policy in the UK will only increase and government will need to construct policy more creatively if it is to maximise the benefits and minimise the losses from migration.

Note

[1] There is a predicted net gain of 4.1 million migrants in the next 24 years (GAD, 2007).

Bibliography

Abbas, T. (2005) *Muslim Britain: Communities under pressure*, London: Zed Books.

Ager, A. and Strang, A. (2004) *Indicators of refugee integration: An indicator framework*, London: Home Office.

Aleinikoff, T. and Klusmeyer, D. (2002) *Citizenship policies for an age of migration*, Washington DC: Carnegie and MPI.

Amnesty International (1999) *The most vulnerable of all: The treatment of unaccompanied refugee children in the UK*.

Amnesty International (2005) *Seeking asylum is not a crime: detention of people who have sought asylum*, London: Amnesty International UK.

Anderson, B. and Rogaly, B. (2004) *Forced labour and migration to the UK*, COMPAS and TUC.

Anderson, B., Ruhs, M., Rogaly, B. and Spencer, S. (2006) *Fair enough? Central and East European migrants in low-wage employment in the UK*, Oxford: COMPAS.

Archbishop's Council (2005) *A place of refuge: A positive approach to asylum seekers and refugees in the UK*, London: Church House Publishing.

Arrango, J. (2000) 'Explaining migration: A critical view', *International Social Science Journal*, 165, pp 283–296.

Aryeetey, B. (2004) 'Policy Transfer in the immigration sector: Is lesson drawing shaping the management of high skilled labour migration into the EU?', unpublished MRes thesis.

Atos Consulting (2004) *A review of resourcing and management of immigration enforcement*.

Audit Commission (2000) *Another country: Implementing dispersal under the Immigration and Asylum Act 1999*, Abingdon: Audit Commission Publications, http://www.asylumsupport.info/publications/auditcommission/another.pdf.

Audit Commission (2002) *Directions in diversity: current opinion and good practice*.

Back, L., Keith, M., Khan, A., Shukra, K. and Solomos, J. (2002a) 'New Labour's white heart: politics, multiculturalism and the return of assimilation', *Political Quarterly*, vol 73, no 4, pp 445–54.

Back, L., Keith, M., Khan, A., Shukra, K. and Solomos, J. (2002b) 'The return of assimilation: race, multiculturalism and New Labour', *Sociological Research Online*, vol 7, no 2.

Balls, E. (2006) 'The PSA framework in CSR 2007', speech by Economic Secretary to the Treasury, Ed Balls, MP, at the SMF Business Forum, 17 October 2006.

Bank of England (2004) Minutes of Monetary Policy Committee meeting, 5 and 6 May 2004, www.bankofengland.co.uk.

Banton, M. (2001) 'National Integration in France and Britain', *Journal of Ethnic and Migration Studies*, vol 27, no 1, pp 151-168

Barnow, B. (1992) 'The effect of performance standards on state and local programs', in Manski, C. and Garfinkel, L. (1992) *Evaluating welfare and training programmes*, Harvard University Press.

Bauböck, R. and Rundell, J. (1998) *Blurred boundaries: Migration, ethnicity and citizenship*, Aldershot: Ashgate.

Bauer, T., Lofstrom, M. and Zimmermann, K. (2001) *Immigration policy, assimilation of immigrants and natives' sentiments towards immigrants: Evidence from 12 OECD countries*, Working paper no 33, San Diego: University of California, www.ccis-ucsd.org/publications/wrkg33.pdf.

BBC (2002) 'Short history of immigration', http://news.bbc.co.uk/hi/english/static/in_depth/uk/2002/race/short_history_of_immigration.stm#1914.

BBC (2004) 'The real story (documentary on Oakington Immigration Reception Centre)', screened at 9 pm 2 March 2005.

BBC News (2004) Interview with Charles Clarke, Radio 4, 16 December 2004, http://www.bbc.co.uk/radio4/today/listenagain/zthursday_20041216.shtml.

BBC News (2006a) 'Immigration system unfit – Reid', http://news.bbc.co.uk/2/hi/uk_news/politics/5007148.stm.

BBC News (2006b) 'Reid outlines immigration plans', http://news.bbc.co.uk/2/hi/uk_news/5212130.stm.

BBC News (2006c) 'Blair goes on ID offensive', http://news.bbc.co.uk/2/hi/uk_news/politics/6120220.stm.

BBC Politics (1999) 'Straw: Asylum is European problem', http://news.bbc.co.uk/2/hi/uk_news/politics/430656.stm.

BBC Politics (2004) 'Blair to end immigration abuse', http://news.bbc.co.uk/1/hi/uk_politics/3601829.stm.

Beckett, M. (2006) 'Trans-national terrorism: Defeating the threat', speech to the Royal United Services Institute, 9 November 2006.

Bercow, J. (2005) *Incoming assets: Why Tories should change policy on immigration and asylum*, London: SMF.

Bevir, M. and Rhodes, R. (2001) *Interpreting British governance*, Oxford: Oxford University Press.

Bhavnani, R, Mirza, H.S. and Meetoo, V. (2005) *Tackling the roots of racism: Lessons for success*, Bristol: The Policy Press.

BID (Bail for Immigration Detainees) (2003) *BID information sheet: Children in detention*, London: BID.

BID (2005) *Fit to be detained? Challenging the detention of asylum seekers and migrants with health needs*, London: BID.

BID and Asylum Aid (2005) *Justice denied: Asylum and immigration legal aid – a system in crisis*, London: BID..

Birkland, T. (2001) *An introduction to the policy process: theories, concepts, and models of public policymaking*, New York: M.E. Sharpe.

Blair, T. (1999) Beveridge lecture, 18 March 1999, Toynbee Hall, London.

Blair, T. (2004a) Speech to Confederation of British Industry on migration, 26 April 2004.

Blair, T. (2004b) Speech to the Labour Party Conference, 28 September 2004, http://news.bbc.co.uk/1/hi/uk_politics/3697434.stm.

Blair, T. (2005) Prime Minister's briefing, 5 August 2005, http://www.number-10.gov.uk/output/page8041.asp.

Blair, T. (2006a) Speech to the Labour Party Conference, 26 September 2006, http://www.labour.org.uk/index.php?id=news2005&ux_news[id]=primeminister&cHash=7e84d2fbb8.

Blair, T. (2006b) *Our nation's future – multiculturalism and integration*, http://www.number-10.gov.uk/output/Page10549.asp.

Bloch, A. (2000) 'Refugee settlement in Britain: the impact of policy on participation', *Journal of Ethnic and Migration Studies*, vol 26, no 1, pp 75–88.

Bloch, A. (2004) *Making it work*, Asylum and Migration Working Paper II, London: Institute for Public Policy Research.

Blunkett, D. (2004) *New challenges for race equality and community cohesion in the 21st century*, London: Institute for Public Policy Research.

Bommes, M and Kolb, H (2004) 'Economic Integration, Work, Entrepreneurship', *State of the art cluster report B4*, Osnabruck: IMIS.

Bosswick, W. and Heckman, F. (2006) *Integration of immigrants: Contribution of local and regional authorities*, Bamberg: EFMS.

Boswell, C. (2007) 'Migration control in Europe after 9/11: Explaining the absence of securitization', *Journal of Common Market Studies* (forthcoming).

Bridges, L., Meszaros, G. and Sunkin, M. (1995) *Judicial review in perspective*, London: Cavendish.

Brown, G. (2006a) 'The future of Britishness', speech to the Fabian New Year Conference, 14 January 2006.

Brown, G. (2006b) 'Meeting the terrorist challenge', speech to the Royal United Services Institute, 13 February 2006.

Browne, A. (2002) *Do we need mass immigration?* London: Civitas.

Bruegel, I. and Natam, E. (2002) *Maintaining contact: What happens after detained asylum seekers get bail?*, www.biduk.org.

Buck, B. (2001) *Dispersed: Housing and supporting asylum seekers and refugees in Scotland*, Edinburgh: Shelter Scotland.

Budget Statement (2003) and pre-budget report, December 2003, www.hm-treasury.gov.uk.

Burchardt, T., LeGrand, J. and Piachaud, D. (2002) *Understanding social exclusion*, Oxford: Oxford University Press.

Burchardt, T. (2005) 'Selective inclusion: asylum seekers and other marginalised groups' in J. Hills and K. Stewart (eds) *A more equal society? New Labour, poverty, inequality and exclusion*, Bristol: The Policy Press.

Burnett, J. (2004) 'Community, cohesion and the state', *Race and Class*, vol 45, no 3, pp 1–18.

Burnley Task Force (2002) *Report of the Burnley Task Force, chaired by Lord Clarke*.

Buzan, B., Waever, O., and De Wilde, J. (1998) *Security: A new framework for analysis*, Boulder: Lynne Rienner.

CAB (Citizens Advice Bureau) (2004) *Nowhere to turn: CAB evidence on the exploitation of migrant workers*, London: CAB.

CAB (2005) 'Home from home? Experiences of migrant workers in rural parts of the UK, and the impact on local service providers', CAB evidence briefing by Brian McLaughlin, CAB.

CAB (2006) *Shaming destitution: NASS section 4 support for failed asylum seekers who are temporarily unable to leave the UK*, by Richard Dunstan, London: CAB.

Cabinet Office (1999) *Modernising government*, Cm 4310, London: Stationery Office.

Cabinet Office (2002) *Better government services: Executive agencies in the 21st century*, London: Cabinet Office.

Cabinet Office (2006) *Capability review of the Home Office*, London: Cabinet Office.

Cabinet Office (2007) Website of the Cabinet Office, www.cabinetoffice.gov.uk.

Cantle, T. (2001) *Community cohesion: A report of the Independent Review Team, chaired by Ted Cantle*, London: Home Office.

Carter, M. and El-Hassan, A. (2003) *Between NASS and a hard place*, London: Housing Associations Charities Trust.

Castles, S. (2004) 'Why migration policies fail', *Ethnic and Racial Studies*, vol 27, no 2, pp 205–227.

Castles, S., Korac, M., Vasta, E. and Vertovec, S. (2002) *Integration: Mapping the field*, Home Office online report 28/03, London: Home Office.

Castles, S. and Miller, M. (2003) *The age of migration: international population movements in the modern world*, 3rd edition, Basingstoke: Macmillan.

CBI (Confederation of British Industry) (2006) 'CBI welcomes government approach to Romanian and Bulgarian workers', CBI press release, 24 October 2006.

Children's Commissioner (2005) 'An announced visit to Yarl's Wood removal centre 31st October 2005', Professor Al Aynsley-Green, Children's Commissioner.

Chimni, B. (2000) *International refugee law: A reader*, London: Sage.

Churches' Commission for Racial Justice (2005) *Response by the Churches' Commission for Racial Justice to the UK government's document 'Controlling our borders: Making migration work for Britain, the five year strategy for asylum and immigration'*.

Clarke, C. (2006) 'Stepping forward together', *Parliament Magazine*, 28 January 2006, pp 58–59.

Clarke, J. and Salt, J. (2003) 'Work permits and foreign labour in the UK: a statistical review', *Labour Market Trends*, pp 563–575.

CLG (Communities and Local Government) (2007) *Preventing violent extremism – winning hearts and minds*, London: DCLG.

Coe, J., Fricke, H. and Kingham, T. (2004) *Public attitudes campaigning*, London: CRE, http://www.cre.gov.uk/downloads/asylum_attitudes_report.pdf.

Cohen, R. (1994) *Frontiers of identity: The British and the others*, London: Longman.

Cohen, S. (2002a) *Folk devils and moral panics*, 3rd edition, London: Routledge.

Cohen, S. (2002b) 'Dining with the devil: the 1999 Immigration and Asylum Act and the voluntary sector', in S. Cohen, B. Humphries and E. Mynott (eds) *From immigration controls to welfare controls*, London: Routledge, pp 141–157.

COI Communications (2004) 'Campaign on immigration: Report of qualitative research' (unpublished).

Cole, I. and Robinson, D. (2003) *Somali housing experiences in England*, Sheffield: Sheffield Hallam University.

Congleton, R. (2002) 'The median voter model', in *Encyclopaedia of public choice*, Dordrecht/London: Kluwer Academic.

Conservative Party (1997) *You can only be sure with the Conservative Party*, the Conservative Manifesto 1997.

Conservative Party (2001) *Time for common sense*, the Conservative Manifesto 2001.

Conservative Party (2005) *Are you thinking what we're thinking? It's time for action*, the Conservative Election Manifesto 2005.

Constitutional Affairs Committee (2005) *Legal aid: asylum appeals*, 5th report of Session 2004–2005, House of Commons, HC 276-I, London: Stationery Office.

Cornelius, W., Tsuda, T., Martin, P., and Hollifield, J. (eds) (2004) *Controlling immigration: a global perspective*, 2nd edition, Stanford: Stanford University Press.

Corry, D. (1996) *Economics and EU migration policy*, London: ippr.

Coussey, M. (2004) *Annual report of the Independent Race Monitor 2003/4*, London: Home Office.

Coussey, M. (2005) *Annual report of the Independent Race Monitor 2004/5*, London: Home Office.

CPAG (Child Poverty Action Group) (2002) *Migration and social security*, London: CPAG.

CPMS (2001) *Better policy making*, London: Cabinet Office.

Craig, G., Dawson, A., Hutton, S., Roberts, N. and Wilkinson, M. (2004) *Local impacts of international migration: The information base*, Hull: University of Hull.

Crawley, H. (2005) *Evidence on attitudes to asylum and immigration: What we know, don't know and need to know*, Working paper no 23, Oxford: Centre on Migration, Policy and Society.

CRE (Commission for Racial Equality) (1985) *Immigration control procedures: Report of a formal investigation*, London: CRE.

CTBI (Churches Together in Britain and Ireland) (2003) *Asylum voices: Churches Commission for Racial Justice*, ed Bradstock and Trotman, London: CTBI.

Davis, D. and Green, D. (2006) *Controlling economic migration*, London: Conservative Party.

DCA (2003) *Judicial statistics 2002*, London: HMSO.

DCA (2005) *Judicial statistics 2004*, Cm 6565, London: HMSO.

DCA (2006a) *Judicial statistics 2005 (revised)*, Cm 6903, London: HMSO.

DCA (2006b) *Review of the implementation of the Human Rights Act*, London: HMSO.

Deakin, N. (1970) *Colour, citizenship and British society*, London: Panther.

Demos (2003) *People flow: Managing migration in a new European commonwealth*, by T. Veenkamp, T. Bentley and A. Buonfino, London: Demos.

DFID (Department for International Development) (2003) *Migrant remittances to developing countries: Overview and introduction to issues for pro-poor financial services*, Bannock Consulting.

DFID (2007) *Moving out of poverty – making migration work better for poor people*, London: DFID.

Dixit, A. (2002) 'Incentives and organisations in the public sector: An interpretative review', *Journal of Human Resources*, vol 37 no 4, pp 696–727.

Dobson, J., Koser, K., Mclaughlan, G. and Salt, J., with Clarke, J., Pinkerton, C., and Salt, I. (2001) *International migration and the United Kingdom*, RDS occasional paper no 75, London: Home Office.

Dolowitz, D. (1997) 'British employment policy in the 1980s: learning from the American experience', *Governance* vol 10, no 1, pp 23–42.

Dolowitz, D. and Marsh, D. (1996) 'Who learns what from whom: a review of the policy transfer literature', *Political Studies* vol 44, pp 343–35.

Dorey, P. (2005) *Policy-making in Britain: An introduction*, London: Sage.

Dowding, K. (1995) 'Model or metaphor? A critical review of the policy network approach', *Political Studies* vol 43, no 1, pp 136-158

Downs, A. (1957) *An economic theory of democracy*, New York: Harper Collins.

DSS (Department of Social Security) (1999) *Opportunity for all: Tackling poverty and social exclusion*, first annual report 1999, Cm 4445, London: DSS.

DSS (2000) *Opportunity for all: One year on: making a difference*, Second annual report 2000, Cm 4865, London: DSS.

DTI (Department of Trade and Industry)(1998) *Our competitive future: Building the knowledge driven economy*, Cm 4176, London: DTI.

Dudley, J. and Woollacot, S. (2004) *Persons granted British citizenship United Kingdom 2003*, London: ONS.

Duffy, B. (2004) *Can we have trust and diversity?*, London: MORI.

Dummett, A. and Nicol, A. (1990) *Subjects, citizens, aliens and others*, London: Weidenfeld.

Dummett, M. (2001) *On immigration and refugees*, London: Routledge.

Dunn, L. and Somerville, W. (2004) 'Integration through employment', *Inclusion*, Working paper 2, London: CESI, www.cesi.org.uk.

Dustmann, C., Fabbri, F., Preston I. and Wadsworth J. (2003) *The local labour market effects of immigration in the UK*, Home Office Online Report 06/03.

Dustmann, C. and Preston, I. (2003) 'Racial and economic factors in attitudes to immigration', London: UCL & IFS., http://doku.iab.de/grauepap/2003/coll_dustmann.pdf.

Duvell, F. and Jordan, B. (2003) 'Immigration control and the management of economic migration in the United Kingdom: organisational culture, implementation, enforcement and identity processes in public services', *Journal of Ethnic and Migration Studies*, vol 29, no 2, pp 299–336.

DWP (Department for Work and Pensions) (2001) *Opportunity for all*, 3rd annual report 2001, Cm 5260, London: DWP.

DWP (2002) *Opportunity for all*, 4th annual report 2002, Cm 5598, London: DWP.

DWP (2003a) *Working to rebuild lives: A preliminary report towards a refugee employment strategy*, London: DWP.

DWP (2003c) *Opportunity for all*, 5th annual report 2003, Cm 5956, London: DWP.

DWP (2004a) *Building on New Deal: Local solutions meeting individual needs*, London: DWP.

DWP (2004b) *Opportunity for all*, 6th annual report 2004, Cm 6239, London: DWP.

DWP (2005a) *Opportunity for all*, 7th annual report 2004, Cm 6673, London: DWP.

DWP (2005b) *Working to rebuild lives: A refugee employment strategy*, London: DWP.

DWP (2007) *Accession monitoring report: May 2004–December 2006*, Joint on-line report, London: DWP, http://www.ind.homeoffice. gov.uk/6353/aboutus/accessionmonitoringreport10.pdf.

Ellison, N. and Pierson, C. (2003) *Developments in British social policy 2*, Houndsmill: Palgrave MacMillan.

Employability Forum (2003) *Employing refugees: Some organisations' experiences*, http://www.employabilityforum.co.uk/pdf/ies_refugee_ exp.pdf.

Ensor, J. and Shah, A. (2005) 'United Kingdom', in J. Niessen, Y. Schibel and C. Thompson (eds), *Current immigration debates in Europe: A publication of the European Migration Dialogue*, Brussels: Migration Policy Group.

Ernst and Young. (2006) *ITEM Club spring 2006 forecast*, London: Ernst and Young.

ESRC (Economic and Social Research Council) (2006a) *Globalisation, population mobility and impact of migration on population*, http://www. esrc.ac.uk/ESRCInfoCentre/Images/ESRC_Seminar_Global_tcm6- 16062.pdf (ESRC website: www.esrc.ac.uk).

ESRC (2006b) *The 'shadow state', citizenship and transnationalism: Examining the role of voluntary sector organisations for refugees and labour migrants in the UK*, RES 000-22-0297, Professor Allan Findlay and Dr Nicholas Fyfe, ESRC website: www.esrc.ac.uk.

EU (2003) *COM 2003 336 final, Communication from the Commission to the Council, the European Parliament, the European Economic and Social Committee and the Committee of the Regions on immigration, integration and employment*, Brussels: European Commission.

EU Council (2006) *Presidency conclusions of the Brussels European Council 14/15 December 2006*, 169879/06, Brussels: Council of the European Union.

European Union Committee (2005) *Economic migration to the EU*, House of Lords, HL Paper 58.

European Union Committee (2006) *Behind closed doors: The meeting of the G6 interior ministers at Heiligendamn*, House of Lords, HL Paper 221.

European Union Committee (2007) *After Heiligendamm: Doors ajar at Stratford-upon-Avon, House of Lords*, HL Paper 32.

Evans, M. (1999) *Policy networks: A British perspective*, Working paper no 16, York: University of York.

Evans, Y., Herbert, J., Datta, K., May, J., McLlwaine, C. and Wills, J. (2005) *Making the city work: Low paid employment in London*. London: Queen Mary University.

Favell, A. (1998) *Philosophies of integration: Immigration and the idea of citizenship in France and Britain*, Basingstoke: Macmillan Press.

Fazel, M. and Stein, A. (2004) 'UK immigration law disregards the best interests of children', *The Lancet*, vol 363, pp 1749–50.

Fazel, M. and Silove, D. (2006) 'Detention of refugees' *British Medical Journal*, vol 332, pp 251–2.

FCO (Foreign and Commonwealth Office) (2003) *UK international priorities: A strategy for the FCO*, Cm 6052, London: FCO.

FCO (2006a) *Active diplomacy for a changing world: The UK's international priorities*, Cm 6762, London: FCO.

FCO (2006b) *Foreign and Commonwealth Office departmental report 2006*, Cm 6823, London: FCO.

Feeney, A. (2000) 'Refugee employment', *Journal of Local Economy*, vol 15, no 4, pp 343–9.

Findlay, A., Harrison, R., Houston, D., and Mason, C. (2003) *An investigation of migration patterns in relation to the Scottish economy, a report to Scottish Enterprise from the Centre for Applied Population Research*, Dundee: University of Dundee.

Finn, D. (2003) 'Employment policy and the New Deals, in Ellison and Pierson, Developments', in *British Social Policy 2*, Palgrave Macmillan, pp 111–28.

Finney, N and Peach, E. (2005) *Attitudes toward asylum seekers, refugees and other immigrants: A literature review for the Commission for Racial Equality*, London: CRE, http://www.cre.gov.uk/downloads/asylum_icar_report.pdf.

Fitzpatrick, P. (2005) 'Asylum seeker families', in G. Preston (ed.) *At greatest risk: The children most likely to be poor*, London: CPAG, pp 92–109.

Flynn, D. (2003) *Tough as old boots? Asylum, immigration and the paradox of New Labour policy*, IRP discussion paper, JCWI.

Flynn, D. (2005a) *A historical note on Labour migration policy in the UK*, Liverpool: Institute of Employment Rights.

Flynn, D. (2005b) 'New borders, new management: the dilemmas of modern immigration policies', *Journal of Ethnic and Racial Studies*, vol 28, no 3, pp 463–90.

Foot, P. (1969) *The Rise of Enoch Powell*, Penguin.

Franklin, B. (2004) *Packaging politics: Political communications in Britain's media democracy*, 2nd edition, London: Arnold.

Fredman, S. and Spencer, S. (2006) *Delivering equality: Towards an outcome-based positive duty*, submission to the Cabinet Office Equality Review and to the Discrimination Law Review, June 2006.

Freeman, G. (2004) Commentary, in W. Cornelius, T. Tsuda, P. Martin and J. Hollifield (eds) *Controlling immigration: a global perspective*, 2nd edition, Stanford, CA: Stanford University Press, pp 334–337.

Frijters, P., Shields, M., and Wheatley Price, S. (2003) *Immigrant job search in the UK: Evidence from panel data* http://ideas.repec.org/p/iza/izadps/dp902.html.

FSB (Federation of Small Businesses) (2006) 'Business fears a mess over new EU entrants', FSB press release, 24 October 2006.

GAD (Government Actuary's Department) (2007) GAD website: http://www.gad.gov.uk.

Galbraith, J.K. (1979) *The nature of mass poverty*, Cambridge, MA: Harvard University Press.

Garbaye, R. (2005) *Getting into local power: the politics of ethnic minorities in British and French cities*, Oxford: Blackwell Publishing.

Gardner, C. (2006) *Can the government manage migration? A study of UK legislation from 1996–2006*, Working paper no 28, Oxford: COMPAS.

Garrard, J. (1971) *The English and Immigration: A comparative study of the Jewish Influx 1880-1910*, Oxford: OUP.

Geddes, A. (2003) *The politics of migration and immigration in Europe*, London: SAGE.

Geddes, A. (2005) 'Getting the best of both worlds? Britain, the EU and migration policy', *International Affairs*, vol 81, no 4, pp 723–40.

German Presidency Press Release (2007) 'Informal EU ministers' meetings in Germany begin with the conference of justice and home affairs ministers in Dresden', 9 January.

Giddens, A. and Diamond, P. (2005) *The new egalitarianism*, Cambridge: Polity Press.

Gilbert, A. and Koser, K. (2003) *Information dissemination to potential asylum applicants in countries of origin and transit*, Home Office findings 220, London: Home Office.

GLA (Greater London Authority) (2004) *Destitution by design: Withdrawal of support from in-country asylum applicants: an impact assessment for London*, London: GLA.

GLA (2005a) *Country of birth and labour market outcomes in London*, DMAG Briefing 2005/1, London: GLA.

GLA (2005b) *Into the labyrinth: Legal advice for asylum seekers in London*, London: GLA.

Glover, S., Gott, C., Loizillon, A., Portes, J., Price, R. and Spencer, S. (2001) *Migration: An economic and social analysis*, Research Development and Statistics Directorate occasional paper no 67, London: Home Office.

Goodhart, D. (2004) *Too diverse?*, www.prospect-magazine.co.uk.

Goodwin-Gill, G. (1996) *The refugee in international law*, 2nd edition. Oxford: Clarendon Press.

Gordon, I., Lewis, J., and Young, K. (1977) 'Perspectives on policy analysis', *Public Administration Bulletin*, vol 25, pp 26-35.

Gott, C. and Johnson, K. (2002) *The migrant population in the UK: Fiscal effects*, RDS occasional paper 77.

Goulbourne, H. (1998) *Race relations in Britain since 1945*, Basingstoke: Macmillan.

Green, A. (2005) *Draft report, local integration of immigrants into the labour market: UK case study – the case of refugees in London*, LDA, OECD, LEED, London: LDA.

Green, S. (2002) *Immigration, asylum and citizenship: Towards an agenda for policy learning between Britain and Germany*, London: Anglo-German Foundation.

Griffiths, D. (2001) *English language training for refugees in London*, Home Office online report 14/03.

Griffiths, D., Sigona, N., and Zetter, R. (2006) *Refugee community organisations and dispersal: Networks, resources and social capital*, Bristol: The Policy Press.

Grillo, R. (2005) 'Saltdean can't cope: Protests against asylum-seekers in an English seaside suburb', *Ethnic and Racial Studies*, vol 28, no 2, pp 235–60.

Guardian (2002) Vikram Dodd, 'Race watchdog is ill informed, claims minister', 17 May, http://www.guardian.co.uk/uk_news/story/0,3604,717013,00.html.

Guardian (2005) Special Investigation, 10 and 11 January.

Guardian (2006) 'Reid shifts 440 police officers to target illegal immigrants', 21 November, http://politics.guardian.co.uk/homeaffairs/story/0,,1953095,00.html.

Guiraudon, V. and Joppke, C. (2001) *Controlling a new migration world*, London: Routledge.

Hale, S. (2002) 'Professor MacMurray and Mr Blair: The strange case of the communitarian guru that never was', *Political Quarterly*, vol 73, no 2, pp 16–30.

Hall, P. and Taylor, R. (1996) 'Political science and the three new institutionalisms', *Political Studies*, vol 44, pp 936–57.

Hall, S. (1981) 'The whites of their eyes. Racist ideologies and the media', in M. Alvarado and J. Thompson (eds) (1990) *The media reader*, London: BFI Publishing.

Halman, L. (2001) *The European values study: A third wave source book of the 1999/2000, European values study surveys*, Tilburg: EVS/WORC/Tilburg University..

Hammar, T. (1985) *European immigration policy: A comparative study*, New York: Cambridge University Press.

Hampshire, J. and Saggar, S. (2005) *Migration, integration, and security in the UK since July 7*, Migration Information Source, 1 March 2005, www.migrationinformation.org.

Hansard (1997-2007), http://www.publications.parliament.uk/pa/pahansard.htm

Hansen, R. (1999) 'The Kenyan Asians, British politics, and the Commonwealth Immigrants Act 1968', *Historical Journal*, vol 42, pp 809–34.

Hansen, R. (2000) *Citizenship and immigration in post-war Britain: The institutional origins of a multicultural nation*, Oxford: OUP.

Hansen, R. (2003) 'Migration to Europe since 1945: Its history and its lessons', in S. Spencer (ed) *The Politics of Migration*, Oxford: Blackwell, pp 25–39.

Hansen, R. (2004) Commentary in W. Cornelius, T. Tsuda, P. Martin and J. Hollifield (eds) *Controlling immigration: a global perspective*, 2nd edition, Stanford, CA: Stanford University Press, pp 338–42.

Hantrais, L. (2000) *Social policy in the European Union*, 2nd edition, London: Palgrave.

Haque, R. (2002) *Migrants in the UK: a descriptive analysis of their characteristics and labour market performance*, London: DWP.

Harris, M. (2003) *Tomorrow is another country*, London: Civitas.

Harvey, C. (2001) *Seeking asylum in the UK: Problems and prospects*, London: Butterworths.

Hassan, L. (2000) 'Deterrence measures and the preservation of asylum in the United Kingdom and the United States', *Journal of Refugee Studies*, vol 13, no 2, pp 184–204.

Hatton, T. and Wheatley Price, S. (1999) *Migration, migrants and policy in the United Kingdom*, Discussion paper no 81, Bonn: IZA.

Hay, C. (2002) *Political analysis: A critical introduction*, Basingstoke: Palgrave.

Held, D., McGrew, A., Goldblatt, D. and Perraton, J. (1999) *Global transformations: Politics, economics and culture*, Cambridge: Polity Press.

Held, D. and McGrew, A. (2003) *Global transformations reader: An introduction to the globalisation debate*, 2nd edition, Cambridge: Polity Press.

Herlitz, L. (2005) *A review of the recent literature on the impact of immigration on the UK*, Pilot research study for the European Migration Network, Croydon: IRSS.

Hill, M. (1997) *The policy process: A reader*, 2nd edition, Prentice Hall/ Harvester Wheatsheaf.

Hill, M. (2005) *The public policy process*, 4th edition, Essex: Pearson Education Limited.

Hills, J. (2002) 'Does a focus on "social exclusion" change the policy response?', in T. Burchardt, J. LeGrand and D. Piachaud (eds) *Understanding social exclusion*, Oxford: OUP.

Hills, J. (2004) 'From outcomes to opportunities?', LSE lecture, 5 March 2004.

Hills, J. and Stewart, K. (2005) *A more equal society? New Labour, poverty, inequality and exclusion*, Bristol: The Policy Press.

Hirst, P. and Thompson, G. (1996) *Globalisation in question: The international economy and the possibilities of governance*, Cambridge: Polity Press.

HM Chief Inspector of Prisons (2004) *Report on the unannounced inspections of four short-term holding facilities: Communications House, London; Lunar House, Croydon; Electric House, Croydon; Dallas Court, Manchester*, London: Her Majesty's Inspectorate of Prisons.

HM Chief Inspector of Prisons (2005) *Report on the unannounced inspections of four short-term non-residential holding facilities: Gatwick Airport, North Terminal; Gatwick Airport, South Terminal; London City Airport; Dover Asylum Screening Centre*, London: Her Majesty's Inspectorate of Prisons.

HM Chief Inspector of Prisons (2006a) *Report on the unannounced inspections of three short-term non-residential immigration holding facilities: Calais Seaport, Coquelles Freight, Coquelles Tourist, France, 2–3 August 2005*, London: Her Majesty's Inspectorate of Prisons.

HM Chief Inspector of Prisons (2006b) *Report on the unannounced inspections of five short-term non-residential holding facilities: Queen's Building and Terminals 1–4, Heathrow, 10–13 October 2005*, London: Her Majesty's Inspectorate of Prisons.

HMSO (1965) *Immigration from the Commonwealth*, Cm 2739, London: HMSO.

HMT (1999) *Pre-Budget report, 9 November 1999*, London: HMT.

HMT (2003) *The Green Book: Appraisal and evaluation in central government*, London: HMT.

HMT (HM Treasury) (2006a) *Long-term opportunities and challenges for the UK: analysis for the 2007 comprehensive spending review*, London: HMT.

HMT (2006b) *Pre-Budget report, 6 December 2006*, London: HMT.

Hollifield, J. (2000) 'The politics of international migration: How can we "bring the state back in"?' in C. Brettell and J. Hollifield (eds) *Migration theory: Talking across disciplines*, London: Routledge, pp 137–85.

Home Affairs Select Committee (2002) *Questions and answers 1–30, hearing with John Gieve, arising from the content of the Home Office Annual Report 2001–02*.

Home Affairs Select Committee (2003) *Asylum removals*, 4th report, HC654.

Home Affairs Select Committee (2005) *Home Office target setting 2004*, 3rd report of Session 2004–2005, HC 320.

Home Affairs Select Committee (2006a) *The work of the Home Office*, written evidence, Session 2005–06, HC604i.

Home Affairs Select Committee (2006b) *Immigration control*, 5th report of Session 2005–06, vol I-III, HC 755-I-III.

Home Office (1998) *Fairer, faster and firmer: A modern approach to immigration and asylum*, Cm 4018, London: Stationery Office.

Home Office (2000) *Full and equal citizens – A strategy for the integration of refugees into the United Kingdom*, London: Home Office.

Home Office (2001) *Building cohesive communities: A report of the Ministerial Group on Public Order and Community Cohesion*, London: Home Office.

Home Office (2002a) *Secure borders, safe haven: Integration with diversity in modern Britain*, Cm 5387, London: Stationery Office.

Home Office (2002b) *The migrant population in the UK: Fiscal effects*, RDS occasional paper 77, London: Home Office.

Home Office (2003a) *New international approaches to asylum processing and protection*, London: Home Office.

Home Office (2003b) *The new and the old: The report of the 'Life in the United Kingdom' Advisory Group*, London: Home Office.

Home Office (2003c) *Prevention of illegal working, proposed changes to document list under Section 8 of the 1996 Asylum and Immigration Act*, Consultation document, London: Home Office.

Home Office (2003d) *Building a picture of community cohesion: A guide for local authorities and their partners*, London: Home Office.

Home Office (2003e) *Home Office departmental report 2003*, Cm 5908, London: Stationery Office.

Home Office (2003f) *Accommodation centres for asylum seekers, some frequently asked questions*, London: Home Office.

Home Office (2004a) *One step ahead: A 21st century strategy to defeat organised crime*, White Paper consultation document, Cm 6167, London: Stationery Office.

Home Office (2004b) *Confident communities in a secure Britain, Home Office strategic plan 2004–2008*, Cm 6287, London: Stationery Office.

Home Office (2004c) *Home Office annual report 2003–04*, Cm 6208, London: Stationery Office.

Home Office (2005a) *Controlling our borders: Making migration work for Britain, Home Office five year strategy for asylum and immigration*, Cm 6472, London: Stationery Office.

Home Office (2005b) *Improving opportunity, strengthening society: The government's strategy to increase race equality and community cohesion*, London: Home Office.

Home Office (2005c) *Integration matters: A national refugee strategy*, London: Home Office.

Home Office (2005d) *Selective admission: Making migration work for Britain*, consultation document, London: Home Office.

Home Office (2005e) *Home Office annual report 2004–2005*, Cm 6528, London: Stationery Office.

Home Office (2005f) *SR 2004 PSA targets*, technical notes, first published 29 July 2004 and updated 27 July 2005, http://www.homeoffice.gov.uk/documents/psa-technical-note-SR04-jul-05?view=Binary.

Home Office (2005g) *'Preventing extremism together' Working Groups*, August, London: Home Office.

Home Office (2006a) *A points-based system: Making migration work for Britain*, Cm 6741, London: Stationery Office.

Home Office (2006b) *A points-based system: making migration work for Britain, Partial regulatory impact assessment*, London: Stationery Office.

Home Office (2006c) *New asylum model update*, Issue no 1, London: Home Office.

Home Office (2006d) *Fair, effective, transparent and trusted: Rebuilding confidence in our immigration system*, London: Home Office.

Home Office (2006e) *Countering international terrorism: the United Kingdom's strategy*, Cm 6888, London: Stationery Office.

Home Office (2006f) *Control of immigration: Statistics, United Kingdom 2006*, Cm 6904, London: Stationery Office.

Home Office (2006g) *A consultation on establishing a Migration Advisory Committee*, London: Home Office.

Home Office (2006h) *The Home Office departmental report*, Cm 6818, London: Stationery Office.

Home Office (2006i) *Borders, immigration and identity action plan: Using the national identity scheme to strengthen our borders and enforce compliance within the UK*, London: Home Office.

Home Office (2006j) *Strategic action plan for the national identity scheme: Safeguarding your identity*, London: Home Office.

Home Office (2006k) *The government reply to the fifth report from the Home Affairs Committee Session 2005–06 HC 775, Immigration Control*, Cm 6910, London: Stationery Office.

Home Office (2007a) *Enforcing the rules: A strategy to ensure and enforce compliance with our immigration laws*, London: Home Office.

Home Office (2007b) *Securing the UK Border: Our vision and strategy for the future*, London: Home Office.

Home Office (2007c) *Public performance target: removing more failed asylum seekers than new anticipated unfounded applications*, London: Home Office.

Home Office (2007d) *Asylum statistics: 4th Quarter 2006*, London: Home Office, http://www.homeoffice.gov.uk/rds/pdfs07/asylumq406.pdf.

Home Office Press Release (2000) 25 July 2000.

Home Office Press Release (2003a) 11 March 2003.

Home Office Press Release (2003b) 22 December 2003.

Home Office Press Release (2003c) 4 December 2003.

Home Office Press Release (2004) 26 April 2004.

Home Office Press Release (2005a) 23 August 2005.

Home Office Press Release (2005b) 22 November 2005.

Home Office Press Release (2005c) 19 December 2005.

Home Office Press Release (2006a) 18 January 2006.

Home Office Press Release (2006b) 10 March 2006.

Home Office Press Release (2006c) 1 March 2006.

House of Commons (2003) *Asylum and Immigration: The 2003 Bill*, Research Paper 03/88, 11 December 2003.

House of Commons (2004) *Migration and development: How to make migration work for poverty reduction*, Report of the 6th Session, HC 79-1.

Hudson, J. and Lowe, S. (2004) *Understanding the policy process: Analysing welfare policy and practice*, Bristol: The Policy Press.

Hussain, A. (2001) *British immigration policy under the Conservative government*, Aldershot: Ashgate.

ICAR (Information Centre about Asylum and Refugees) (2005a) *Attitudes towards asylum seekers, refugees and other immigrants: A literature review for the CRE*, London: CRE.

ICAR (2005b) *Key issues: Public opinion on asylum and refugee issues*, ICAR Navigation Guide by Nissa Finney.

ILPA (Immigration Law Practitioners Association) (2004) *Asylum: A guide to recent legislation*, 4th edition, London: Immigration Law Practitioner's Association.

Institute of Directors (2007) 'Business leader's survey on migrant workers', Press release, 30 January 2007.

ippr (Institute for Public Policy Research) (2003) *States of conflict: Causes and patterns of forced migration to the EU and policy responses*, by S. Castles, H. Crawley and S. Loughna.

ippr (2004a) *Labour migration to the UK: an ippr fact file*, www.ippr.org.uk.

ippr (2004b) *Brain strain: Optimising highly skilled migration from developing countries*, Asylum and Migration working paper 3, London: ippr.

ippr (2006a) *EU enlargement: Bulgaria and Romania – migration implications for the UK, an ippr factfile* www.ippr.org.uk.

ippr (2006b) *Migration and development: Opportunities and challenges for policymakers*, Paper prepared for IOM conference, 15/16 March, Brussels.

Jackson, P. and Penrose, J. (1993) *Constructions of race, place and nation*, London: UCL Press.

Jacobson, D. (1997) *Rights across borders: Immigration and the decline of citizenship*, Baltimore: John Hopkins University Press.

James, O. (2004) 'The UK core executive's use of public service agreements as a tool of governance', *Public Administration*, vol 82, no 2, pp 397–419.

JCHR (Joint Committee on Human Rights) (2004a) *Asylum and Immigration (Treatment of Claimants etc.) Bill*, 5th report of Session 2003–04, HL Paper 35/ HC 304.

JCHR (2004b) *Asylum and Immigration (Treatment of Claimants etc.) Bill: New Clauses*, 14th report of Session 2003–04, HL Paper 130/ HC 828.

JCHR (2004c) *The international covenant on economic, social and cultural rights*, 21st report of Session 2003–04, HL Paper 183/ HC 1188.

JCHR (2004d) *Scrutiny of bills: Final progress report*, 23rd report of Session 2003–04, HL Paper 210/ HC 1282.

JCHR (2005a) *The Convention on the Elimination of Racial Discrimination*, 14th report of Session 2004–05, HL Paper 88/ HC 471.

JCHR (2005b) *Review of international human rights instruments*, 17th report of Session 2004–05, HL Paper 99/ HC 264.

JCHR (2007) *The treatment of asylum seekers*, 10th report of Session 2006–07, HL Paper 81-I/ HC 60-I.

Joint Council for the Welfare of Immigrants (2006) *Immigration, nationality and refugee law handbook*, London: JCWI.

Jones, A. (1998) *The child welfare implications of UK immigration and asylum policy*, Manchester: Manchester Metropolitan University.

Joppke, C. (1999) *Immigration and the nation state: the United States, Germany and Great Britain*, Oxford: OUP.

Jordan, B. and Duvell, F. (2003), *Migration: The boundaries of equality and justice*, Cambridge: Polity Press.

Joseph Rowntree Foundation (2005) *Developing communities containing dispersed refugee people seeking asylum, Findings document*, York: JRF.

Justice (1999) *Immigration and Asylum Bill: Human rights compliance*, Justice, www.justice.org.uk.

Justice (2002) *Asylum: Changing policy and practice in the UK, EU and selected countries*, London: Justice.

Kalia, K. (2004) 'A reaction to tabloid pressure? Examining Britain's decision to impose benefit restrictions on labour migrants from the new EU member states' (unpublished).

Kay, D. and Miles, R. (1992) *Refugees or migrants workers: European volunteer workers in Britain 1946–1951*, London: Routledge.

Kaye, R. (1998) 'Redefining the refugee: the UK media portrayal of asylum seekers', in K. Koser and H. Lutz (eds) *The new migration in Europe: Social constructions and social realities*, Basingstoke: Macmillan.

Kelly, L. and Joly, D. (1999) *Refugees' reception and settlement in Britain*, York: JRF.

Kempton, J. (2002) *Migrants in the UK: Their characteristics and labour market outcomes and impacts*, RDS occasional paper no 82, London: Home Office.

Koser, K. and Lutz, H. (1998) *The new migration in Europe: Social constructions and social realities*, Basingstoke: Macmillan.

Koser, K. and Pinkerton, C. (2002) *The social networks of asylum seekers and the dissemination of information about countries of asylum*, Home Office Findings 165, London: Home Office.

Krasner, S. (1988) 'Sovereignty: an institutional perspective', *Comparative Political Studies*, vol 21, pp 66–94.

Kyambi, S. (2005) *Beyond Black and White: Mapping new immigrant communities*, London: ippr.

Labour Party (1997) *New Labour: Because Britain deserves better*, Labour's manifesto 1997.

Labour Party (2001) *Ambitions for Britain: Labour's manifesto 2001*.

Labour Party (2005a) *Britain forward not back*, The Labour party manifesto 2005.

Labour Party (2005b) *Labour's top 50 achievements: Our top 50 achievements since being elected in 1997*, October 2005, www.labour.org.uk.

Lahav, G. (2000) 'The rise of nonstate actors in migration regulation in the United States and Europe: changing the gatekeepers of bringing back the state?', in N. Foner, R. Rumbaut and S. Gold (eds) *Immigration research for a new century: Multidisciplinary perspectives*, New York, NY: Russell Sage Foundation.

Lambert, H. (1999) 'Protection against refoulement from Europe: human rights law comes to the rescue', in *International and Comparative Law Quarterly*, vol 48, no 3, 515-544.

Lasswell, H. (1948) *Power and personality*, New York: W.W. Norton.

Laumann, E. and Knoke, D. (1987) *The organisational state*, Madison: University of Winsconsin.

Lavenex, S. (2002) *Labour mobility in the General Agreement on Trade in Services. (GATS) – Background Paper*, Working Paper 1/2002, PEMINT.

Lavenex, S. (2004) 'Towards an international framework for labour mobility? The General Agreement on Trade in Service (GATS)', in M. Bommes, K. Hoesch, U. Hunger and H. Kolb (eds) *Organisational recruitment and patterns of migration: Interdependencies in an integrating Europe*, Osnabruck: IMES-Beitrage, pp 23–47.

Lawrence, F. (2004) *Not on the label: What really goes into the food on your plate*, Harmondsworth: Penguin.

Lawrence, F. (2006) 'Carry on gangmaster', in *Guardian*, Friday 27 January.

Layton-Henry, Z. (1981) *A report on British immigration policy since 1945*, Warwick: Warwick University.

Layton-Henry, Z. (1984) *The politics of race in Britain*, London: Allen and Unwin.

Layton-Henry, Z. (1992) *The politics of immigration: Immigration, race, and race relations in post-war Britain*, Oxford: Blackwell.

Layton-Henry, Z. (2004) 'Britain from immigration control to migration management', in W. Cornelius, T. Tsuda, P. Martin and J. Hollifield (eds) *Controlling immigration: A global perspective*, 2nd edition, Stanford, CA: Stanford University Press, pp 297–333.

Layton-Henry, Z. (2006) 'Patterns of migration – a problem or opportunity?' Podcast from the University of Warwick, 18 May 2006, http://www.podcastdirectory.com/podshows/435016.

Layton-Henry, Z. and Rich, P. (1986) *Race, government and politics in Britain*, Basingstoke: Macmillan.

Layton-Henry, Z. and Wilpert, C. (2003) *Challenging racism in Britain and Germany*, Basingstoke: Palgrave.

LCD (Lord Chancellor's Department) (2001) *Judicial statistics 2000*, London: LCD.

Lee, A. and Mulgan, G. (2001) *Better policy delivery and design: a discussion paper*, London: Cabinet Office.

Leigh, L. and Beyani, C. (1996) *Blackstone's guide to the Asylum and Immigration Act 1996*, London: Blackstone.

Leiken, R. (2005) 'Europe's angry Muslims', *Foreign Affairs*, vol 84, no 4, pp 120-35.

Levitas, R. (1998) *The inclusive society? Social exclusion and New Labour*, Basingstoke: Macmillan.

Lewis, H. (2007) *Destitution in Leeds*, York: JRCT.

Lewis, M. (2005) *Asylum: Understanding public attitudes*, London: ippr.

Liberty (2004) *Briefing on legal aid provisions in Clause 14 of the Asylum and Immigration (Treatment of Claimants etc) Bill in the House of Lords*, London: Liberty.

Lipsky, M. (1971) 'Street level bureaucracy and the analysis of urban reform', *Urban Affairs Quarterly*, vol 6, pp 391–409.

Lipsky, M. (1979) *Street level bureaucracy,* New York: Russell Sage Foundation.

Lister, R. (2001) 'New Labour: a study in ambiguity from a position of ambivalence' *Critical Social Policy*, vol 24, no 4, pp 425–47.

Little, K. (1947) *Negroes in Britain: A study of racial relations in English society*, London: Kegan Paul.

Loizillon, A. (2004) 'Principal labour migration schemes in the United Kingdom' in OECD *Migration for employment: Bilateral agreements at a crossroads*, OECD: Paris.

MacDonald, I. and Webber, F. (2001) *MacDonald's immigration law and practice*, 5th edition, London: Reed Elsevier.

McCleish, J., Cutler, S., and Stancer, C. (2002) *A crying shame: pregnant asylum seekers and their babies in detention*. London: Maternity Alliance, BID, and London Detainee Support Group.

McCombs, M. (1994) 'News influence on our pictures of the world', in J. Bryant and D. Zillmann (eds) *Media effects: Advances in theory and research*, Hove: Lawrence Erlbaum, pp 1–15.

McGhee, D. (2006) 'Getting 'host' communities on board: Finding the balance between "managed migration" and "managed settlement" in community cohesion strategies', *Journal of Ethnic and Migration Studies*, vol 32, no 1, pp 111–27.

McKee, R. (2004) 'Mistreatment of claimants? A section-by-section survey of the 2004 Act', *Tottel's Journal of Immigration and Asylum Law*, vol 18, no 4, pp 229–42.

McLaren, L. and Johnson, M. (2004) 'Understanding the rising tide of anti-immigrant sentiment', *British Social Attitudes 21st Report*, London: Sage, pp 169–200.

March, J. and Olsen, J. (1989) *Rediscovering institutions*, New York: Free Press.

March, J. and Olsen, J. (1996) 'Institutional perspectives on political institutions', *Governance*, vol 9, no 3, pp 248–264.

Marsh, D. and Rhodes, R. (1992) *Policy networks in British government*, Oxford: Clarendon Press.

Marsh, D., Richards, D., and Smith, M.J. (2000) 'Re-assessing the role of departmental cabinet ministers', *Public Administration*, vol 78, no 2, pp 305–26.

Marsh, D., Richards, D., and Smith, M.J. (2001) *Changing patterns of governance in the United Kingdom*, Basingstoke: Palgrave.

Marsh, D. and Smith, M. (2000) 'Understanding policy networks: Towards a dialectical approach', *Political Studies*, vol 28, pp 4–21.

Marshall, T.H. (1964) 'Citizenship and social class', in *Class, citizenship and social development: Essays by T.H. Marshall*, New York: Doubleday.

Massey, D. (1999) *Worlds in motion: Understanding international migration at the end of the millennium*, Oxford: OUP.

Maxwell, R. (2006) 'Muslims, South Asians and the British mainstream: a national identity crisis?', *West European Politics*, vol 29, no 4, pp 736-56.

Messina, A. (1989) *Race and party competition in Britain*, Oxford: Clarendon Press.

Minogue, M. (1983) 'Theory and practice in public policy and administration', *Policy and Politics*, vol 11, pp 63–85.

Mitchell, J. and Pain, N. (2003) *The determinants of international migration into the UK: A panel based modelling approach*, NIESR discussion paper no 216, London: National Institute of Economic and Social Research.

Moch, L. (1994) *Moving Europeans: Migration in Western Europe since 1650*, Bloomington: Indiana University Press.

MORI (2007) *MORI political monitor: 'The most important issues facing Britain today'*, London: MORI.

Morris, L. (2002) 'Britain's asylum and immigration regime: the shifting contours of rights', *Journal of Ethnic and Migration Studies*, vol 28, no 3, pp 409–25.

Morris, L. (2004) *The control of rights: the rights of workers and asylum seekers under managed migration*, IRP discussion paper, London: JCWI.

Munz, R. (1996) 'A continent of migration: European mass migration in the twentieth century', *New Community*, vol 22, no 2, pp 287–300.

NACAB (National Association of Citizens Advice Bureaux) (2000) *A person before the law*, London: Citizens Advice Bureaux.

Nandy, L. (2005) 'The impact of government policy on asylum-seeking and refugee children', *Children & Society*, vol 19, pp 1–4.

National Audit Office (2001) *Better policy-making: Ensuring policies deliver value for money*, Session 2001–2002, HC 289.

National Audit Office (2004a) *Visa entry to the United Kingdom: The entry clearance operation*, HC 367.

National Audit Office (2004b) *Improving the speed and quality of asylum decisions*, HC 535.

National Audit Office (2005a) *Returning failed asylum seekers*, Session 2005–06, HC 76.

National Audit Office (2005b) *National Asylum Support Service: The provision of accommodation for asylum seekers*, Session 2005–06, HC 130.

Noble, G., Barnish, A., Finch, E. and Griffith, D. (2004) *A review of the operation of the National Asylum Support Service*, London: Home Office.

Norris, P. (2001) 'New Labour and public opinion: The third way as centrism?' in S. White (ed) *New Labour: The progressive future?*, London: Macmillan, pp 32–44.

OECD (1997) *Enhancing the effectiveness of active labour market policies: A streamlined public employment service*, Paris: OECD.

Office of the Deputy Prime Minister: Housing, Planning, Local Government and the Regions Committee (2004) *Social Cohesion*, Sixth Report of Session 2003-04, HC 55-1.

Ognjenovic, M. and Somerville, W. (2004) *The benefits of migration*, working brief issue 152, London: CESI.

Oldham Independent Panel Review (2001) *One Oldham, one future, panel report, chaired by David Ritchie*, Oldham: Oldham Metropolitan Borough Council.

ONS (Office of National Statistics) (2003) *National Statistics quality review on international migration (Implementation plan)*, London: ONS.

ONS (2006) *Report of the Inter-departmental Task Force on Migration Statistics*, London: ONS.

ONS (2007) Website of the Office of National Statistics, http://www.statistics.gov.uk/

O'Reilly, W. (2001) 'The Naturalization Act of 1709 and the settlement of Germans in Britain, Ireland and the colonies', in R. Vigne and C. Littleton, *From strangers to citizens: the integration of immigrant communities in Britain, Ireland and colonial America, 1550–1750*, Brighton: Sussex Academic Press.

Osborne, D. and Gaebler, T. (1992) *Reinventing government*, New York: Penguin.

Papademetriou, D. (2006) *Europe and its immigrants in the 21st century: A new deal or a continuing dialogue of the deaf?* Washington DC: MPI.

Papademetriou, D. and O'Neil, K. (2006) 'Selecting economic migrants', in D. Papademetriou (ed) *Europe and its immigrants in the 21st century: A new deal or a continuing dialogue of the deaf?* Washington DC: MPI, pp 223–56.

Parekh, B. (1988) 'Integrating minorities', in T. Blackstone, B. Parekh, and P. Sanders (eds), *Race in Britain: A developing agenda*, London: Routledge.

Parekh, B. (2000) *The future of multi-ethnic Britain*, London: Runnymede Trust/Profile Books.

Parsons, W. (1995) *Public policy: An introduction to the theory and practice of policy analysis*, London: Edward Elgar.

Paul, K. (1997) *Whitewashing Britain: Race and citizenship in the postwar era*, Ithaca, NY: Cornell University Press.

Peach, G. (1968) *West Indian migration to Britain*, London: OUP.

Pearce, N. (2005) 'Goodbye to multiculturalism, but hello to what?' *Parliamentary Brief*, vol 10, no 3, pp 7–8.

Penrose, J. (2002) *Poverty and asylum in the UK*, Oxford: Oxfam and Refugee Council.

Pensions Commission (2004) *Pensions: Challenges and choices, first report of the Pensions Commission*, London: Stationery Office.

Phillips, D. (2006) 'Moving towards integration: the housing of asylum seekers and refugees in Britain', *Housing Studies*, vol 21, no 4, pp 539–53.

Phillips, M. and Phillips, T. (1998) *Windrush: The irresistible rise of multiracial Britain*, London: HarperCollins.

Plaut, G. (1995) *Asylum: A moral dilemma*, Westport: Praeger.

Pleasence, P. (2002) *The first Legal Services Research Centre's survey of legal need,* London: Legal Services Research Centre.

Pollard, S. (2005) *David Blunkett*, London: Hodder and Stoughton.

Pollitt, C. (2003) 'Joined-up government: a survey', *Political Studies Review*, vol 1, pp 34–49.

Portes, J. and French, S. (2006) *The impact of free movement of workers from central and eastern Europe on the UK labour market: early evidence*, Working Paper 18, London: DWP.

Powell, M. (2002) *Evaluating New Labour's welfare reforms*, Bristol: The Policy Press.

Prime Minister's Strategy Unit (2005) *Strategic audit: Progress and challenges*, London: Cabinet Office.

Prisons and Probation Ombudsman for England and Wales (2004) *Investigation into allegations of racism, abuse and violence at Yarl's Wood removal centre*, London: Prisons and Probation Ombudsman.

Prisons and Probation Ombudsman for England and Wales (2005) *Inquiry into allegations of racism and mistreatment of detainees at Oakington immigration reception centre and while under escort*, London: Prisons and Probation Ombudsman.

Propper, C. and Wilson, D. (2003) 'The use and usefulness of performance measures in the public sector', *Oxford Review of Economic Policy*, vol 19, no 2, pp 250–67.

Public Accounts Select Committee (2000) *Home Office: The Immigration and Nationality Directorate's casework programme*, 7th report of Session 1999–2000.

Public Accounts Select Committee (2005) *Foreign and Commonwealth Office: Visa entry to the UK: the entry clearance operation*, 7th report of Session 2004–05, HC 312.

Public Administration Select Committee (2003) *On target? Government by measurement*, 5th report of Session 2002–03, HC 62-I.

Putnam, R. (2000) *Bowling alone: The collapse and revival of American community*, Simon and Schuster.

Rawlings, R. (2005) 'Review, revenge and retreat', *Modern Law Review*, vol 68, no 3, pp 378–410.

Refugee Council (2002) *A case for change: How refugee children in England are missing out, First findings from the monitoring project of the Refugee Children Consortium*, London: Refugee Council.

Refugee Council (2004) *Hungry and homeless: the impact of the withdrawal of state support on asylum seekers, refugee communities and the voluntary sector*, London: Refugee Council.

Refugee Council (2005) *Refugee Council briefing: New asylum model, September 2005*, London: Refugee Council.

Refugee Media Action Group (2006) *Seeking asylum: A report on the living conditions of asylum seekers in London*, London: Migrant Resource Centre.

Refugee Survival Trust (2005) *'What's going on?' A study into destitution and poverty faced by asylum seekers and refugees in Scotland*, Scotland: Refugee Survival Trust.

Reid, J. (2006) 'I stand with the public', Speech to the Labour Party Conference, 28 September 2006.

Rentoul, J. (1995) *Tony Blair*, London: Warner Books.

Rhodes, R. (1995) 'From prime ministerial power to core executive', in R. Rhodes and P. Dunleavy (eds) (1995) *Prime minister, cabinet and core executive*, Basingstoke: Macmillan, pp 11-37

Rhodes, R. (2000) 'The governance narrative: Key findings and lessons from the ESRC's Whitehall Programme', *Public Administration*, vol 78, pp 345–63.

Rhodes, R., Carmichael, P., McMillan, J. and Massey, A. (2003) *Decentralizing the Civil Service: From unitary state to differentiated polity in the United Kingdom*, Buckingham: Open University Press.

Richards, D. and Smith, M. (2002) *Governance and public policy in the United Kingdom*, Oxford: OUP.

Richmond, A. (1954) *Colour prejudice in Britain: A study of West Indian workers in Liverpool, 1941–1951*, London: Routledge and Kegan Paul.

Robinson, D. (2005) 'The search for community cohesion: Key themes and dominant concepts of the public policy agenda', *Urban Studies*, vol 42, no 8, pp 1411–27.

Robinson, D. and Reeve, K. (2006) *Neighbourhood experiences of new immigration: Reflections from the evidence base*, York: JRF.

Robinson, V. (1999) *Migration and public policy*, Cheltenham: Edward Elgar.

Robinson, V. and Segrott, J. (2002) *Understanding the decision-making of asylum seekers*, Home Office Research Study 243, London: Home Office.

Robinson, V., Andersson, R. and Musterd, S. (2003) *Spreading the 'burden'? A review of policies to disperse asylum seekers and refugees*, Bristol: The Policy Press.

Rogers, N. (2004) 'A dereliction of the duty of care: human rights and responsibilities owed to migrants and refugees', Garden Court Chambers, Paper delivered at the Human Rights Law 6th Annual Law Conference, 15 October 2004, London.

Rohl, K. (2005) *Fleeing violence and poverty: non-refoulement obligations under the European Convention of Human Rights*, Working paper 111, UNHCR.

Rollason, N. (2002) 'International mobility of highly skilled workers: the UK perspective', in OECD (ed) *International mobility of the highly skilled*, Paris: OECD, http://www1.oecd.org/publications/e-book/9202011E.PDF.

RSA Migration Commission (2005) *Migration: A Welcome Opportunity, A new way forward by the RSA Migration Commission*, London: RSA.

Rudiger, A. and Spencer, S. (2003) 'Meeting the challenge: Equality, diversity and cohesion in the European Union', Joint European Commission/OECD conference on the economic effects and social aspect of migration, Brussels.

Rutter, J. (2003) *Working with refugee children*, York: JRF.

Saggar, S. (1992) *The politics of race in Britain*, London: Harvester Wheatsheaf.

Saggar, S. (1998) *Race and British electoral politics*, London: UCL Press.

Saggar, S. (1999) 'Immigration and minority policy debate in Britain: Multicultural political narratives contested', in A. Geddes and A. Favell, (eds) *The politics of belonging: Migrants and minorities in contemporary Europe*, Aldershot: Ashgate, pp 42–59.

Saggar, S. and Drean, J. (2001) *British public attitudes and ethnic minorities*, London: Cabinet Office.

Salinsky, M. and Dell, S. (2001) *Protection not prison: torture survivors detained in the UK*, London: Medical Foundation for the Care of Victims of Torture.

Salt, J. (2001) *Current trends in international migration*, Brussels: European Commission.

Salt, J. (2006) *International migration and the United Kingdom: report of the United Kingdom SOPEMI correspondent to the OECD*, London: UCL Migration Research Unit.

Salt, J. and Clarke, J. (2005) 'Migration matters', *Prospect*, vol 110.

Salt, J. and Millar, J. (2006) *Foreign labour in the United Kingdom: current patterns and trends, Labour Market Trends*, London: ONS, pp 335–55.

Sassen, S. (1999a) *Globalization and its discontents*, New York: New Press.

Sassen, S. (1999b) *Guests and aliens*, New York: New Press.

Schain, M. (2006) 'The extreme-right and immigration policy-making: Measuring direct and indirect effects', *West European Politics*, vol 29, no 2, pp 270–89.

Schuster, L and Solomos, J. (2001) 'Asylum, refuge and public policy: current trends and future dilemmas', *Sociological Research Online*, vol 6, no 1.

Schuster, L. and Solomos, J. (2004) 'Race, immigration and asylum: New Labour's agenda and its consequences', *Ethnicities*, vol 4, no 2, pp 267–300.

Seldon, A. (2004) *Blair*, Simon and Schuster.

Singh, G. (2002) CRE 25th anniversary speech, 16 May 2002.

Shelter (2004) *The black and minority ethnic housing crisis*, London: Shelter.

Sivanandan, A. (2006) 'Britain's shame', *Catalyst Magazine*, July, www.catalystmagazine.org.

Smith, M.J. (1993) *Pressure, power and policy*, Hemel Hempstead: Harvester Wheatsheaf.

Smith, R. (1988) 'Political jurisprudence, the "new institutionalism" and the future of public law', *American Political Science Review*, vol 82, pp 89–108.

Solomos, J. (1998) *'Race' and racism in Britain*, 2nd edition, London: Macmillan.

Solomos, J. and Back, L. (1996) *Racism and society*, London: Macmillan.

Somerville, W. (2003) 'International migration to the UK', *Working Brief*, vol 142, London: CESI.

Somerville, W. (2004a) *The newcomers handbook, 2004*, London: CESI.

Somerville, W. (2004b) 'Migration and employment', *Working Brief*, vol 150, London: CESI.

Somerville, W. (2004c) 'Illegal working uncovered', *Working Brief*, vol 156, London: CESI.

Somerville, W. (2004d) *The welfare to work handbook*, 2nd edition, London: CESI.

Somerville, W. (2006a) *Success and failure under Labour: Problems of priorities and performance in migration policy*, IRP working paper 3, London: JCWI.

Somerville, W. (2006b) *Working in the UK: The second edition of the newcomers handbook*, London: CESI.

Somerville, W. (2006c) 'Employment', in S.Spencer (ed) *Refugees and other new migrants: a review of the evidence on successful approaches to integration*, pp 37–51, London: Home Office.

Somerville, W. (2007) 'Brown's immigration challenge', *The Guardian*, Saturday 30 June, http://commentisfree.guardian.co.uk/willsomerville/.

Soysal, Y. (1994) *Limits of citizenship*, Chicago: University of Chicago Press.

Spencer, I. (1997) *British immigration policy since 1939: The making of multi-racial Britain*, London: Routledge.

Spencer, S. (1994) *Strangers and citizens: a positive approach to migrants and refugees*, London: ippr/Rivers Oran Press.

Spencer, S. (2002) 'Recent changes and future prospects in UK migration policy', Paper presented at Ladenburger Discourse on Migration, 14–15 February.

Spencer, S. (2003) *The politics of migration*, Oxford: Blackwell.

Sriskandarajah, D., Cooley, L. and Reed, L. (2005) *Paying their way: The fiscal contribution of immigrants to the UK*, London: ippr.

Sriskandarajah, D. and Drew, C. (2006) *Brits abroad: Mapping the scale and nature of British emigration*, London: ippr.

Statham, P. (2003) 'Understanding anti-asylum rhetoric: Restrictive politics or racist publics?', *Political Quarterly*, vol 74, no 1, pp 163–77.

Statham, P. and Geddes, A. (2006) 'Elites and the "organised public": WHO drives British immigration policy and in which direction?', *West European Politics*, vol 29, no 2, pp 248–69.

Stewart, E. (2004) 'Deficiencies in UK asylum data: practical and theoretical challenges', *Journal of Refugee Studies*, vol 17, no 1, pp 29–49.

Stone, D. (2001) 'Think tanks, global lesson-drawing and networking social policy ideas', *Global Social Policy*, vol 1, pp 338–60.

Strategy Unit (2003) *Ethnic minorities in the labour market*, London: Cabinet Office.

Sutton, K. (2004) *Inquiry into handling of ECAA applications from Bulgaria and Romania*, London: Home Office.

Symes, M. (2004) 'The application of ECHR rights', in *Immigration and asylum law: A commentary on the House of Lords in* Ullah and Do; *and* Razgar, www.ein.org.uk.

Temple, B. and Moran, R. with Fayas, N., Haboninana, S., McCabe, F., Mohamed, Z., Noori, A. and Rahman, N. (2005) *Learning to live together: Developing communities containing dispersed refugee people seeking asylum*, York: JRF.

Thorp, A. (2007) *UK Borders Bill*, research paper 07/11, House of Commons Library.

Times, The (2004) 'Three steps we will take for a fairer asylum system', Tony Blair, 16 September 2004.

Timmins, N. (2001) *The five giants: A biography of the welfare state*, 2nd edition, London: HarperCollins.

Torpey, J. (1998) 'Coming and going: On the state's monopolisation of the legitimate 'means of movement', *Sociological Theory*, vol 16, no 3, pp 239–59.

Torpey, J. (1999) *The invention of the passport: Surveillance, citizenship and the state*, Cambridge: Cambridge University Press.

Toynbee, P. (2002) 'We need a fortress: mass migration is a fact of life, and the defence of Europe's borders is essential for a fair society', *Guardian Comment*, Friday 21 June.

Treasury Committee (2005) Oral evidence taken before the Treasury Committee, Thursday 24 March 2005, Questions 38–40 to Mervyn King, relating to the February 2005 Bank of England Inflation Report.

Trott, P. (2005) 'Working, business, investment and retirement in the UK', in *MacDonald's Law and Practice*, 6th edition, London: Sweet & Maxwell, pp 505–78.

TUC (Trade Union Congress) (2002) *Migrant workers – a TUC guide*, London: TUC.

UKVisas (2004) *UK Visas annual report 2004*, Foreign and Commonwealth Office and Home Office.

UKLGIG (2004) *UK Lesbian & Gay Immigration Group briefing document on asylum*, www.uklgig.org.uk.

UNDP (United Nations Development Programme) (2000) *Replacement migration: is it a solution to declining and ageing populations?* New York: UN.

Van Selm, J. (2005) *Where migration policy is made: starting to expose the labyrinth of national institutional settings for migration policymaking and implementation*, Global Migration Perspectives No 37, Geneva: GCIM, www.gcim.org .

Vertovec, S. (2006) *The emergence of super diversity in Britain*, Centre on Migration, Policy and Society, Working paper no 25, Oxford: COMPAS.

Vertovec, S. and Wessendorf, S. (2005) *Migration and cultural, religious, and linguistic diversity in Europe: An overview of issues and trends*, Working paper no 18, Oxford: COMPAS.

Ward, K. (2004) *Key issues: UK asylum law and process*, London: ICAR.

Weil, P. (1995) *La France et ses étrangers: L'aventure d'une politique de l'immigration de 1938 à nos jours*, Paris: Gallimard.

Wheatley Price, S. (2001) 'The unemployment experience of male immigrants in England', *Applied Economics*, vol 33, pp 201–15.

Williams, R. (2004) *Refugees: Renewing the vision: An NGO working paper on improving the asylum system*, London: Refugee Council.

Wilson, R. (2001) *Dispersed: A study of services for asylum seekers in West Yorkshire December 1999–March 2001*, York: JRF.

Winder, R. (2004) *Bloody foreigners: The story of immigration to Britain*, Little Brown.

Woodbridge, J. (2005) *Sizing the unauthorised (illegal) migrant population in the United Kingdom in 2001*, Home Office Online Report 29/05, London: Home Office, http://www.homeoffice.gov.uk/rds/pdfs05/rdsolr2905.pdf .

Working Group on Forced Marriage (2000) *A choice by right*, The Report of the Working Group on Forced Marriage, London: Home Office.

Zetter, R. (2002) *Survey on policy and practice related to refugee integration*, Oxford Brookes.

Zetter R., Griffiths, D., Ferretti, S., and Pearl, M. (2003) *An assessment of the impact of asylum policies in Europe 1990–2000*, Home Office Research Study 259, London: Home Office.

Zolberg, A. (1989) 'The next waves: migration theory for a changing world', *International Migration Review*, vol 23, no 3, pp 403-430.

Zucconi, M. (2004) 'Migration and security as an issue in US–European relations', in J. Tirman (ed) *The maze of fear: Security and migration after 9/11*, New York: New Press.

Index

Page references for notes are followed by n